ALSO BY TERRENCE REAL

I Don't Want to Talk About It:
Overcoming the Secret Legacy of Male Depression

How Can I Get Through to You?

Reconnecting Men and Women

Terrence Real

SCRIBNER
New York   London   Toronto   Sydney   Singapore

SCRIBNER
1230 Avenue of the Americas
New York, NY 10020

a/v

For information about special discounts for bulk purchases,
please contact Simon & Schuster Special Sales:
1-800-465-6798 or *business@simonandschuster.com*

DESIGNED BY ERICH HOBBING

Text set in Janson

Manufactured in the United States of America

10 9 8 7 6 5 4 3 2 1

Library of Congress Cataloging-in-Publication Data is available.

ISBN 0-684-86877-6

To Belinda,
the jewel in the petal,
the object of my desire.

What have we given?
My friend, blood shaking my heart
The awful daring of a moment's surrender
Which an age of prudence can never retract
By this, and only this, we have existed.

—T. S. Eliot

We ourselves cannot put any magic spells on this world.
The world is its own magic.

—Shunryu Suzuki-Roshi

ACKNOWLEDGMENTS

I did not write this book alone, but with guidance and sustenance from many. First among them is Carol Gilligan. Over the past several years, our collaboration with couples transformed my vision of what men and women are capable of. Many of the critical ideas found here have been shaped by that association, and every idea has been touched by it. You are my fellow cartographer. But more than this, it is the lessons of our friendship that have lent me the most clarity and courage. Thank you for standing together with me.

Cheryl Richardson is my spiritual sister. Her insight, practicality, and sheer wattage have been abundant enough to empower both of us. Her positive energy ripples through these pages. Thank you for teaching me so much about generosity. Beth Vesel, my literary agent, has been intellectual companion, bellwether, and friend. At Scribner, Gillian Blake left her imprint on every aspect of this work. With unerring editorial instincts, she saw, and helped realize, a vision. I want to thank Pat Eisemann for her encouragement and savvy. And gratitude goes to the presiding spirit of Nan Graham, whose belief in me, and whose guidance, has been invaluable. You are the occasion I have tried to rise to. My association with Pia Mellody, teacher, healer, dear friend, continues to enrich. This work rests upon hers. I want also to thank the Meadows, in particular Pat Mellody and Lonnie Werdersky, for their support. Thanks go to the legendary Olga Silverstein, who sits beside me each time I see a couple or family, to Mel Bucholtz for helping bring me into right relationship to this work, and to Ed Shea for his unstinting help. I am grateful to my assistant, Liz Grabiner, for assistance throughout the project, especially with the notes. I want to thank friends, old and new, for their love and patience. And finally, thanks to my family, to Justin and Alexander, who daily inspire, and to my wife, Belinda, who claims to have been put on this earth to, among other things, help me with my narcissism, a difficult task by any account. I hope to keep making it worth your while.

CONTENTS

AUTHOR'S NOTE

All of the cases described in this book are composites. They have been deliberately scrambled in order to protect my clients' rights of confidentiality and privacy. No client found in this book corresponds to any actual person, living or dead.

How Can I Get Through to You?

INTRODUCTION

The relationship between men and women is in trouble, and it has been for over a generation. The relatively stable divorce rate over the past few decades indicates that the advent of couple's therapy in the 1950s has so far yielded nothing potent enough to affect the fate of the roughly one out of two couples who will see their marriage dissolve. We have enjoyed a period of unheralded creativity and prosperity. We marvel at new advances in technology and science that lengthen and strengthen our lives every day. No generation in history has taken so seriously issues of health and well-being—both for ourselves and our children. And yet, nonetheless, we have never been lonelier. Our sense of community is breaking down, our sense of belonging has seldom felt weaker, and, silhouetted against this backdrop, couples that once loved one another have never had a more difficult time holding fast.

For over forty years the enormously influential women's movement has examined the oppression of girls and women in our society, the corrosive force leveled against our daughters to make them conform—and the psychological cost of girls' compliance. We have just begun to extend similar empathy and support to our sons. And even now, as I write, it seems easier for us as a culture to empathize with boys than with grown men. But if we are to heal the enmity between the sexes—collectively as a culture or individually in our own marriages—we must begin to understand the forces that shape, and misshape, our husbands. The idea of opening our hearts to men will strike some women as opening the door to disempowerment. Being "soft" on men means to many a facile excuse for diffi-

cult, even dangerous behavior. There has been a split in our cultural
attitude toward men. For a generation, feminists have held men
responsible for privileged, insensitive, and at times offensive behaviors. But most feminists have not spoken to men's subjective experience of pain. Psychologists and those in the men's movement, by
contrast, have begun to look at the cultural gauntlet through which
our sons must pass, and the damage it does to them. But, in all
their empathy, they rarely acknowledge the power men wield. One
camp speaks of the violence men do, the other of the violence done
to them. If men and women are to learn how to preserve the natural
state of love and respect each deserves, both aspects of masculinity
must be addressed—the wounding and the wound.

Since the publication of my previous book, *I Don't Want to Talk
About It: Overcoming the Secret Legacy of Male Depression*, I have spent
a fair amount of time on the road, speaking and giving workshops
throughout the country to both health professionals and to the general public about men and what ails them. Wherever I have gone, I
have been struck by a burgeoning desire, almost a sense of urgency,
about "figuring men out"—how we can help struggling sons, husbands, fathers, in much the same way that women collectively
began helping daughters, wives, and mothers a generation ago.

The latest research on boys and their development tells us that,
despite our raised consciousness and good intentions, boys today, no
less than ever before, are permeated with an inescapable set of
highly constricting rules. Those boys who try to "step out of the box"
place themselves in harm's way since, even today, our culture's tolerance for young men who deviate from what we deem masculine is
limited, and our intolerance expresses itself in singularly ugly ways.
The great bind is that those boys who do not resist, who choose or
who are coerced to comply, do not escape either. Avoiding attack
from without, those who adopt the traditions of male stoicism and
"self-reliance" risk injury to the deepest and most alive aspects of
their own being. The consequence of opposition is psychological and
often physical brutality. The consequence of compliance is emotional
truncation, numbness, and isolation.

"Good-bye, Justin," I say as I drop my thirteen-year-old off at school in the morning. Unlike his ten-year-old brother, Alexander, Justin averts his face from my farewell kiss, concerned that we will be observed. Though Justin is ebullient and vivacious at home, his expression visibly hardens as the low-slung school buildings come into view; his voice drops to a near monotone. I watch my son dampen down, toughen up. I watch him try to fit in. Despite his best efforts to hide his openness, older boys, bullies, have picked up the scent of emotional vulnerability in him, like a pheromone, and episodically over the years they have tortured him for it. The school protects Justin, and his mother and I arm him, as best we can. But in the mean game of inclusion/exclusion, ridicule and praise, in the socialization fields of the playground, Justin knows better than anyone that it is he alone who must make his way. Who am I to tell my son that he should keep his heart open as he threads his path to the classroom? And who am I to tell him that he should not? I don't begrudge Justin the emotional armor he dons each morning, the mask of feeling less, caring less, than he really does. It just makes me sad.

In the voices of those I work with in therapy, the men and women in the workshops I lead throughout the country, I hear a hunger for a way out of the dilemma of traditional masculinity, a roadmap toward something brighter, more whole.

If we weren't awake to the violence entwined with masculinity before, startling eruptions like those in Littleton, Colorado; Atlanta, Georgia; Santee, California, have made it difficult to ignore. "The fears of the father are transferred to the son. It was from my father to me and from me to my son. He already had it . . . I had to take him with me." So wrote a seemingly normal Atlanta stockbroker before he took his son's life, along with the lives of nine innocent people.

The alarming rise in men's violence and in boys' violence at first seems incomprehensible. But there is an old saying in Alcoholics Anonymous: "Hurt people hurt people." The transmutation of agony into rage, fear into attack, is neither foreign nor new to manhood. As a teacher and practitioner of family therapy for the past twenty years, I have seen the wages of what I call "toxic masculinity"—the legacies of drinking, womanizing, depression, and fury—

sweep through whole generations like a fire in the wood, taking down everyone in its path until one man in one generation is graced with the courage to turn and face his demons, stemming the tide of injury passed from father to son. I write this book as one contribution to that force of courage and grace. I write as an emissary of a revolution, with the express purpose of engaging as many of you as I can to join in, to empower yourselves and those around you to shake off the illusions we have lived within for centuries. For, surprising as it might seem, what so profoundly alienates men is no different than what has disenfranchised women—the system of patriarchy.

When the term *patriarchy* first entered the popular vernacular back in the 1960s and '70s, it conjured up images of male chauvinist pigs and radical, angry, bra-burning women. It was taken to mean the oppression of women by men. But early feminists like Betty Friedan and Gloria Steinem also understood that the dynamics they unearthed did harm to both genders. The revolution of which I consider myself an emissary stands on the ground laid by that generation of women, and seeks to extend its insights.

In my work with men and women I distinguish between *political patriarchy*, which is the sexism that has been the target of most feminist writing, and what I term *psychological patriarchy*. *Psychological patriarchy* goes beyond the relationship between actual men and women—as individuals or as a class. *Psychological patriarchy is the dynamic between those qualities deemed "masculine" and "feminine" in which half of our human traits are exalted while the other half is devalued. Both men and women participate in this tortured value system.* Psychological patriarchy is a "dance of contempt," a perverse form of connection that replaces true intimacy with complex, covert layers of dominance and submission, collusion and manipulation. It is the unacknowledged paradigm of relationship that has suffused Western civilization generation after generation, deforming both sexes, and destroying the passionate bond between them.

Here is the good news: the latest empirical research on both early infant relations and on adult optimal health indicates that, as a species, we are inherently wired for, and operate best in, a state of active, authentic connectedness. Even the tiniest infants, both male and female, show themselves eager, active participants in intimacy. Studies demonstrate that young children are innately connection-seeking, naturally sensitive readers of others' emotions, inherently compassionate and honest. In another domain, research on resilience, both physical and mental, reveals that rich authentic connection is one of the most salient factors in continued good health, outweighing such decisive forces as nutrition, exercise, even the absence of smoking. *We enter life whole and connected, and we operate best when richly attached. Intimacy is our natural state as a species, our birthright.* And yet, while the push away from genuine closeness occurs at different points in their development, and in critically different ways, neither boys nor girls are allowed to maintain healthy relatedness for very long.

As a culture, with no malevolent intent, following strictures we have all been raised within, we force our children out of the wholeness and connectedness in which they begin their lives. Instead of cultivating intimacy, turning nascent aptitudes into mature skills, we teach boys and girls, in complimentary ways, to bury their deepest selves, to stop speaking, or attending to, the truth, to hold in mistrust, or even in disdain, the state of closeness we all, by our natures, most crave. *We live in an antirelational, vulnerability-despising culture, one that not only fails to nurture the skills of connection but actively fears them.* Few of us have emerged from healthy, psychologically responsive families because the patriarchal norms all families live within are profoundly skewed against emotional sensitivity. While you may have your particular story and I may have mine, what we most likely share is longing, a sense of inner emptiness. Part of that emptiness is spiritual, existential, our "human condition." But a great part of the troubling sense of dis-ease comes from a profound missing of the abundant well-being we find in authentic connection. The wound of being torn from that state represents nothing less than the core environmental contribution to most psychiatric and behavioral disorders. Some of us react to this internal deficiency with depression, others with fear. Some try to fill it with food, or erase it with achievement, or alcohol, or desperate romance. Some of us feel victimized by our own misery, projecting onto others the resources we lack and hating them for it, lashing out in torrents of hurt, helpless, rage. We starve, we glut, we kill ourselves, we kill others. We don black trenchcoats and plan media-adoring shooting sprees. All in reaction to the great deformity, the thing we should have gotten and did not get.

We enter life as children, the poet Wordsworth tells us, "Not in entire forgetfulness, / And not in utter nakedness, / But trailing clouds of Glory." The men and women whose stories I tell have not forgotten that. Unwilling heroes, they are in crisis and, as any family therapist knows, in crisis lies opportunity. Unlike some others content to live lives of quieter desperation, these fortunate ones have allowed themselves to be thrown to the wall. They have come to a choice-point in which they must risk either change or disaster. It is not uncommon for the men and women who enter my office to present themselves initially as victims, but I see them as just the opposite. In the core of their dissatisfaction, their refusal to "adjust," lie unrecognized seeds of resistance. Angry, lonely, bruised, addicted, they carry within themselves intimations of passion once possessed, like clouds of glory, no matter how dimly recalled. And they share this in common—they want it back.

It is time to recognize that patriarchy does damage not just to girls and women but also to boys and men, that the psychological violence leveled against our children does harm to each sex and renders sustained, truthful connection between the sexes virtually impossible. It is time for men to come in from the cold. And for a generation of women, who have labored so mightily to reclaim their power, to now bring their full selves back into relationship with their lovers and husbands. Men and women will not completely love one another until both recover the state of integrity in which they began their lives. From there, each must proceed to hone and nurture qualities and skills that may well have stopped growing from the age of three, four, or five. The cultivation of our nascent relational skills is the kind of help all of us as children deserve but few of us receive. Instead, girls are taught to submerge their own needs in the service of others, while boys are taught to ignore their own and anyone else's needs in the service of the great god, achievement.

A generation ago, women across the West united in an unparalleled collective movement to support one another in reclaiming the half of their humanity—assertion, public competence, independence—that patriarchy denied them. Now, empowered, they are insisting on levels of relational skill from their spouses that men have in no way been prepared to deliver. They are also concerned for their sons—desperately wishing for means to help keep them intact, and yet mistrustful of their own influence.

It is men's turn to recapture that half of our humanity—receptivity, emotional expressiveness, dependency—that has been denied to us. But the reclamation of wholeness is a process even more fraught for men than it has been for women, more difficult, and more profoundly threatening to the culture at large. The work of relational recovery does not say "Men are intrinsically this, and women are intrinsically that, so therefore one should learn to accept or accommodate . . ." It says, "Most of what you have learned about being a man, being a woman, being in love, is wrong. Throw it out! Go back to the beginning! Turn your ear to a deeper, younger, voice that has never left you . . . and learn."

CHAPTER ONE

Love on the Ropes:
Men and Women in Crisis

Women marry men hoping they will change. They don't.
Men marry women hoping they won't change. They do.
—BETTIN ARNDT

"I've always felt our relationship was a threesome," says Steve Conroy, crossing thin legs sheathed in worsted wool, black socks reaching not quite high enough, cordovan loafers with tassels. His style is pure Beacon Hill, his voice soft, modulated. "Our little ménage à trois has consisted of me, Mag, and Maggie's misery."

"Oh, *nice*, Steve," Maggie snorts, on cue. Short, blond, muscular, she seems coiled for action.

Steve stares down at his hands folded together in helplessness; his forehead puckers with concern.

My wife, Belinda, also a family therapist, has a saying: "Beware of 'nice' men with 'bitchy' wives."

"Her misery?" I pursue.

Steve nods, ruefully. "It's rare to see my wife happy."

"It's rare to see her happy with *you*, maybe." Maggie takes the bait.

"Asshole," I finish for her.

"Pardon me?" Maggie turns to me, flushed.

" 'It's rare to see me happy with *you*, maybe, asshole,' " I paraphrase.

Maggie pulls her head back a few inches, as if smelling something disagreeable. "I never said that," she tells me softly.

I nod, turning to Steve. "Is she always this easy?"

"I'm not sure I take your meaning . . ."

"This goad-able?"

"Look." The concerned frown reappears. "I have no interest here in . . ."

I take a breath, regroup. The covert hostility flying around the room is getting to me. When I ask Steve how his wife's "misery" manifests itself, he hesitates, and, studying him for a moment, I sense that his reluctance is more than a move in their game. He really is afraid of her. On the other side, Steve's negative image of Maggie traps her like tarpaper. The more violently she protests, the more he stands confirmed as the victim of her irrationality. For eighteen years, Steve has managed to outflank his wife like this. Enormously successful in the world, ever reasonable at home, often beleaguered by his wife's high emotions, steadfast, patient Steve has only one problem—Maggie wants to leave him.

"I love Steve," Maggie declares. "I'll always love him. But not in the way I need to, not anymore," she trails off, seeming more worn out than angry.

Steve has no idea why his wife wants to quit their marriage, even though—watching from the outside—I can recognize their troubled dance within a few minutes of our first encounter.

"I just don't feel connected," Maggie tries to explain. "I used to fight it. Years ago. I'd try to talk. I'd arrange little dinners. I'd beg Steve to open up . . ."

"You'd throw things," Steve adds helpfully.

Maggie looks at Steve sideways and then sighs. "Sometimes I'd be measured, sometimes I'd be wild," she says, like a nursery rhyme. "Sometimes I'd be seductive, sometimes I'd be cold."

"There was a little girl who had a little curl," I chime in.

"Yes, but then one day the little *woman* looked at herself in the mirror and came to a big realization."

"Which was?" I ask.

Maggie leans toward me in her chair and confides in a stage whisper, "*It doesn't matter.* It doesn't matter *what* I do. With Steve, what you see is what you get. This is as open as my husband is going to become." She leans back again. "I don't know what I am to Steve. I don't know *who* he thinks he needs to ward off. To be honest, at this point, I don't care. I'm just tired of it, whatever it is. All right, Doctor?"

"Call me Terry."

"You win, Steve." She pushes right through me. "Here's the white flag, okay? 'Uncle.' I surrender. I'm a bitch, okay? I admit it. There. Can we all go home now?"

I raise an eyebrow toward Steve.

"What am *I* supposed to do?" he complains. "Forgive me if I don't feel quite as vile as her portrait suggests. For years now Maggie has complained that I am 'shut down.' But, frankly, I just don't buy it. Actually," Steve says, crossing his legs, "for a guy, I think I'm pretty romantic."

Maggie laughs.

"You want to put that into words?" I ask her.

"By romantic . . ." Maggie looks at her husband. "Steve means flowers and music whenever he feels like having sex."

"You know, that really is unfair . . ." Steve begins.

"Anyway, what's wrong with that?" I ask Maggie, heading him off.

"Nothing," she says, "as long as it doesn't take the place of other ways to be close."

"Like?" I prompt.

Maggie's eyes dart over the room, anywhere but at Steve. "Like *listening* to me!" she says.

"But Maggie," Steve whines, "once again, you simply don't . . ."

"Like," I ask Maggie, "as in now, for example?"

"Now, just hold on a second." Steve's voice rises.

"Is this how it is at home?" I ask her, ignoring him. "How it's been?"

Maggie's head drops; she nods. I can't tell if she's crying.

Finally, Steve's reasonableness cracks. "Do I get to speak here?"

He vibrates with indignation, hands outstretched, warding off the two of us. "Do *I* have a voice?"

"Not yet," I answer softly, trying to catch Maggie's eye. "So," I continue, "this is how it is?" She nods, beginning to cry while Steve fumes.

"If I push him," she says, her voice small, "which I don't anymore."

"How long?" I ask. Steve impatiently shifts in his chair.

"Steve," I say, an aside. "I can be nice to you right now, or I can do my best to salvage your marriage. What's your preference?"

He opens his mouth, shuts it, and then waves me on.

"How long?" I resume, turning to Maggie.

"How long has he been treating me like this?" she asks.

"How long since you gave up?"

"Years." Maggie begins to cry in earnest. "Years."

I lean back, sobered, sad. "I'm sorry," I tell them both. "I'm sorry you've had to go through this." Maggie cries harder. Steve looks to the side, upset as well. "And you tried therapy?" I ask.

"Yes." Maggie nods vigorously. "Twice, no, three times, really. But . . ."

"But no one took him on." I finish the sentence for her. She nods.

I lean toward her. "And if I do, Maggie?" I ask. "If Steve changes? I mean really changes. Are you even open to it at this point, or is it a forgone conclusion that—"

"No!" Maggie wails. "I *want* this to work. I *want* to love him. Three children, eighteen years!" She folds in, crying hard, angry and hurt. "Don't you think I've *tried?*"

"Okay," I soothe. "Okay, Maggie. I've got it. Breathe a little. I've got it."

Now Steve charges in, furious, oblivious to his wife's tears. "She asks me to cut back on my work. I say, 'Okay, I will.' And I do. She wants me to be more involved with the kids. I don't turn around like a lot of—"

"Steve," I interrupt, speaking gently. "Are you aware of your wife crying a few inches next to you?"

"Of course I'm aware," he blusters, offended. "And you accuse me of condescension! What kind of cretin do you take me for? I *do* respond to my wife. That's precisely the point. I work hard. I tend to our children—"

"That's all to the good," I stop him. "It really is. I am not being glib about that. But it just doesn't seem to be good enough, Steve. I'm sorry. I believe you are trying, trying hard in fact. But it's just not the fundamental thing."

"What I'm attempting to say . . ." Steve tries plowing on.

"The fundamental thing," I continue, "is that, real or imagined, your wife experiences you as someone who, though you don't mean her harm, is nevertheless in day-to-day life simply too selfish and in your own way too controlling to live with."

Steve stops short. "I can't believe this!" he says, his voice a whisper. "You don't even *know* me."

"Do you think I'm wrong?" I ask him. "*Do* you? Watch this." Steve is speechless. I turn to Maggie, "Am I?"

She shakes her head vehemently.

"Then maybe you'd better tell him yourself."

"Steve," she says turning to him. "My darling. Idiot! I've *been* telling you. I've used those very words—for years!"

Steve contemplates us both for a long moment, eyes squinting as if in bright light. Then, to my surprise, he suddenly smiles. A shrewd businessman, Steve is, in fact, nobody's fool. He knows, for example, when he's been had. I notice he stands in possession of a truly disarming grin. What causes him to back down now? Because he has correctly assessed that within minutes I have gained access to something he has been living without and very much wants—Maggie's goodwill.

"Nice smile," I say, breathing again. "So, what are you feeling?"

"Like I've just lost controlling interest of the board." His smile broadens.

"And how is that for you?" I ask.

"Well, I guess we'll just have to see, won't we?" he replies. We let that one sit between us for a while. "So now what?" Steve breaks the silence. "What do I need to do?"

I find myself matching his smile with one of my own. "Now,

that's the most refreshing question I've heard so far today," I answer. "So, listen. I have good news and bad news. Which do you want first?"

"Oh, you decide," he offers magnanimously, the tension between us dissipating.

"What happened to all that anger just a moment ago?" I ask.

Steve grins again. "Well," he says, "sizing things up, I suppose I decided that it was just . . . too irrational. You were giving me some news?" he prompts.

"Fine," I answer. "Here's how it is. The good news is that I think I can help you, if you're willing to do the work. Unless there's some curveball I don't know about, my guess is we have a fair shot at turning this around."

"And?"

"The bad news is that you have to do what I tell you."

"Which bridge will I need to dive off of?"

"None, most likely. I think you'll find most of what I coach you to do eminently reasonable. But it may be uncomfortable a little, Steve. Maybe even uncomfortable a lot."

"Hey, I'm a captured market," he says. "Bring it on."

"Are you sure?" I ask.

"Yes," he answers simply, seriously.

Now it is my turn to contemplate him for a moment. "Why?" I ask.

"Eighteen years," Steve replies without a pause. "My family, my home. You don't think I care about that?"

"And Maggie?" I ask.

"Sure Maggie," he says. "Of course Maggie."

"What about her?"

Steve turns to his wife, as she burrows and cries. For the first time in the session, he seems really to look at her. As he answers, his gaze finally matches the softness of his voice. "Maggie's the woman I love," he tells me, eyes shining.

She looks up at him.

"And those tears in your eyes, Steve," I amplify. "If they could speak, what would they say to her?"

"That she's the most important person in the world," he tells me, softer than ever, unable to say it to her directly. "I don't want to lose her."

I offer him my hand. "Good work," I tell him.

"But this isn't that different . . . ," he starts.

I put a finger to my lips and he stills. "This is a nice moment," I tell him. "Let it be."

Maggie was right about Steve. Even though he had no idea what she was trying to tell him, and had no conscious malevolence, nevertheless, Steve would eventually push any partner to the brink his wife now stood upon. And, while some other wife might have gone down quietly instead of swinging, like Maggie, sooner or later, most women would have gone down. And with them, the marriage, the real marriage, their passion, no matter if the conjugal shell remained intact or imploded, as it was about to do here. And the saddest part of it all was how much Steve really did love her, not even "deep down," but all the way through. Maggie knew her husband loved her, suspected how devastated he would be if she left. But she could no longer feel his love. He would not let her. Their marriage was like a beautiful garden Steve adored but rarely tended. Their enemy was not blatant violence, other women, or alcohol. Their enemy was simple rot.

The medieval alchemists said, "To make gold, one must first have a drop of gold." Within minutes of our initial session, Steve and Maggie were able to shift from helpless recrimination to a shared moment of tenderness. Fragile, fleeting, as dependent upon the therapy as someone on a respirator, their capacity to touch and be touched had survived, buried perhaps, but not extinguished. The sheen in Steve's eyes as he professed his love, and the way Maggie's body relaxed when she heard it—these were the drops of gold I was looking for. I call this process "moving the couple back into connection." No one could predict the fate of their marriage, but these early signs augured well. There is another old saying, "Hope is the remembrance of the future." Steve and Maggie had it in them to remember a future, their love, at least for an instant. If they could do that, then the odds were that with hard work, they could remember it for an hour or two, perhaps a whole day. This is how couples heal, building up from such small instances of recovery. Finding these moments, sometimes creating them—through teaching, encouraging, exhorting—is the essence of my job. In the trenches with Maggie and Steve I have one paramount question: How can I help them recover? But, after twenty years as a couple's therapist, after meeting hundreds of pairs who struggle like Maggie and Steve, a broader question presents itself. What is it exactly that must be recovered, and how did it come to be lost to begin with?

Like most couples I see, Maggie and Steve did not start off in such disrepair. Quite the contrary, their earliest days were spent in that marvelous state of joy called "falling in love." "The first time I saw Maggie," Steve tells me in one session, "I thought I was looking at a thousand-watt chandelier. I mean, look at her. Does she light up a room or what?"

"You sure haven't been treating her like a thousand-watt chandelier lately," I observe.

"No." He looks down, sheepish. "No, I guess not."

"I loved Steve's energy, I just *loved* it," Maggie says in another session, glancing fondly at him. "He literally swept me off my feet. Right into the dustbin."

The answer to the question "What must Maggie and Steve recover?" is simple—their love. They each still love one another inside, but in the wear and tear of everyday life, that crucial emotion is rapidly becoming too bruised to be of much use to them. Maggie might still love Steve even on the day she files for divorce; she just won't love him enough to live with him any longer. Were that day to arrive, Steve would probably feel, like so many of the men I treat, confused, angry, and betrayed.

In his relationship to Maggie, Steve reminds me of an ancient Sumerian poet who once complained to his gods, "I would gladly do what it is you require of me—if only I knew what it was!" And Maggie brings to mind the angry wife in a *New Yorker* cartoon who exclaims to her puzzled husband in front of their marriage counselor, "Of *course* you don't know why we're here. *That's* why we're here!"

"He doesn't *get* it!" cries Maggie. "What does she *want* from me?" complains Steve. Their essential lines are so familiar, so quintessentially male and female, it is all I can do not to smile, until I recall how high the stakes are; their marriage, three children.

One of the few stable statistics in our fast-changing world is our rate of divorce, which has hovered between 40 and 50 percent for the last thirty years. Any two people who marry face a grim 50 to 60 percent chance of survival. And if that weren't sobering enough, one needs to ask further: Of those who remain together, how many do so happily, as opposed to those who stay for external reasons, like their children, finances, religion, or fatigue? Conservatively, we can estimate that at least one out of three, perhaps one out of two, of those couples left standing do not relish their lives together. Maggie, Steve, and their children are real people, not emblems. But variations of their story play themselves out every day in homes across the West, crossing ethnic and economic lines.

These are hard times for lovers, and beyond that, for relations between men and women in general. No matter if one looks at the confusion and bitterness triggered by issues of sexual harassment, the anger of many divorced fathers at the court's handling of custody, the backlash against the women's movement, or the debacle of Bill Clinton's affairs and their aftermath—we are surrounded by indications, at both the individual and at the social level, that the connection between men and women has rarely been so full of tension, even bitterness. Something has gone awry.

Maggie has some keen observations on the state of male/female relations in the person of a limited but well-observed sample—her husband. She perches at the edge of her seat, in one session, impatiently flipping the bangs of her pageboy away from her eyes. "You want me to give you a clear, concise example of why I cannot tolerate living with this man?" she offers.

"Sounds good," I tell her, thinking, Pert, I'll bet that's what they used to call her. Pert. But she hardly looks pert any longer; "grimly determined" would be more appropriate. Maggie gathers her thoughts for a moment, and then smirks, an appealing trace of malice in the lines of her smile.

"So, here's the scene." She starts warming to the exercise. "Steve has been gone for three days on a business trip, and he's due to leave again the next morning. I've had a tough week at the bank myself. I'm officially part of their accounting department and it's heading toward tax time—not our favorite season. Plus . . ." she smiles, "I've had the kids. Steve comes bounding in looking like Tigger—before they put Tigger on Ritalin, that is. You know, like, 'Hi, honey, I'm home! Let heaven and nature sing!' Meanwhile, I'm on the phone with this other mom trying to arrange a play-date for Suzie. I'm spoon-feeding oatmeal into little Mariana. Billy sees his dad and crashes over a chair running to him. All hell breaks loose. I have been trying to reach this other mom for three days solid, and we're now *this* close to settling plans. So, I give Steve a look like, 'Could you *please* just deal with the kids for a second while I finish this?' And you know what?"

"He doesn't?" I offer obediently.

"Right you are." Maggie smiles. "Steve does *not* help out. Steve does *not* let me finish. What Steve does is he gives Billy a perfunctory pat on the head and he begins reeling off a list of the things *I* need to attend to . . ."

"*We* need," Steve protests, but Maggie is on a roll, and brooks no interruptions.

"I give him a look," she continues, "that says, 'Steve, *please!*' But our Steve gives me a look right back, don't you?" She nods to her husband. "A look I have seen quite a few times before. A look that manages somehow to be very much bigger and very much darker and a whole lot more scary than mine could ever be."

"Oh, I don't know about that," Steve begins, and quickly stops on the blunt end of a glare from his wife.

"And so," Maggie goes on, "I excuse myself, nicely, abruptly. I piss off my friend. I hang up the phone. I stare up at my husband, and his scary look that starts to seem downright pathetic, and then I just sort of collapse inside, like someone just kicked out the backs of my knees. I find myself with my cheek down in a cold pile of oatmeal on the table top, banging my hand wrapped around some grimy little spoon, saying, 'Steve. Steve! You win, honey. Okay! You have my full, my un*fucking*divided attention.' And my husband looks at me like, "What the hell?' And, in a way, I don't blame him, really. And yet there is another part of me that looks up at his bewildered, pissed-off, doughy little face and thinks, 'I will *never* love you again, Steven. I will *never, ever* in one *million* years feel the way I used to again.' And if he had reached out to touch me at that moment, I swear I could just as easily—"

"Okay, Maggie. I think we get it." I turn to Steve. "And what did you do?"

Steve assumes his usual stance, "What could I do? I mean—"

"We'll talk about what you could have done in a minute. Right now the question is what did you do."

"Well, I got mad, I guess." Steve sulks.

"You pouted," I infer from his present reaction.

"Words passed between us," he allows.

Words passed, I think to myself. What a bland little phrase that is. Steve tells me he'd spoken a few "words" to Maggie, who evidently spoke a few "words" right back. Then, as had become their custom, they gave one another a wide berth for the rest of the evening. Later that night, unbeknownst to either, each lay awake on the far side of the bed, too hurt and angry to sleep, too defeated to talk, thinking of how it once had been between them, imagining other lovers.

Steve and Maggie are not bad people. They are great parents; they know how to have friends, be good neighbors. How can they manage so well in every relationship except the one that matters the most? Is there some natural law of marital entropy? Some ubiquitous centripetal force pulling decent people away from one another? Of the thousands of statistics about marriage churned out by social research each year, the one I find most depressing is that in all couples, rich and poor, happy and unhappy, one of the most reliable predictors of marital dissatisfaction is simple longevity. The longer couples live together, the lower their reported contentment.

"Our souls are love," wrote Yeats, "and a continual farewell." Or

as Maggie described it once in more ordinary terms, "My feelings
for Steve are like a balloon that's been leaking air for years. I don't
hate my husband anymore. I did for a while. But I don't even have
that much left in me. I'm just out of air."

Our cultural upbringing has not left us so ill equipped that we are
prevented from falling in love. But a great many of us emerge as
adults unprepared for the task of *staying in love*. I know that was true
for me. After spending years as both a patient and a therapist, learning to heal deep internal wounds, I found myself wanting to embrace
intimacy and yet thoroughly ignorant about how one goes about it.
Just as I went into the field of psychotherapy in order to restore my
damaged self, I moved toward a specialty in couple's therapy to learn
how people relate to one another. From the vantage point of twenty
years' hindsight, I no longer feel ashamed of my deficiencies, any
more than my own patients should. "Where were you supposed to
have learned relational skills?" I ask a guy like Steve, or myself
twenty years ago. "The culture at large has little wisdom to offer, and
your dysfunctional family wasn't going to give you the help you
needed either."

The problem for contemporary men and women is that whether or
not we possess good relationship skills, they seem suddenly required.
In part, the current crisis can be traced to a relatively new expectation that marriage afford emotional closeness. Throughout most of
Western history, marriage was prized for providing stability, not intimacy. Nobles joined in matrimony for political gain, commoners for
support in their demanding lives. Many marriages were arranged.
People spoke of husbands and wives almost exclusively in terms of
their roles—someone to help with the cooking and cleaning, raise the
children, manage the farm. The cosmos with God at their head, the
state with the king as its ruler, and the family with the man as its chief
all echoed the same patriarchal order. Demands for connection, passion, emotional support would have been seen by most as irrelevant,
even indulgent. Such observations are well-trodden ground. What
may come as a bit of a surprise, however, is the realization that for a
great many people such a pragmatic view of marriage remained

relatively unchanged from the time of the Middle Ages to just a generation ago. We might even say that the current crisis in marriage begins precisely with that vision's demise.

"Yes, I was annoyed," admits Steve, "when Maggie wouldn't hang up the phone."

"Annoyed?" I push a little.

"All right, more than annoyed. I mean, you work hard. You've been in hotel rooms . . ."

"Say, 'I,'" I tell Steve.

"Huh?"

"Listen, here's the first little trick. Don't say, '*You* sleep in hotel rooms . . .' I haven't been in hotel rooms lately, you have. Say, 'I.'"

"Ugh," Steve grunts, inspecting me for a moment, as if to say, "For *this* I'm paying good money?" But he does what I ask of him.

"*I*," he emphasizes, "have been in hotel rooms, sweating it out. Meetings, presentations. Nothing ungodly, let's be clear, you just . . . *I* just miss my wife and kids. I think of them all the way back on the plane. I imagine how it will be when I get home."

"Not quite the greeting you had in mind." I can see his point. "Home is the sailor, home from the sea," I think to myself. Odysseus returns to faithful Penelope. "The husband/father unit has returned," quips a middle-aged everyman in another *New Yorker* cartoon, "ready for interaction!"

When Steve bounds in, slaps down his valise, and opens his arms in the expectation of immediate deference and attention, he behaves no differently than his father might have, or his father's father before him. If Maggie's mother had tried to explain to one of her contemporaries that she was leaving her husband over such trifling behavior, she would have been seen as wildly immature, perhaps a touch mad. But Steve's "chronic selfishness, insensitivity, and control" now stand a hairsbreadth away from costing him his marriage. The first thing to notice about the current crisis is that it is not triggered because of changes in the man, nor even changes in both of them. *The crisis starts with Maggie.* It is women who buy magazines with headlines that promise "Ten things to do to keep your marriage hot." It is women who fuel the self-help industry. And it is women, by and large, who end their marriages. In fact, over 70 percent of divorces are initiated by wives. Most men, like Steve, are not dissatisfied with the status quo, and they are not dreadfully unhappy in their marriages; *they are unhappy with their wives' unhappiness.* If their partners could just ease their complaints, most men tell me, they'd be fine. Wives like Maggie, by contrast, often live in a state of chronic resentment. How did men and women's experience of marriage become so divergent? My first therapeutic "intervention" with Maggie and Steve is a history lesson.

Since the coming of urbanization, gender roles have been rigidly defined as man-the-breadwinner and woman-the-caretaker. The family's social and economic status derived exclusively from the male, while women and children siphoned off and fulfilled most psychological demands. Women's participation in the workforce, changing economic resources, and thirty years of feminism have forever changed that landscape. A generation ago, a man like Steve would have pulled into the driveway exhausted after work, kicked off his shoes, picked up the paper, and "relaxed." Nowadays, his tired spouse pulls into the driveway right behind him. Both need care and support; each would do well with a traditional wife, though neither has it in them to be one. As women move into the public domain, a demand naturally arises for men to carry more weight, both logistically and psychologically, in the domestic arena. The problem is that while many men try, for now at least, the majority simply does not know how. Vague pronouncements and headlines in the news about men and women's "changing roles" do not quite tell the whole tale. While the old roles may be changing, they are not changing gracefully, and they are not changing at equal rates for both sexes. One reason for the current crisis in gender relations is simply that in the last thirty years, *women's roles have radically transformed while men's have not.* Society—including the field of psychotherapy—has yet to deal with the ramifications of this asymmetry. The crunch goes well beyond issues of who does the dishes. In the story Maggie tells, she does want Steve to put his needs aside and help her with the children. But, more than that, Maggie wants Steve to "read" her emotionally, to look beyond himself to the needs of those around him. In other sessions,

Maggie augments these requests with the wish that Steve "share who he is inside, what he's feeling," an invitation sure to send many men psychologically heading for the hills. I ask Steve, "So, what are the five most dreaded words in any man's life?"

"Okay, I'll bite," he answers.

"Honey, we have to talk," I say.

"Sorry." Maggie won't be put off. "Call me a demanding witch if you need to, but I need more from my marriage than just, 'Hi, dear. How was your day?' "

Sensitivity to others, the capacity to identify and share his feelings, a willingness to put his needs aside in the service of the family, these are the qualities Maggie wants from Steve. *In short, Maggie needs her husband to respond more like a traditional woman.* She is far from alone. Women across the West are rightly insisting that men step into levels of familial involvement, of sensitivity and responsibility, that were unheard of a generation ago. The problem is that when Steve claims not to grasp what Maggie wants of him, he is telling the truth. Empathy, sensitivity, knowing what he feels and wants, speaking with a vulnerable heart, even introspection itself—these skills belong to a world Steve left behind a long time ago. They are the very "feminine" qualities that most boys, even in these enlightened times, have had stamped out of them. In our culture, boys and men are not now, nor have they ever been, raised to be intimate. They are raised to be competitive performers.

Women's insistence upon a level of emotional competence from their partners that men are ill equipped to meet places both wives and husbands in complementary double binds—catch-22s which not only fail to make things better but most often ensure that things will get worse. The problem for women is this: since their expectations for closeness often exceed their partner's level of skill, or even desire, the chances are good that if a wife does not teach her partner how she wants to be treated, over time she will not like the treatment she receives. On the other hand, if she speaks out, the chances are good that she will be seen as a stereotypically "bad" woman—demanding, nagging, complaining.

"As far as I'm concerned, we're here now," Maggie tells us one session, "because years ago Steve withdrew, and the deal for me was that if I didn't go after him, I didn't get him. On the other hand, if I complained, or demanded more, I still didn't get him, only now it was my own fault because I was a bitch."

The bind for a man like Steve is that while he may be too "politically correct" to say it aloud, he has little patience for wifely instructions on shaping up, although, if he did have ears to hear, Maggie would prove worth listening to. In order to comprehend what Maggie wants of him, Steve would require the very relational qualities and skills—receptivity, flexibility, empathy—that she needs to teach him about. Developmentally, he can't get out of the starting gate without being near the finish line.

This difficult knot for both men and women stems from a profound asymmetry in their interpersonal abilities. While both genders are relationally wounded, and both need to heal, *their injuries are not equal.* By raising girls to know more about and want more from their relationships, we set up adult women to be either unfulfilled or "overfunctioning," or, as is most often the case, both at the same time. By raising boys to know less about and want less from their relationships, we set up men to feel beleaguered and unappreciated. Fair or unfair, the political reality of family life means that Maggie is in no real position to be her husband's relational coach, while Steve stands in desperate need of some coaching. If they could work out this conundrum on their own, they would have by now. *Steve and Maggie need help from without.* And this is precisely where conventional therapy fails them. Conventional therapy does not give men and women the tools they need to work through this difficult time of transition, because most therapy retreats from acknowledging that such a critical difference in men and women's relational desires and abilities even exists. The silence about this disparity in intimacy skills amounts to a whitewash, one that reminds me of the whitewash about the issue of male depression I wrote about in my previous book. By ignoring that we traditionally raise girls to focus their energies on maintaining connection while we raise boys to focus on achievement, by acting as if both genders come to marriage—or marriage counseling—equally motivated and equally competent, psychology has shied away from addressing the "dead elephant sitting in the middle of the room," the unnamed truth that lies at the heart of current marital dissatisfaction. *Women are unhappy in their marriages because they want men to be more related than most men know how to be. And men are unhappy in their marriages because their women seem so unhappy with them.* Any therapy, psychological theory, or self-help model that does not deal with this central impasse will miss the boat, failing women like Maggie, and consequently, men like Steve as well.

CHAPTER TWO

Echo Speaks:
Empowering the Woman

When I assert that women are more relationally skilled than most of their mates, I am not claiming that women enjoy a state of good relational health—they do not. I maintain only that many women are less damaged than their male partners. Neither men nor women pass through the gauntlet of socialization unscathed. Our culture teaches neither boys nor girls how to have a healthy relationship with themselves or with others. It is axiomatic that one cannot sustain intimacy without the capacity for self-esteem. But a consistent ability to cherish the self is a rare commodity in our society. Real self-esteem comes from within; it is the existential, spiritual truth that we have value and worth intrinsically, because we are here and breathing, not because of anything we have or can do, nor how others regard us. Traditional socialization teaches girls to filter their sense of self-worth through connection to others, often at great cost to themselves, while it teaches boys to filter their sense of self-worth through their performance. Neither sex learns about true intimacy. This patriarchal arrangement is epitomized in the Greek myth of Narcissus and Echo. Narcissus, a cold-hearted, beautiful youth, falls in love with no one, though many are entranced by him. The great goddess Hera hears the complaints of her love-struck nymphs and decides to punish the young man for his pride. One day while out hunting, Narcissus stumbles upon an enchanted well where he gazes upon the most seductive face he has ever laid eyes upon. Immediately smitten, he reaches out for the glorious nymph whom he imagines lives in the well. Each time he grasps for it, the beautiful image dissolves. Even his sighs cause his lover's retreat. Unable to sleep, eat, or withdraw, he pines, frozen to the spot, until he dies of thirst and hunger. But Narcissus is not alone. There is, indeed, a nymph present, though she is not in the well. The wood nymph Echo suffered a horrifying transfiguration of her own when she had the misfortune of meeting Hera while the goddess's husband, the great Zeus, dallied with Echo's sisters and friends in the forest. Knowing how wrathful Hera would be if she discovered her husband and his lovers, Echo deliberately detained Hera with empty words and pleasant chatter. In that moment, Echo chose loyalty to the father over the mother, protecting Zeus, the ultimate patriarch, by lying. The consequence of her choice is swift and apt. Hera deprives Echo of her voice—almost. Echo can speak, but only for others. She can make sounds, even words, but none of her own.

Narcissus is an emblem of disconnection. Unable to requite love before Hera's curse, he becomes addicted to false love ever after. He stands rooted over the well not because he has too much self-love but because he has far too little. It is not his self he is bewitched by, but his image. Narcissus at the well stands for any man more in love with his accolades, his performance, his stock options, than his own being. But if Narcissus is merely the reflection of a whole human being, Echo is the reflection of his reflection. Enamored by the young man, yet unable to speak, Echo pines for Narcissus, just as he pines for his own shadow. Each time he sighs, she sighs. "If only you could come here!" Narcissus laments to the beautiful boy. "Here! Here!" behind him Echo urgently, futilely calls.

Maggie Conroy had spent most of her life under Hera's curse. Like many wives of her generation, she had reached out longingly toward her husband's back, while he huddled over the pool of his ambition. "Somewhere in the early years of our marriage," Maggie tells me in one session. "I felt that Steve made a unilateral, irreversible decision that his career came first, over and above the family, and over and above his relationship to me. My career didn't even blip on his screen. He was always a great father to the children, when he was with us. But there just wasn't enough of him to go around. Not just physically, but energy-wise, emotionally. I tried to fight it. I really tried. But it just seemed to make things worse."

As Steve experienced it, mostly what Maggie meant by "trying" was complaint. "I don't think I was aware of it," he confesses, "but it starts to feel easier to stay at work than to come home when you know . . . when I know," he corrects, "that what I'm in for is a ration of bullshit."

But Maggie resents Steve's portrait. "I tried every which way but Sunday, Steven," she protests. "Sure, I complained. But I also tried to be nice. Candlelight dinners. 'Let's go out.' "

"I think I stopped wanting to be alone with you because I was afraid that . . ."

"So, what am I supposed to do with *that?*" Maggie scornfully cuts him short. "Go hang myself?"

"Hey, look," Steve answers, spreading his hands, angry. "You say you want to hear my feelings. I'm just trying to tell you how I felt."

"Well, fine. Thanks, but I mean, really," Maggie says, "if I dare to tell *you* how I feel, I'm a complainer, and even if I'm nice to you, you have to avoid me because I *might* complain?"

On this point, I am on Maggie's side. "As I see it," I tell her, "where you went wrong wasn't in speaking out, but in not speaking out enough."

"Oh, great," she snorts. "Take the teetering car and push it all the way over the cliff."

"Here's the moment," I go on, "where it seems to all head south. In that scene you shared before, when you're on the phone and Steve comes in from his business trip expecting to be catered to?" She nods, wary of where I may be heading. "You're clear as a bell that you wanted to finish that conversation with the other mom."

"Yes," she says.

"But you allowed yourself to be intimidated. You said—"

"I remember what I said, Terry."

"That dark look on his face—"

"What about it?"

"That's my question to you. What about it made you put your own needs aside?"

"Like, what was I afraid he'd do?" she asks.

I nod.

"Well, it's not like he'd *beat* me or anything," she says.

"So, what was it?" I press.

Maggie crosses her legs and fidgets with her foot. "Jesus," she says. "I don't know. Haven't you ever lived with somebody? It depends on the day, his mood, whether his boss pissed him off or not. One day, it wouldn't mean anything, another day, there might be yelling, or stomping around . . ."

"He'd stomp around?" I pursue.

"Well, " she corrects, "Steve isn't usually all that obvious, you know. That's more me. What Steve does is what I call 'putting out a stink.' You know. Not talking to me, like for days? Being short with the kids. You just *know* how pissed off he is. Like we're all walking around with tension headaches and he hasn't said one nasty thing."

"You recognize yourself in any of this?" I ask Steve.

"Well," he equivocates, "in some aspects."

"Good," I push on, before he has a chance to recant. "So, Maggie," I confirm, "this is it? This is what you're afraid of?"

"Well, yeah," she answers.

"Well, it does sound pretty awful," I agree. "I guess the next question is what do *you* do?"

She frowns at me, incredulous, "What do *I* do? What do you mean, what do I do? I get off the damn phone is what I do. *Hello!* Isn't this where we came in? I do what Steven wants me to do!"

"And then hate him for it," I add softly.

She shakes her head, her eyes filling up. She points a finger at me, smiling while she tears. "I *knew* you were going to do this to me," she says. "Yes," she confesses after a pause. "Part of me has grown to hate him."

"And how do you make him pay, Maggie?"

"Oh, *please.*" She dismisses the question.

I won't be shaken off. "How does the anger come out?"

Maggie shakes her head, still crying soundlessly, too overcome, she conveys, to be bothered with my questions. Silently, I note her imperiousness but decide to choose my battles. Instead of pressing her further, I ask Steve, who affects not to understand what I'm talking about.

"I've always thought we've done pretty well together," he trots out, the soul of lucidity.

"Steve," I confront him. "Come on. Maggie's been angry for years. You look at her before you dare even open your mouth." He flushes, but I don't care. I have had it with his retreat into obliviousness. "Try again, Steve. How has your wife made you pay?"

"Well." He coughs, glancing at Maggie, stopping himself, then glancing at me to see if I noticed it.

"Why did you need to check her out, just now?" I ask him. "What are you afraid of?"

"Well." Steve pauses. "You know, maybe setting her off."

"Keep going."

"Getting her mad, you know." He smiles. "Maggie can raise a stink in her own right, let me tell you."

"Is this funny?" I push him.

"No." He loses the smile. "No, not at all."

"So, she gets mad," I continue. "Angry and silent, like you, you mean?"

"Well, no." Steve can't stop that winning smile. "No, Maggie's quite verbal at those times, let me assure you."

"And beside those extreme times," I ask, "payback in more ordinary ways?"

"I've always *thought* generally we've been fine . . ." Steve trails off. He tries winding up to deliver his accustomed obtuse routine, but he can't quite find the heart to follow through with it. Suddenly, Steve looks collapsed, pained.

"What are you feeling?" I ask him gently.

He starts something glib, and then thinks better of it. "Actually," he admits. "I'm feeling rather sad."

"About?"

"About all *this*," he says. "About how lonely I am, if you really want to know. I feel lonely just sitting here with the two of you."

"Now you're talking," I mutter.

"I feel lonely at home, to tell you the truth. One of the few places I don't feel lonely anymore is in the office."

"How's your sex life?" I help him.

"Fine," he says, clearing his throat. "When we have one. We haven't had much of one lately, of course . . ."

"Lately?"

"Well, a year, maybe two . . ."

"Maybe four," pipes in Maggie.

"How affectionate is she?" I press on.

"In general, you mean, or to me?"

I lean toward him. "How loved have you been feeling, Steve?"

He blinks at me and turns away from both of us, toward the wall. His hand moves up to his eyes. "I always cover my face when I cry," he says finally, still with his back to us. "Why do I do that?"

We sit together in silence.

"My father used to do it, too. The few times I ever saw him cry, which believe me . . ."

"What are you feeling, Steve?"

He pauses. "Just overwhelmed, I guess." He turns around and faces his wife. "I'm so sorry, Maggie. I really am sorry. I don't know how we got here. Look at us!" He smiles at her as she cries, gazing back at him. "A couple of . . ." Steve's words dry up.

"Sounds like you've missed your wife," I offer as they face one another.

"I wish we could go back," he tells her.

"To?" I ask.

"The way it once was," he answers.

"Not the way it was, Steven," Maggie says tenderly.

"I only meant . . ."

"The way it could be," she continues.

Maggie is right. Neither she nor Steve can ever go back. Nor can we as a culture. The genie of women's empowerment will not return to the bottle, and we wouldn't want it to. But if the conundrum for men like Steve is that they have not changed much from the role they were raised with, the dilemma for women like Maggie is that, while they may have changed profoundly, they still may not have changed enough. Maggie is far enough removed from the values and limitations of her mother's generation to want something different from her man, but, in dozens of small moments, like the incident on the telephone she described, Maggie remains too intimidated by Steve to command all that she wants. Like most contemporary women, Maggie is in an uneasy state of transition. A generation ago, a wife might not have felt so acutely the tension engendered by Steve's demands. His expectations that she drop her concerns and tend to him would have been the norm. On the other side, it may turn out that our daughters, or certainly their daughters, having been raised on feminism—whether they know it or not—might be less willing to allow themselves to be put off by a husband's "dark look." There are some encouraging signs to that effect in the younger couples I treat. But while younger women may be less easily backed away from their needs than their older counterparts, when pushed hard enough, the vast majority of the wives and girlfriends I encounter, whether in their twenties or fifties, will begrudgingly capitulate, at least for a time. They are caught, as Maggie was, between two mores of womanhood, the old and the new. Maggie is still enough under the sway of tradition to back down from the threat of Steve's wrath. But she has been sufficiently suffused with the new that she bitterly resents her subservience. The cost of her unwilling surrender is love. "I will *never* feel the way I once felt about you," she tells us she had thought in the moments after she gave in. Maggie's words fall on the ear like a pledge, as in some old melodrama—the last holdout of angry will against her experience of subjugation.

In her classic study *The Second Shift*, sociologist Arlie Hochschild interviewed full-time working couples about how they divided the housework and childcare. Across America, the men and women Hochschild questioned described a wide variety of arrangements, from quite traditional (the wife did it all) to egalitarian (a 50-50 split). When Hochschild sent in research teams with video cameras and stopwatches, however, she found that, despite the broad range in couples' self-reports, the truth was that in virtually all cases, working women performed the lion's share of housework—their "second shift." That the bulk of the domestic labor fell to wives intrigued Hochschild, but captivating her even more was the question of why these women, no less than their husbands, seemed to be in a state of denial about it. It doesn't take much to imagine why men might "selectively remember." But why the women as well? Reviewing her data, Hochschild arrived at a disturbing conclusion. What drove these women to minimize the imbalance in their domestic arrangements was the same force driving Maggie to back down to Steve—fear.

The wives Hochschild studied were neither hysterical nor paranoid. Some husbands, faced with a partner they experience as too angry, or too demanding, or just "too much" in a thousand small ways, will, just as women worry, simply back out, finding someone younger, prettier, and more compliant. And when husbands do leave, research indicates, their standard of living tends to rise slightly, while that of the woman and children can drop as much as an average of 60 percent. There is a stark political reality to women's silence.

Angela is a feisty, plain-speaking mother of four children who range in age from three to fifteen. Her husband, Bill, is a decent guy, mostly. He's a sensitive lover, a steady provider, and an alcoholic. Bill has always been moody when drinking, but as his consumption has increased over the years, so has the intensity of his meanness. Angela finds herself particularly worried about the effects of Bill's sarcasm on their children, but she's convinced that if she pushes her husband he will simply abandon her, taking his much-needed paycheck along with him. I suggest that she might attend Al-Anon, the AA group for spouses of alcoholics, but Angela roundly dismisses the idea.

"There are a lot of wise women across America who live with active drunks," I tell her, "and manage to make a life for themselves and their kids. It's a very tough road. But you wouldn't be the first or the last person to pick it. Al-Anon can help you with tools to manage. You can find some support there."

Angela sneers. "Support for what? I just want what's best for my children. Is Al-Anon going to teach me how to get Bill sober?"

"No, it can't," I say.

"Or be less mean?" I shake my head. "And when my husband storms off and my kids are on welfare, is Al-Anon going to find me a job?"

"I thought the idea was to not have Bill storm off," I say.

"Yeah, that's right. 'Cause I am not going to *deal* with him, that's why. But now, if I go off to some meeting where everybody's sitting around talking all day long about their situation, how they feel about this and that, you think that's gonna make it easier on me to go home and *not* deal with him? Is that what you're saying?" She shakes her head. "I need to go somewhere to learn how to see *less* of what's going on, not more."

I rub my eyes, feeling suddenly tired, stalling for something to say. "I guess the question, then, is why have you come here?" I finally get out. "I mean, how can I help you?"

"Damned if I know," she mutters.

We sit together in silence for a moment, heavy, inert. "See, I think you came here because you're in pain," I tell her. "I think you're lonely in your marriage. And you're worried about Bill. And it scares you to see him go after your kids."

"Yeah, that's all true," she says, sounding tired herself and frustrated with me. "But I'm even more scared at the thought of no food on my table, no man in my house, and my kids out on the corner with a bunch of young hoodlums."

I felt chastened by Angela's directness. Fancy middle-class shrink, what the hell did I presume to know about her life? I told her how I was feeling, adding that I'd be happy to talk from time to time, but it was hard to imagine a therapy which had as its goal helping her see *less* about herself and her situation. She thought that was pretty funny, and told me she'd enjoyed meeting me anyway, though I hadn't done her much good and I shouldn't expect to hear from her anytime soon. I didn't.

What changed Angela's mind, about five months later, was the death of her cat. Bill, drunk, couldn't get the irksome young pet out of his chair. And on his third angry swipe—despite Angela's protests and their kids' desperate wails—the chair toppled over, breaking the cat's spine. Bill was distraught at "the accident," though not enough to take responsibility for it. Angela didn't confront her husband, even then. But she did come back to see me, and she started going to Al-Anon. Just as she had predicted, talking about her husband's drinking did not make it easier for her to keep her mouth shut. She began speaking out and, then, also as she had foreseen, Bill answered with his feet. "He went out for that long pack of cigarettes. You know that one?" she asked me. "That *long* pack." The rest, however, turned out to be less grim than she had imagined. Angela got a job as a waitress at night. Neighbors and friends helped her with childcare, as did her oldest son, who proved more responsible than she had expected. And after close to three months on his own, Bill said he wanted to come back. Angela's first requirement was that he see me, and her second was AA and sobriety. Bill was no fool. He had had his few months of bingeing and was ready to stop. The son of an alcoholic, he belonged to a family riddled with addictions. One sister had died of an over-dose, several of his brothers were in recovery. At Angela's instigation, a core group of the sober men in Bill's family met with me for an ad hoc strategy session. Afterward, they sat down with Bill on their own for "a little conversation." Evidently, it helped.

"Angela can be a real pain in the ass," Bill confides in me during our first session. He looks with mock balefulness at his wife, who gazes down at the floor. "But I miss being home. And there's no real excuse for dragging my children through all this shit."

"Sounds like you know close up what it means to be the kid of an alcoholic," I suggest.

"Okay." He sighs hard. "I'll give it a chance." Looking at Angela, he addresses me. "Contrary to what some people may think, I *am* a good man."

"You're better than good when you're sober," Angela sniffs, still not looking at him.

"Yeah, well," he faces her. "We're working on it."

Six months have passed since that first meeting with Bill and, so far, he has remained sober; he has been the good man he wants to be. Angela and their children are proud of him. Will it last? "Damned if I know," Bill confessed the last time I saw him. And if he doesn't stay in recovery, will Bill find the strength to take the next step, which would probably mean rehab? Will Angela hold fast—both to her conviction and to their relationship? I have no idea. And I wouldn't trust anyone who pretended to. But I do know this: while the success of their marriage is uncertain if Angela, as she puts it, "deals," its failure seems guaranteed, over time, if she does not.

Angela and Maggie, though from radically different backgrounds, both face essentially the same choice. *"Explode or corrode"* is the expression I use with women clients. If a wife truly demands that her emotional needs be met, she may indeed put her marriage on the line. On the other hand, few women who back away from their needs manage to bury their resentment. Their unspoken anger spills out as occasional rage and everyday coolness. Feeling uncherished, many wives unwittingly shut down their own sense of pleasure, as well as their willingness to please their partners. And even if women try to accept and forgive, eventually passion drains away from the marriage along with their authenticity. It is impossible to maintain real connection and overaccommodate at the same time. Vitality mixes poorly with inauthenticity. I cannot tell you how many long-suffering women I have seen who, over the years, tolerated their husbands' verbal abuse, unilateral decisions, wholesale withdrawal—only to find themselves, in middle age, dumped for younger women anyway. So much for the rewards of patience! I do not mean to be glib about the agonizing dilemma inherent in these situations, and, truly, who can say what is right or wrong for another? But I do ask my clients to remember this: if there are dangers in speaking, there are also dangers in not speaking. Avoiding conflict may not be a safer choice in the long run, only a quieter one.

When Angela chooses inaction while her husband goes after their kids, when Maggie accommodates Steve and loathes it, each is reaping the bitter fruit of her childhood socialization as a girl. Research tells us that all human beings start off in what researcher Judith Bardwick once called "the relational/affiliative mode"—expressive, dependent, deeply embedded in the matrix of emotional connection to others. Pioneer researcher Carol Gilligan and a generation of writers following her have shown that in early adolescence, society thrusts upon girls the traditionally feminine mores of accommodation. The girls in Gilligan's study, who had for years shown themselves to be articulate, even astute, about one another's personalities and relationships suddenly, by ten to thirteen, seemed to render themselves dumb—in both senses of the word. To be a "popular girl," to be "likeable," "good," suddenly takes hold as a preeminent value. And "good" girls don't make waves. At the edge of adolescence our daughters fall under the "tyranny of the kind and nice." They learn the ideal, to paraphrase David Habersham, of "pretty, polite, and not too bright." "Girls," Gilligan writes, "lose relationship in the service of maintaining relationships." In her famous phrase, girls lose their "voice."

"If you ask an eight-year-old girl what she wants on her pizza," Catherine Steiner-Adair of the Harvard Eating Disorders Center once explained, "chances are she will tell you. 'I'll have extra cheese and peppers.' By the time that same girl reaches eleven or twelve, the answer becomes, 'I don't know.' And when you ask her at thirteen, what do you get? 'What would *you* like on the pizza?'"

There is a word for that transition from "Extra cheese and peppers" through "I don't know" to "What would *you* like?" The term is trauma. It is no coincidence that the loss of voice in early adolescence corresponds with the first outbreak of many mental-health problems—eating disorders, depression, significant drops in self-esteem. Clearly, adapting to the traditional role is not good for girls' emotional well-being.

In my work with women, I examine not just the impact of the loss of voice on the women themselves, but also on their relationships. By focusing primarily on the cost to the individual, the woman's movement has, thus far, paid little attention to some of the more troubling aspects of compliance with the traditional role.

As I work with men it has become clear to me that for the women's movement to gain credibility with both sexes, it must step down from earlier patterns of rhetoric I facetiously summarize as "Women are relational and men are rocks." When I claimed earlier that the traditional socialization of girls and boys does damage to both, I meant this: *You cannot speak of women as oppressed without speaking, then, of the consequences. You cannot say that women learn to be indirect without then saying that they learn to manipulate. You cannot say that they stop telling the truth without saying that they lie. Men know very well that women lie to them, manage them, and virtually every man I have ever spoken to feels some measure of mistrust and bitterness about it.* We will not heal the profound and abiding enmity between the sexes until we start naming the truth on all sides—including the truth about women's covert aggression. If we acknowledge women's disempowerment we must also reference their rage toward their subjugators, rage that, no matter how graciously disguised, in the close quarters of marital life, rarely misses its mark. Women maintain connection, but do they maintain *healthy* connection?

Quite often, if I'm speaking to a group, a guy in the back of the room stands up at this point to let me know about his "objections" to my claims. His remark usually sounds something like this: "Mr. Real. If you think women have been cowed into silence, I suggest you spend a few evenings over at my house! Docile is not the description that first comes to mind when describing my wife."

"Well, maybe you're just lucky," I might answer, "or maybe your wife fits into a common pattern." While it is true that some women, like Angela, do succeed in almost completely burying their needs and resentments, most of the wives and girlfriends I've seen over the years fit into the more common pattern of "stash and blow." That's a cycle wherein, after weeks of silence or mild sniping and coolness, one Thursday evening the man comes home an hour late, or he leaves the lid off the mayonnaise jar, and then four months of unspoken resentment comes flooding into the room. While a wife may have it in her to blow up from time to time, even to rage, there is a great difference between histrionics and clear, firm limits. Maggie "lost it" from time to time, but until therapy, she was unwilling to "mean it."

Men know the difference between blowing off steam and a real limit. Husbands are practiced in the art of battening down the hatches until their partner's "mood" passes over ("Must be that time of the month"). Men are adept at ducking below the wave of their wives' complaints, coming out the other side, and then going about whatever it was they had planned to do anyway. The therapist's job is to help the woman move from the position of "all bark but no bite" to one of "talk softly but carry a big stick." The issue isn't simply whether or not a woman speaks, but whether she speaks effectively. It is true that setting real limits initially throws the couple into an even greater crisis. But from a family therapy perspective, that is good.

One of the great paradoxes of intimacy is that in order to sustain passionate connection, one must be willing to "go to the mats" from time to time. Keeping relationships vital requires us to put them to the test periodically. "No" means "no." In a later session, as Angela tries out "this new woman-thing" as she calls it, Bill starts reeling off the limitations of his busy schedule, all the things she should not expect of him in the next few months. Angela stops listening, bending over instead to poke around on the floor, looking as though she were hallucinating.

"What the *hell* are you doing?" Bill finally notices.

"Looking for my bottom line," she replies.

There is a word for people who are completely incapable of setting limits. We call them slaves. And, in the long run, slaves rarely make for loving partners. As "diplomacy" replaces forthright conflict, as girls learn the rules of becoming "good women," many are taught to fear that even reasonable limits may not be tolerated, may incur abandonment. Such fears are by no means groundless. And yet, I tell wives like Maggie and Angela that they may have more power in their marriages than they might at first think. After all, Steve stayed, and Bill came back, even braving AA to do it. Despite all of their flaws and difficulties, these men don't want to walk out on their own lives, leave their wives and children. They want to come home.

CHAPTER THREE

Bringing Men in from the Cold

Show me the meaning of being lonely
Is this the feeling
I need to walk with
Tell me why I can't be there where you are
There's something missing in my heart.

—BACKSTREET BOYS

Here is the moment. A man and woman fall madly in love. Their connection is palpable. Anyone around them can feel it. At some point she turns to him saying some version of "Let's thoroughly give ourselves over to this." "Let's move in," she might say, or "Let's get married. Let's honor our extraordinary love," at which point the man turns to her and replies with some version of, "Now, what love are you referring to, exactly?"

How many women and men have at one point in their lives played out some rendering of this moment? She knows that what she has experienced is real. She knows he is lying, that he feels their closeness as surely as she does. But no amount of railing, crying, or screaming succeeds in getting him to admit it. He withdraws, leaving her feeling that she must be crazy.

Here is the moment. A young couple holds one another in bed, drifting, talking. It is obvious that they have just made love. She is sad because she'll be leaving the East Coast soon to go to California. She asks him to come with her. He declines. "But why?" she persists. "We love each other." He evades, burbling some nonsense. And then she asks the unspeakable question. Looking him in the eye she dares utter these words: "What are you afraid of?" Her name is Skylar and the scene is from the film *Good Will Hunting*.

Skylar is a young woman and her question would not have been so easily asked by someone of an older generation. Her daring in asking what her lover fears may be new, but Will's response is as old as patriarchy. He becomes enraged.

"You don't want me," he tells her.

"Yes I do," she protests.

"No you don't," he insists. "You're going to go off to Stanford and marry some rich doctor prick your mother will approve of and laugh with the other trust fund babies about how you went slumming too once."

Now Skylar gets angry. "What is your obsession with my money?" she challenges. "My father died when I was thirteen and he left us with this money. So, okay, I'm glad for it. But don't you think a day doesn't go by when I don't miss him? That I wouldn't trade in the money, give it all back, if I could be with him, for just one day? But I can't and that's my life and I deal with it. So don't you put your *shit* on me! Look, I know you're scared." She softens, reaching out to him. "You're afraid if you love me I won't love you back. Well, I'm afraid too. But, fuck it, I want to give it a shot."

But the more she pleads, the more aggressive her lover becomes.

"You don't really want to know me," Will tells her.

"Yes I do," she protests.

"What? What do you want to know? You want to know that I don't have any brothers? That I grew up in a fucking orphanage? That these are fucking burn marks where they put cigarettes out on me? That this isn't fucking surgery, the motherfuckers stabbed me? You don't want to know that shit, Skylar."

"Yes I do," she cries.

"No you don't!" he screams as she weeps.

"I *do* want to know," she wails. "I love you. I want to help you."

"Help me? Help me? What, have I got a fucking sign on my back saying 'Save me'?"

"No," she cries. "I just want to love you."

"Don't bullshit me," he rages, pounding the wall with his fist, inches from her face. "Don't *bullshit* me!"

Kissing his face, Skylar whispers, "Tell me you don't love me. Say that and I won't call, I won't be in your life anymore."

The young man looks her dead in the eyes. "I don't love you," he lies.

What in the world has just happened to this young couple? How did they move so quickly, so violently from the soft place of closeness at the start of the scene to the self-destruction at the end? I have played this vignette to therapists throughout the country, asking them this question and the answer is always the same. Will, feeling mistrustful, feeling somehow unworthy of love, backs away from its promise, cloaking himself instead in rage. But why? What drives him to pursue such a mad course of action? He tells us why, if we listen closely. Within the framework of "You don't want to know," Will, in fact, informs Skylar of all the things he claims she will have no interest in. He reveals the deepest, most hidden part of his being. His protest is, in fact, a catalogue of his wounds. "You don't want to know that I grew up an orphan, that these are burn marks, that the motherfuckers stabbed me . . ." Triggered by the stimulus of Skylar's love, what surges out of Will, wrapped in rage, is a recitation of past trauma.

Here is the problem Will and his lover face in this moment: love hurts. Not just in its absence, but equally in the simplicity of its presence. Love acts like a giant magnet that pulls out of us, like iron filings, every recorded injury, every scar. *The prospect of deep connection stimulates a visceral recall of each instance of disconnection we have encountered.* Confronting the prospect of intimacy, Will becomes flooded with pain, mistrust, and fear. The technical term for his feeling of unworthiness is shame. Having about a millisecond's worth of tolerance for his own feelings, Will flips from being shame-filled, "less than," up into grandiosity, "better than." He quickly shuttles from helplessness to dominance. The transmutation of pain into rage is an all-too-accustomed track for many men. But why is Will so easily flooded to begin with? If the vulnerability that accompanies closeness threatens Will, it also threatens Skylar. She has lost her father. Her life has not been free of suffering. "I'm afraid, too," she proclaims. "But, fuck it, I want to give it a shot." How is it that Skylar has the resources to bear the fear love engenders while Will first flies into rage and then merely flies? As an abused orphan, Will's particular history is far more brutal than that of his privileged girlfriend, but there are too many Skylars and Wills to write their confrontation off as unique, or even anomalous. *If women contend more easily than men with deep relational wounds it is because they often have less to contend with.*

While both boys and girls are pushed out of their natural state of intimacy, that forced exile hits boys much earlier in their development. Girls at eleven, twelve, thirteen show a remarkable lucidity about what they will themselves to stop being lucid about, a kind of Orwellian "doublethink." It is this doubleness that is both the gift and curse of traditional femininity. No such envelope of lucidity surrounds boys' injuries. Recent research tells us that boys from all walks of life evidence a clear, measurable decrease in expressiveness and connection by the ages of three, four, and five. By the time most boys hit kindergarten they show significant drops in their willingness to express strong emotion, openly demonstrate their dependency. Before our sons learn how to read, they have read the stoic code of masculinity. Trauma encountered at age three, four, or five has very different consequences than trauma met at eleven, twelve, or thirteen. The injuries run deeper and they are more overwhelming. The younger child has not the cognitive skills, the language, nor the social resources of a preteen. If Skylar is scared, at least she knows it. She can put it into language, understand it, reach out for help. Trauma research indicates that the surest indicator of resilience in the face of deep psychological hurt consists of precisely these skills—the capacity to "frame" the injury, to comprehend it, along with an ability to move beyond isolation. Will, like most men in our culture, has been raised with impaired access to all of these skills. The same code of stoicism that creates boys' wounds forbids them to acknowledge or deal with them. As one of my patients once put it, "First, they cut your legs off, and then they lop off your arms so you can't reach out for help."

In his work on couples, researcher John Gottman "wired up" men and women to a variety of instruments designed to measure changes in their autonomic nervous system—heartbeat, temperature, perspiration. Gottman and his team were surprised to find that during times of conflict or distress, the men in their sample, though outwardly stoic, showed more pronounced signs of physiological upset. Their hearts beat faster, their bodies pumped out more adrenaline than those of their wives, even while the women showed greater outward signs of emotion. Gottman went so far as to claim empirical evidence that men, if anything, experience emotion more strongly than women do. Perhaps, Gottman mused, it is the surfeit of feeling, not its lack, that causes so much male withdrawal. Other researchers attempted to replicate Gottman's findings and could not. Gottman's claim, for the moment, remains controversial. But even if it does prove true, increased physical arousal in men during times of high emotion does not necessarily lead to the conclusion that men are inherently, biologically wired for avoidance. Anyone feeling strong emotion without commensurate cognitive skills to process his feelings would wind up in a state of hyperarousal. This is precisely the insight that lies at the core of most trauma treatment regimes. By definition, trauma breaks through our capacity to understand, to make sense, and most treatment protocols aim to restore such cognitive capacities. It is predictable that men, wounded early, and bereft of the skills of introspection, would be prone to hyperarousal.

One reason Will chooses to avoid pain is that, as a man, he may be more flooded with it than a woman, and possess less capacity to manage it. But there is also another reason why Will runs away—he can. For all of men's vaunted stoicism in the face of physical distress, many of the men I have treated over the years are babies when it comes to bearing emotional discomfort. Men are socialized to mistrust feelings, particularly difficult feelings, to experience them as threatening, overwhelming, and of little value. It takes a lot to teach men to, as they say in AA, "Don't just *do* something, *stand* there!" In stark contrast lies the traditional culture of girls and women, who are taught early that suffering is a requisite skill in the armamentarium of any "good woman." When confronting pain in close relationships, men have an option to withdraw that is not a part of most women's repertoire.

In *Maternal Thinking*, psychologist Sara Ruddick meditates on the psychological qualities inherent in mothering. Ruddick recounts the story of one of her clients, who arrived breathless and sleepless for an appointment early one morning. This young woman, with a colicky first baby who had not stopped crying for three straight days, had spent the preceding night riding the subway cars of Manhattan with her infant in her arms. After seventy-two hours of helpless frustration, contending with the restimulated fault lines of her own violent childhood, this young mother feared that, left alone with her child, she would "throw her out the window." And so she fortified her resources by keeping them both out in public. What Ruddick noticed about her heroic client is that she did not give herself an "out." Calling a friend, leaving the child with a relative—for good or ill, abdicating full responsibility for her baby simply did not appear to this mother as a viable choice. The notion that discomfort needs to be borne is the emotional equivalent of male stoicism in the face of physical pain, exhaustion, or fear. In the traditional arrangement, it is not—as it is often portrayed—that one sex is strong while the other is weak, but rather that each sex is groomed to be strong in its respective domain and each allowed to be weak in the other's. Historically, we have not asked women to beat off wild animals, and we have not asked men to sit with wild feelings.

As our culture changes, as women in record number support one another in doing the psychological, political, spiritual work of crossing the line into that forbidden zone of male competence, men collectively find themselves faced with the challenge—and the opportunity—of crossing in the other direction, reclaiming connection. But, as Will Hunting shows us, a man cannot connect with others and remain cut off from his own heart. Intimacy generates too many raw feelings. Contending with them is requisite work for staying close. Yet the stoicism of disconnection, the strategy of avoiding one's feelings, is precisely the value in which boys are schooled. The skills needed to tolerate strong emotions are both daunting and unfamiliar to many men. Empathy to oneself and others lies in a realm that has remained devalued and unexplored—the domain of women. Men cannot bring to the work of intimacy the tools that have accomplished so much in the world. A man cannot "fix" his relationships or outsmart his own feelings. Love's labors are of a different order.

What pushes Will Hunting away from the truth, what drives him to destroy his own happiness, is the "one-two punch" of first his wounds and then his willingness to mishandle them. Both the roots of Will's pain and also his entitlement to run from it, inflicting it, instead, on those he most cares for, lie at the heart of patriarchy—the masculine code into which all boys are inducted.

"Look." Jack Connelly faces me in his chair, a middle-aged Will Hunting lacking much of Will's charm. Short, stocky, tough, even though he now lives in a fancy suburb, Jack remains indelibly a "Southie"—blue-collar South Boston Irish-American—down to the ends of his battered wing tips. He looks like a block of cement poured into a suit. "You don't yank my chain and I won't yank yours," he begins.

"Fair enough," I say, thinking that if this is Jack's *entrée* to shared intimacies it could use some polish.

"We both know how great Tracy is. She's terrific. Tracy is one of the finest, sweetest girls . . . A great mother. She's involved in a ton of community work. She's fun to be with. It isn't even that I don't love her. I do love her. I will always love Tracy."

"It's just that you don't love her enough." I try helping him along.

"No," Jack corrects. "It's that I no longer love her in *that* way. You know what I mean? 'In that way'?"

"Tell me," I say.

"I think you know." He shifts in his chair. "I'll bet I'm not the first person in here who ever sounded like this."

"Tell me anyway," I urge.

He looks away. "I have never felt like this in my life before." His rough voice trembles. I feel awkward in the face of raw passion in this unemotional man. "*Never,*" he repeats. "I know I need to go back to Tracy. I know I should. But I just cannot give up on this thing."

I nod. "Does this thing have a name?" I inquire.

"Beth," he says.

"Tell me the story," I ask, and he does. Just as he had imagined, I have, indeed, heard other versions before. Jack runs a medical supply company, a business he inherited from his father. Beth was a sharp, young marketing person with an eye toward Internet sales that helped take his business to a new level. Aggressive, yet still in a subordinate position to her boss; incisive, and yet somehow fragile, Beth seemed to breathe life into Jack's tired routine.

"I found myself having long talks with her about new strategies, new markets. Hey, look, I've been in this business since I was a kid. I used to spend Saturday mornings with my father up on the delivery truck. Suddenly, after all this time, I found myself excited about going to work. It took me a while to admit it wasn't just work I was looking forward to." He pauses, suddenly fatigued. "You know." He shrugs. "What can I say? One thing led to another. We started talking about our lives. She comes from a tough background. Me too, in a way. I talked about my kids, about Tracy. She was a terrific listener. Still is."

"Go on."

"Listen, I knew." He can't look at me. "I knew I was getting wrapped up in this thing. I was just looking for excuses to be with her. But I never thought she . . . So, I don't know, two years ago, maybe. It's late. The place is cleared out. We're sitting and talking and she just smiles at me and says, 'Hey, you wanna kiss?' I mean, Jesus, these young girls. I thought the back of my head would explode. Fly right off and hit the back wall. I don't know how long things would have gone on just like they were if she hadn't said that. But she did, so there it was. There it was, right in front of me. Beautiful. Young. Got that smile, that look in her eye. *Should* I have done it?" Jack muses. "I don't know if I *should* have done it. But I damn well knew I was going to do it. I crossed that line. I've had opportunities before, trust me. But this one, I don't know. This one just reached up and grabbed me. So I did it, and I can't say I'm sorry—even for all the damage it's done. You know why?" he asks.

"Because this thing with Beth has opened up places inside that you didn't even know existed before?" I venture.

He squints at me for a moment. "You fuckin' with me?" he asks.

"Do I look like I'm fucking with you?" I answer.

Jack mulls for a minute. "Yes," he says softly. "That's exactly right. I have opened up to things I never even knew I could feel. Everyone thinks it's about sex." He turns to me. "Hey, listen, I understand. Older guy. Hot young woman. And the sex is incredible, don't get me wrong. But that's not it, not all of it. It sounds hokey, I guess, but it's the feeling. I just feel fucking wonderful, just being with her. I don't know what the feeling is exactly . . ."

"I can guess," I interject.

"Yeah?" he asks, interested.

"It's just a shot," I say.

"Go ahead."

I look at Jack for a moment, gray hair, strong back, the eager, closed expression of his eye. "I think it's tenderness," I tell him. "That's what you've discovered at this late date."

"But Tracy has always been very kind to me," he begins.

"It's not Tracy I'm talking about, Jack. And I don't think it's Beth's tenderness that compels you either. It's yours."

A young boy, no more than ten, rounds the corner of a tree-lined street in Brooklyn. It's March and spring has come early. Black-crusted snow that has lingered all winter, getting filthier and filthier, has burnt off with the same first hot rays of sunlight that make the boy squint as he zooms home, heavy satchel of books slung over his back. It has been a good day. His classes had gone well; he'd nailed a runner at second in an after-school game. Little Jackie was both an athlete and a smart student, though his parents hardly noticed. The youngest of seven, their "baby boy," Jackie felt more like an only child. His next oldest sister, Joanne, was seventeen. Jack had heard about Mom and Dad in that *other* family preceding him. He had heard from his sisters about their fighting, Dad's drinking. But all that was pretty much over by the time he was aware of anything. Like a supernova that had exploded and then shrunk, his parent's marriage was now little more than dead ash. Buoyed by his own thoughts, his myriad small ambitions, Jackie rounds the corner toward his brownstone house and then he encounters it, that feeling of coming home, like walking into a wall. Anxiety, we might call it these days, or exhaustion.

His mother sits alone in the darkened house, curtains drawn, no lights, still in her nightgown from the morning. Jack sighs and steels himself. Breezing past her, he drinks milk straight out of the bottle from their refrigerator.

"How was your day?" the ghost of his mother manages to inquire from the living room.

"Fine," Jackie answers, finishing off half the bottle and wiping his mouth with his sleeve. "And how was *yours*?"

"'How was *yours*?'" she mocks his insolent tone.

"Why don't you put on some clothes, Mother?" He stands above her in the doorway, concerned and disgusted. "Dad will be home soon."

"Ah," she breathes. "Dad will be home soon. I'd better be presentable then."

He comes closer, kneels by her chair. "Come on, Ma," gently guiding her up from her resting place.

She smiles as she looks at him. "Such a good boy," she says, touching his hair.

Dinner is mostly in silence. Jack wolfs his meal down.

"Not so fast, son. Not so fast," his father abjures.

"I have a lot of homework," Jack lies.

"Here's the thing," his father leans toward him, blocking his mother from view. "Ya can't let 'em get ya down." He casts a furtive glance at his wife. "Do ya hear what I'm telling you, boy? Don't let it get to ya, that's all there is. Be a man."

Jack Connelly took his father's advise to heart. For the next forty years he perfected his early talent for living behind walls. Yes, Tracy was a tender woman. She was even tender toward Jack. But she might have saved herself the effort. For the twenty years of their marriage Jack had always respected his wife. He just never let her touch him. Jack kept peace with Tracy, as he kept peace with his own unruly heart—by holding both at bay. Now, no longer young, with grown children, a career with few new surprises, with most of the challenges behind and mortality lying ahead, Jack allowed himself to step off the conveyer belt and reach for something more alive in the smile of a willing young woman.

I did not try to convince Jack that his feelings for Beth were either wrong or untrue. When faced with a situation like Jack's I most often pursue the radical course of taking what my clients say at face value. This was more than adolescent infatuation. Jack Connelly was hardly a frivolous man. If anything, he was weighty, somber. What Jack felt late in his life was important enough that he was willing to leverage his wife and his children for it. Writing it off glibly as "midlife crisis"—whatever that means—would not do. I do not tell Jack that he needs to withdraw from the feelings of vitality and passion he feels with Beth, just the opposite. These feelings are his birthright. They compel him because they are his natural state. The issue is not that they are unreal or unimportant; the issue is that he should have been feeling them all along.

"Jack Connelly," I tell him one session, "has always been a tough guy, stalwart—"

"What's that?"

"A guy who comes through. Shoulder to the wheel. A good businessman. No real drinking. Kids in college. A better husband and father than your own father was by a long shot." I watch his eyes tear despite himself. Before Beth, I wonder how much praise anyone has ever given him. "There was only one thing missing in this grand picture."

"Being?"

"Jack Connelly."

He considers this for a moment, looking woebegone, traces of that little boy in the broad, gray man.

"Jack," I say softly. "I want to take you back, back to that moment with your mother. Will you do that with me?"

"Aw, shit," he says, nodding.

•　　•　　•

We set up the chairs for the psychodrama—this is the couch, and over here is the dining room. We go over it once, then again. We run through a typical role-play induction: How old are you? What are you wearing? Look at your mother. What do you see? Tell her how it feels to see her. Jack goes through the drill, once, twice, but, though he is willing, he is emotionally blocked. An old "trick" floats back to me from early training.

"Jack," I say. "We need to get on our knees."

"Are we praying, now?" he asks. "Am I that far gone?"

"No. We're going to do what we've been doing. Only we'll do it now boy-size."

Jack creaks down onto his knees, obediently looks up at his imagined mother, squares his shoulders. He opens his mouth to speak and nothing comes out. That's more like it, I think, putting my hand between his shoulder blades. He opens his mouth again but says nothing.

"Look at her." I crouch beside him. "Take a long look. What do you see?" He tells me. "And what do you feel as you stare at her?"

"Heavy," Jack says. "Fucking heavy. And dark."

"Tell her," I instruct him, gently. "Say it out loud." I guide Jack through an imagined dialogue with his mother. Looking up at her he speaks from the heart. Haltingly, he begins to say the things he could not, hear what he did not.

"What do you want to tell her?" I say, after a time. "Really tell her?"

"Aw, *shit*." He turns away. Stalwart Jack begins to cry.

"Go on," I urge.

"It's just that . . . It's just . . . Why couldn't ya take care of yourself, Ma? That's all," he tells me, coming out of role.

"Tell *her*," I insist.

"It's just that . . ." Unfamiliar tears stream down his face; he ignores them. "I don't know why you gave up," he tells his mother, halting, holding back the flood of pain that threatens to wash over him. "How could you give up on yourself? Why did you let him *treat* you like that?"

"Tell her what that was like for you," I direct.

"It was godawful, Ma! Don't you understand how awful it was?" he says.

"Don't you understand how helpless I felt?" I suggest.

"Yes," he agrees.

"Repeat it, then," I ask and he does.

"Don't you understand," I go on for him, "how much I loved you?" Jack bends down slowly, unable to resist the pull of his grief. He doubles in on himself, soundless tears.

"Open your throat, Jack," I tell him. "You'll get sick. Open your mouth, make some noise."

"Shit," is all he can say. "*Shit. Shit.*"

"Tell her," I push. "Tell her how much you love her."

"It just breaks me, Ma," his voice trembling. "It breaks me to see you this way."

Somewhere along the way Jack Connelly decided that he would never be vulnerable, like his bitter mother, never allow himself to be overwhelmed—"broken" as he put it—like that young boy. "You sleepwalked through life, Jack," I tell him later. "You were a little kid in a big, stiff suit. You made all the right moves but there was no heart in it."

"And Tracy?" he asks.

"Who is that?" I reply. "A good mother? What did you say? A good charity worker? Who has that woman ever been to you?"

"It's not that she didn't try," he defends her.

"I'm not talking about her," I answer. "I'm talking to you."

"'Never let 'em get to ya,'" Jack quotes his father. "Words can barely describe how much I loathed that man."

"That may be," I reply. "But you know what? His are the rules you have lived by. You've been a loyal son to both of them."

Beth or Tracy? I tell Jack I care less about who he is intimate with than that he is truly intimate with someone. Beth has opened new worlds, but Jack suspects life with her has been something of a vacation. With Tracy he has history, solidity, but has there ever been passion? Neither of these relationships, as they are, offers what I would wish for him. The question is—which one does he want to work on?

"To be honest, I think in some ways there's more between me and Beth, but the problem is shaving my face in the morning."

"Meaning?" I ask.

"I have to look at myself in the mirror," he answers.

"You could grow a beard."

I tell Jack that staying with Tracy out of obligation won't be enough for either of them. It might be different if there were young children involved but his kids are grown. If he stays, it must be because something is there to keep him. Reluctantly, Jack puts aside his relationship with Beth, for at least the time being, in order to try to revivify—or, to be more accurate, to vivify for the first time—his marriage. Between Jack's avoidance and Tracy's compliance, they stopped engaging one another decades ago. All Tracy's policy of not rocking the boat had accomplished was getting her left. She was not shocked by her husband's affair. She had suspected him, erroneously it turns out, of having had affairs for years. But whether Jack was wrapped in the arms of another or wrapped in the details of his account book, Tracy knew he had never been possessed by her.

"Where did you learn to demand so little?" I ask her in our first joint session.

"And just where would I have learned to demand more?" she returns.

Is there enough between Jack and Tracy to hold them together? Time alone will tell. But for either of them to step into intimacy, with one another or anyone else, both must move beyond their assigned gender roles. Tracy must drop the mantle of long suffering self-abnegation and allow herself to become dangerous. She must risk fighting for her real needs and taking on her husband. And Jack must learn to be responsible and passionate at the same time, intimate and sensual with the same person. By taking down his walled-off defense, and caring for the overwhelmed boy he crated inside, Jack reaches past, not just his toxic childhood, but our toxic version of manhood. Both Jack Connelly and Will Hunting are brothers in disowned vulnerability cloaked in overt disdain. Will's contempt is explosive, dramatic. Jack's showed itself more subtly as everyday negligence, coldness, absence. Devaluing women, devaluing intimacy itself, occurs along a range. We call Jack's place on the continuum "taking her for granted," and we call Will's "abuse." Before we can bring men back into intimacy we must understand that coming to occupy a position somewhere along the spectrum of contempt is synonymous with learning to be a man.

CHAPTER FOUR

Psychological Patriarchy:
The Dance of Contempt

As a psychotherapist working with men and women, I have been drawn to examine not just gender's politics but also its dynamics. At the political level, men throughout history have claimed rights for themselves that they have, in most cultures, been loath to grant women—the right to vote, to have access to education, to own property, to not be someone's property. But at the psychological level, the dynamic of patriarchy stretches beyond the oppression of women by men. *Psychological patriarchy* defines the relationship between two sets of human qualities.

The pattern of *psychological patriarchy* can be envisioned as a set of three concentric rings surrounding each of us as individuals, both men and women. The first of these rings is a process in which all the properties granted to us by nature, the elements of one whole personality, are bifurcated. It is as if we as a culture have taken a blank piece of paper and drawn a line down its center declaring all characteristics to the right of the line "masculine," and all of those to the left "feminine." My clients are every bit as capable as I in describing these two domains. On the "masculine" side lie such qualities as strength, logic, aggression, antidependence, goal orientation, and insensitivity. On the "feminine" side lie such qualities as weakness, emotion, yielding, dependence, process orientation, and oversensitivity.

Which one of these two "sides" is healthy? Neither. From the late 1930s throughout much of the '70s and early '80s, sociologists and psychologists labored to prove what everyone understood by "common sense"—that healthy men and women, boys and girls, were "secure" in their "gender identities." Manly men and womanly women, boyish boys and girlish girls were the order of the day. But in 1983, sociologist Joseph Pleck, the father of men's studies, published his tour de force, *The Myth of Masculinity,* in which he carefully sifted through all of the research of the previous four decades on "masculine identity," and systematically demolished it. Meanwhile, social psychologist Sandra Lipsitz Bem, and a generation that followed, began proving that the best predictor of good mental health in both children and adults was not confinement to rigidly defined characteristics but rather access to the whole palette of traits and appetites afforded us by nature. Psychologically whole human beings, who could be both tender and tough, depending on the circumstances, proved to have the best mental health. Initially Bem and her colleagues called this new ideal "androgyny." Late in her career, however, Bem revamped her language. Even the term androgyny, Bem reasoned, implies that such characteristics as empathy or nurturing are inherently female, while others, such as strength, or reasoning, are intrinsically male. After considering the data, she concluded that these are not gendered traits so much as human traits. After years of research, it turns out that what makes for highly adaptive people is their capacity to . . . adapt. Some psychotherapists are perspicacious enough to learn this in the comfort of their own homes and offices. As a suburban, slow learner, I had to journey all the way to Africa before I fully believed it.

No matter how much water we drank, the hot wind and the dust made us thirsty again. I was traveling in Tanzania with my family, Belinda and the boys, Justin and Alexander, then only nine and six. Our friends Judi Wineland and Rick Thomson ran a safari company in Arusha, even though they now lived Stateside with two daughters our boys' age. Our two families were close and when they offered to take us with them in their yearly trip back to their second home, we seized upon it as the chance of a lifetime. We spent the first three weeks in the bush, camping and touring the wildlife reserves. Now we were on a brutal six-hour drive through the desert to the planned climax of the trip, a remote Masai village. Judi and Rick had been involved in this particular village's life for close to twenty years and were counted as friends. Climbing stiffly out of the Bedford, the leviathan truck that was our home, I looked down at the spot we would rest in, nervous about encountering these people. I, who had spent time with Robert Bly, who had read, even written, I blush to admit, about the warrior within, would soon come face-to-face with a living remnant of warrior culture. The Masai subsisted on a diet of milk mixed with blood, killed lions with spears, and circumcised their boys at thirteen with a machete-like knife. Would I be repulsed? Awed by their noble savagery? I was in for a few surprises.

Rick's oldest friend in the village, Samuel, sat on a tree stump, waiting for our arrival, twig from a "toothbrush tree" in his mouth. How he knew of our coming I will never discern. There were hugs and warm introductions all around. "Samuel," I remarked, "Your English is really wonderful."

"You think so?" He smiled. "So is my French, Spanish, German, and Swedish."

"Swedish?" Rick noted, hauling a jerrican from the truck.

"Well," Samuel demurred. "Maybe a word or two." He shrugged. "The tourists."

Later that night, and for the following three nights, Rick, as a favor, asked Samuel to gather the elders of the village to speak with me about things male. No women and no children were allowed. Questions went from English to Swahili to Masai and then back again. The evenings were long, full of dissension and laughter.

"In America, " I said one evening, "there is a big debate now about what makes a good *morani*, a good warrior. Some say a good man is one who is strong and tough, able to be fierce. Yet others say a good *morani* is someone who is gentle and sensitive to others, able to respond with kindness. What are your thoughts? What is most important to know about being a man?"

The question made the rounds through their circle. After much vibrant chatter, one of the smallest, oldest men in the group stood up and pointed his bony finger at me.

"I refuse to tell you what makes a good *morani*," our translator told me. "But I will tell you what makes a great *morani*. When the moment calls for fierceness a good *morani* is very ferocious. And when the moment calls for kindness, a good *morani* is utterly tender. Now, what makes a *great morani* is knowing which moment is which!"

That old man and Sandra Bem would certainly have a lot to talk about.

Whatever wisdom about flexibility we might once have possessed is reclamation work for us now. Our sons learn the code early and well: don't cry, don't be vulnerable; don't show weakness—ultimately, don't show that you care. As a society, we may have some notion that raising whole boys and girls is a good idea, but that doesn't mean that we actually do it. Even though you or I might be committed to raising less straitjacketed kids, the culture at large, while perhaps changing, is still far from changed. Try as we might, in movie theaters, classrooms, playgrounds our sons and daughters are bombarded with traditional messages about masculinity and femininity, hour by hour and day by day.

I took my children to see the film version of *Stuart Little*. At one point, Stuart, the mouse, must leave his adoptive human parents, seemingly forever. His human mother sobs hysterically, flinging her arms around him in a long, sad embrace. Stuart's human father proffers a manly handshake with the emotion-drenched words, "Take care, son."

I asked my kids what they thought of Stuart's adoptive father. They thought he was a good dad. I pointed out the discrepancy between his behavior and his wife's.

"But Dad," Justin, my thirteen-year-old, protested, "fathers don't have to do all that stuff for their kids to know they love them."

"Well, how do they know then?" I asked.

"I don't know," chimed in ten-year-old Alexander. "They just do." This from two boys who could easily expire on the spot if a whole day went by without my telling them how much I cared for them.

The discrepancy between our own family life and that mythic

class of persons, "dads," passed without notice. Did they mean by "dads" men up on movie screens, men living next door, men they aspired to be? Clearly, showing too much emotion, even to a talking mouse, wouldn't do. At best it was deemed unnecessary and at worst it would have seemed, to use a current playground term, "gay." "Gay" is used interchangeably with "wuss," a combination of "wimp" and "pussy," a word readily found in the mouths of eight- and nine-year-old boys throughout the country. So much for our enlightened times.

No matter how politically correct we may be, in their classrooms, on their playgrounds, our kids know the real score. There is little doubt in their minds about the hard line dividing boy-land from girl-land. Our daughters, after a generation of the women's movement, have some modicum of support for daring to transcend their traditional roles. But think for a moment about how unsupported, how completely out on a limb, is a boy who is different. In *I Don't Want to Talk About It*, I wrote in detail about the "everyday violence" that is leveled against our sons, both physical and psychological. While I don't need to repeat that discussion, let me share one of the personal stories I wrote about. When my son Alexander was in his third year his favorite pastime was "dress up." He adored all manner of costume. A single day might find him, in turns, a wizard, a Dracula, a bear. But without doubt my son's most favorite persona was Barbie. And not just any old Barbie, but Barbie the good witch. Psychologist friends, some of whom made their living lecturing on gender issues, could not resist offering unsolicited concern about Alexander's impending "identity issues."

"There's nothing *wrong* with the dress," one friend expressed. "But don't you think he might find it confusing?"

"Hmm," Belinda thought for a moment. "You know, so far he doesn't seem to wonder very much about whether or not he's a *vampire.*"

Singling out Alexander's Barbie costume had nothing to do with his discomfort, but ours. My son was as clear about his games as he was happy in them—for a time.

One day his big brother Justin had a bunch of older boys over for a play-date, and, delighted, Alexander quickly donned his cherished paraphernalia—white dress, silver wand, matching tiara. Whooshing down the stairs he struck a magnificent pose for the big kids, like, "Ta-*da!*" The boys stopped their chatter and looked up, saying nothing. These boys were sensitive, liberal children and not a single word of open ridicule passed their lips. And yet, standing in the room with them, the moment felt molten. I sensed my own face burn red as Alexander turned heel, fled up the stairs, threw off the dress, jammed into a pair of jeans and, as casually as he could, joined the group as they retired downstairs to the woodshop to work on their swords, knives, and guns. That dress has never been touched again.

Without a shred of malevolence, the stare my son received transmitted a message: *You are not to do this.* And the medium that message was broadcast in was a potent emotion: *shame.* At three, Alexander was learning the rules. A ten-second wordless transaction was powerful enough to dissuade my son from that instant forward from what had been a favorite activity. I call such moments of induction the "normal traumatization" of boys.

When I first began looking at gender issues, I believed that violence was a by-product of boyhood socialization. But after listening more closely to men and their families, I have come to believe that violence *is* boyhood socialization. The way we "turn boys into men" is through injury. We sever them from their mothers, research tells us, far too early. We pull them away from their own expressiveness, from their feelings, from sensitivity to others. The very phrase "Be a man" means suck it up and keep going. Disconnection is not fallout from traditional masculinity. Disconnection *is* masculinity.

The first ring of *psychological patriarchy* is "the great divide," the process family therapist Olga Silverstein called "halving." The second ring represents the relationship between the two halves, holding one domain as exalted and the other as devalued. Strength versus weakness, rationality versus emotion, self-reliance versus dependency—are these qualities held as "separate but equal?" Manhood means clinging to one side and disowning the other with all of our might. As sociologist Nancy Chodorow pointed out, unlike femininity, masculinity represents a "negative identity." Being a boy means not being weak, not feeling, not needing—in a word, not being a girl. Of course boys' and men's putative "masculine identity" is "insecure." It is a myth. And yet even the language of disowning, denying, is not strong enough. It is not merely that boys and men are taught to disavow these human qualities; they are actively taught to despise them.

"I want to be a bone," confessed Jeff, a client struggling against physical rage directed at both himself and his family. "Like a Georgia O'Keeffe painting. Some white, gleaming skull in the dessert. Picked clean. Not a scrap of flesh left on me."

"No vulnerability," I say. "No needs. No chance of getting hurt."

"No flesh," Jeff repeats. "Nothing *soft.*" He wrinkles his face around the word, spitting it off his tongue, like a bug.

Will Hunting shrieks, "Help me? *Help me?* What, have I got a fucking sign on my back saying, 'Save me'?"

If Will had screamed that out in my office I might have told him, after he'd simmered down, that his very rage *was* a sandwich board calling out "Save me." And that shutting up and allowing himself to be saved would be a good and brave thing to do. But taking in help, taking in any form of care or nurture, requires men to express those threatening qualities on the left-hand side of the page—emotionality, dependency, vulnerability. Jeff and Will learned in extreme ways what all boys learn, though sometimes less brutally—that vulnerability triggers attack. Will's every stab wound and cigarette burn carried a message, no less than the silent stare directed at my wide-open, three-year-old son. That message reads: *This is what we do to the feminine.*

Once we move beyond seeing the devaluing of the feminine as exclusively played out between the sexes, we come to a sobering, even frightening, vista—patriarchy as psychic landscape, patriarchy as war—an ageless dynamic in which one half of our own being ceaselessly tortures the other.

My grandfather Abe, in a fit of depression, tried to kill himself and his two boys when my father was eleven years old. He closed the garage door, stopped up the vents, put himself and the kids in the car, locked the doors, and turned on the engine. When my father protested, Abe put a comforting arm around his son's shoulders. "Shh," my father remembered Abe saying. "Shh." My father grabbed his young brother, Phil, and kicked the glass out of the car window. It was the defining moment of my father's life. Bereft of the mother who died when he was nine, of the father who proved to be far worse than absent, exiled to another part of town to live with his grandmother, my father at eleven made a deal with himself. He took the black cavernous hole of his longing and buried it. "Abe was a weak man, a passive man," my father told me some fifty years after that day in his life. "I swore I would never be like that." But our fates are not so easily controlled. There is an old saying, "The bigger the front, the bigger the back."

My father was never overtly passive or dependent. His whole demeanor was big, booming, tough. But in his life, he played out his unacknowledged vulnerability with a vengeance, drifting from job to job, always superior to the "idiots" he answered to. It was my mother who held us together—logistically, financially, psychologi-cally—even while managing to appear fragile, and earning the whole family's derision.

Over the years, cloaked in grandiose rage, my father grew ever more covertly dependent. The stage upon which he played out the drama of his death-lock grip on his own vulnerability grew ever more narrow. He gave up on work, on friends, on ambition. Toward the end of his life, after years of my own therapy, I remember daring to ask my father a thoroughly taboo question: "Dad, what are you doing with yourself these days?" My heart pounded in my chest as I braved this simple inquiry, as though I had just asked an alcoholic how much he'd been drinking. My father, nonplussed, looked over the room, a supercilious smile on his face. "Just watching the grass grow, Terry," he announced. "Just watching the grass grow." He meant to suggest, I suppose, that he had lots of plans held close to his vest, but to my shame, he didn't pull it off. Everyone in his hearing knew that his answer was pretty much true. Within months of this exchange my father contracted ALS, Lou Gehrig's disease, and the

dimensions of his struggle with vulnerability shrank to the perime-
ter of his own skin, moving inexorably inward. He lost the use of his
hands, his legs, his arms, his bowels. Eventually, he lost the use of his
lungs and stopped breathing. Early on in the disease's career, my
father worked hard on healing meditations. He would call me up and
enthusiastically read me his new visualization regime. Instead of the
spiritual work of relaxing, releasing, working with the body's natural process, the metaphors my father read to me were all about war,
marching armies of "good cells," rampaging the bad, plundering and
marauding. He recorded these martial tales on tape in his labored
voice and played them back all hours of the night and day to
"empower" himself. From the first time I heard them, I knew he was
a dead man.

For the past twenty years, in a thousand incarnations, I have
treated my father. Though I was not aware of it, looking back I can
only assume that somewhere along the way, I also made a deal. I
would rather devote my life to saving my father than being him.

The essential madness of the patriarchal vision is the delusion of
dominance, what pioneer feminist psychologist Jean Baker Miller has
called the "power over" model of relationship, as distinct from a
model of "being with." It is the hubris of viewing ourselves as above
our surroundings, rather than as a part of them. The Old Testament
God does not merely place Adam within nature's bounty. He gives
Adam dominion over nature. In hindsight, that turns out to have
been a singularly bad idea. The more my father tried to "conquer"
his own vulnerabilities, the more they snuck up from behind and
devoured him. The problem with the agenda of denying half of one's
own humanity is that our humanity rarely cooperates. On the other
hand, if a boy does not fall into step with that agenda, at best he will
not "fit in," and at worst, he will engender outright attack.

"When could it have been?" Paul muses. "Kindergarten, maybe. First
grade? Anyway, I know this is the stupidest thing, but it's therapy,
right? This is the shit I'm supposed to be getting into here?"

"Do it," I tell him.

"So, okay, I had this thing, this monkey. Pal, his name was. You know, one of these deals, had him since birth, all the fur rubbed off, no stuffing, smells like baby puke from five years ago . . ."

"Got it," I say.

"So, we're inseparable. Literally. No Pal, no Paul. That's how that is. Night and day. So, this worked okay in kindergarten. Maybe some flak but, frankly, if there was, it zoomed right over my head. But the next year, first grade I guess it must have been, either they change or I'm more aware, but, no, it couldn't have been so bad before . . . They were, the other kids, they were fucking merciless."

"Go on," I say.

"They taunted me from the minute I set foot in that school," Paul continues. "No letup. None. Jeering at me, making chimp noises, scratching their armpits. 'Monkey,' they called me. 'Hey, Monkey, get over here.' 'Hey, go ask the Monkey.' There was this one kid in particular, Joey Fitterelli. He got me so pissed off one day, I just hauled off and clocked him." Paul laughs. "There we were rolling around on the classroom floor. You know the way young kids fight, wrestling mostly. We both got suspended for that, both of us." He shakes his head. "My parents were fit to be tied. They took Pal away from me for a week." He stops for a minute. "I can't tell you how clearly I remember all this. It felt like eternity, my first nights without Pal. I cried and cried but they wouldn't budge. Then I did a funny thing. I still don't know why. When they handed Pal back to me I marched right over to the kitchen corner and put him on top of the garbage can. Just like that. Not a word. He just sat there, on top of that can till Friday—that's when the garbage went out. Three days Pal sat there. I remember, every day I ran home praying my parents would have rescued him, put him back on my bed. But they didn't. When I ran home that Friday after school he was gone. Just like that. I just stared at the space where he had been sitting. I couldn't believe he was really gone. Like a dead person who you keep waiting to walk back into the room."

"And then?"

"You know, honestly, I feel really stupid telling you all this, but . . ."

"And then?" I repeat.

"Well, it honestly was one of the most important moments of my life. I mean, I remember . . ."

"What?" I ask.

"I remember understanding that this really, really, truly is the way it is. That if you sit and wait for someone to rescue you, you've got a long wait on your hands."

"You learned the way of the world."

"Don't show them your back," Paul tells me. "Don't give them the opportunity. They definitely *will* use it." He glances up at me. "You know those shits called me 'Monkey' till I was in junior high?"

Paul spent most of his time away from the home he no longer trusted, away from his tormentors at school—at the library, at the basketball court. He became a star athlete, a star pupil. He got scholarships to all the right schools, was snapped up by good companies, and blustered his way through no less than three perfect marriages.

"Hey, I think we unearthed it today, Terry," he says and grins at me. "The *nub*," dropping his voice, a sonorous announcer. "*Rosebud!*" he confides.

"Citizen Paul," I pick it up.

"Citizen Pal," he returns and then sighs, deflated.

"What's the sigh?" I ask.

He thinks a minute, serious again. "I guess it's 'What do we do now?'" he tells me.

For a moment, I can almost see the pentimento—little boy, stuffed animal squeezed in a careless headlock, aging entrepreneur. "Fix it," I answer.

The great paradox for girls is that their ticket into relationships is silence, overaccommodation, indirect expression. How can one maintain genuine relationships while not being genuine in them? The paradox for boys is that in order to be worthy of connection, they must prove themselves invulnerable—buttoned-down warriors in the world's emotional marketplace. In the world of boys and men, you are either a winner or a loser, one up or one down, in control or controlled, man enough or a girl. Where in this setup is the capacity to love? Sustaining relationships with others requires a good relationship to ourselves. Healthy self-esteem is an internal sense of worth that pulls one neither into "better than" grandiosity nor "less than" shame. But the essence of *psychological patriarchy* is the nonexistence of such middle ground. If you win, if you inhabit the "masculine" right-hand side of the page; you are exalted. If you lose, if you fall into the "feminine" left-hand column; you are despised and rejected. Neither outcome affords closeness. It is impossible to be intimate from either a "one-up" or a "one-down" position. And neither location affords peace of mind. Your place in this perilous dance is determined solely by your performance. "What have you done for us lately?" is the credo men live by. This is part of what irritates men when women speak in glib terms about male privilege, which feels about as secure and long-lasting to most guys as the quality of their last pitch. The Faustian deal men are forced into is this: You can have inordinate power and privilege up to the second you stop producing. Once someone younger, smarter, faster steps in from the wings, you're finished.

The second ring of psychological patriarchy is a relationship between the two halves of our being that is characterized by contempt. And contempt is why so many men have such trouble staying connected. Since healthy self-esteem—being neither one up nor one down—is not yet a real option, and since riding in the one-down position elicits disdain, in oneself and in others, most men learn to hide the chronic shame that dogs them, fleeing into the better-than position or else simply fleeing, running from their own humanity and from closeness to anyone else along with it. *The relentless internal architecture of grandiosity and shame, better-than, less-than, is nothing less than the dynamic of psychological patriarchy itself played out inside our own skulls.* It is the intrapsychic version of the second ring, the cultural dance of "masculine" and "feminine" that saturates each of us from birth.

CHAPTER FIVE

The Third Ring:
A Conspiracy of Silence

> Many of us know this sensation of conduction from early
> childhood: the mother and father talk to each other
> through the child. The shame of the alcoholic father, for
> example, goes through our body heading east, and the
> anxiety of the dependent mother goes through our body
> heading west. Fury and contempt pass each other, meeting
> somewhere in the son's or daughter's chest.
>
> —ROBERT BLY

A man called me from Idaho and asked for a telephone consult
about his "chronic malaise." I requested that, to prepare for our
conversation, he write a letter giving me whatever background he
thought I should know and an idea of what he would like to make
better. Here is the letter he sent:

Dear Terry,

I've been thinking about writing this "natural history of my
shame" as we called it in our brief conversation. The truth is I
have a hard time getting in touch with not just shame, but any
emotion. In addition, I'm not feeling like I really have a story
to tell that can compete for drama or trauma with many of
those outlined in your book (my mother didn't physically suf-
focate me, I wasn't sexually abused, etc.) What I will do is

relate circumstances of my life to the best of my memory and knowledge.

From an early age (I'm guessing five or six), I can remember being tuned into my mother's emotional despair as it related to my father. Specifically, I can remember sitting up with her late on some nights waiting for my father to come home and terrified about whether he was OK or even would come home. My father, an attorney, would routinely stay out late drinking with "clients"; I learned later (probably in my early twenties) that there was some significant philandering going on as well. I remember an incident one night where my mother was crying desperately and on the phone with various people trying to track my father down. I was sitting on the bed beside her and she shared with me that my father had recently been arrested for driving while drunk, but that his connections in the court had gotten him off. She was clearly scared of what he might be up to. She stated, "Don't tell your father I told you."

This was a pattern repeated throughout my life, with my mother turning to me as the "sensitive" older son and giving me more than a youngster should be called upon to carry. I can remember some particularly dramatic times later on in my early teens where my mom was holed up in her bedroom playing the part of the helpless victim, unable to cope. I was always embroiled with her in these situations. I kept asking, "What's wrong, Mom? What's wrong?" It was my life's mantra.

I can remember a few times, again while I was young, where my mother beat me fairly severely on the legs, back, and butt with a belt, to the point of welts and bruises. I am sure I was "misbehaving" in some manner but, even then, I knew quite distinctly that she was taking something out on me. I can also remember at least one time where she stood in my doorway crying over what she had done—distraught over her own behavior. I felt bad for her.

My father was rarely there for me physically or emotionally. He worked long hours to become "successful" including nights out late "entertaining." When he was home on weekends he would typically retreat into his bedroom to read books or else use his time to play tennis. It was pretty clear that my mother's job was in large part to keep the kids out of his hair so he could recoup. He had been very athletic earlier in his life and made some attempts to move me in that same direction. I disappointed him because I was never that interested in sports, nor did I ever feel particularly adept or confident in that regard. I gravitated toward such things as art, music, coin collecting, and other things he seemed unwilling to show interest in. My whole time growing up and even to this day, I have to sit through my father relating all his stories about being class president in high school, marrying the homecoming queen, the photographs of him in the yearbook, tops in his class at law school, etc., etc. He never cared much about what I was doing and, as you might imagine, I never felt I had a prayer of measuring up. For both of us, it was always about him.

I realize now that a significant amount of my life's energy has been spent trying to gain my father's approval. He is stingy with the time he gives to me and my family, even after our son (his only grandchild) has been born—he generally says he can't afford to take time away from his practice because it's "billable hours." I have never been a priority, even after earning two Ivy League degrees, becoming a "successful" businessperson myself (probably for the wrong reasons). Intellectually, I know it is because he doesn't have it to give. But that doesn't do much to fill up the hole in my chest.

My mother quit college after her first year to marry my father and support him through law school. She was basically a housewife from that time on and, I'm convinced, never had a strong sense of her self. My father often treated her like a doormat. I can remember him verbally abusing her quite viciously and rarely was she able to defend herself—I don't believe I ever recall physical violence. I do remember sitting at the bottom of the stairs on many occasions listening intently to my parents' exchanges, particularly to hear when my name would be invoked as somehow culpable for all these problems.

I know that my lack of self-esteem has affected my life. It made it difficult for me to have confidence with the opposite sex and led to some painful rejections. There have been many instances where I have sold myself short and I've had to struggle to convince myself that I am capable person. Feeling worthy never seems to last very long and, I recognize, is largely determined by positives I glean from outside myself. I do know that I am a caring, sensitive, intelligent person. I've been faithfully married for over seven years and I adore my sons. My wife is very stable and I believe she does feel supported by me. I think she would say she feels good about our marriage. For the most part, we have a peaceful home, although at times my rage bursts out and it pains me to say it gets directed at her—she is very strong and doesn't take my shit. I don't know what I did to deserve her. It is difficult for her to see me in turmoil and struggling with myself. I also know that my struggles deplete energy that I would otherwise have to give her and our kids. She is as supportive as a person could be.

Terry, I want to heal. I am scared about entering the process because I gather that I may have to live through some significant pain to get there. But I'm even more scared of what will happen to me if I don't. I have been to four different therapists and they were all nice people but to tell you the truth, none of them helped very much. None of them touched the heart of it, whatever that means. I'm writing to you—please take this the right way—because in your book, you don't seem so nice. I mean you have a lot of heart but I want someone to grab me by the throat. I don't really need more understanding; I need help. Throw me a lifeline, man. Everything's fine here—the house, the cars, the kids, the marriage. Everything's really, really fine—except that I'm drowning.

I look forward to hearing from you.

Bob

As I read Bob's letter, I am haunted by the image of his mother standing in the doorway, the complex, convoluted, unspeakably sad moment when that little boy, still hurt from his mother's misplaced rage, accepts her mute apology, abandoning his own pain in favor of feeling sorry for her. I remember similar moments from my own childhood. As my father ranted, inches away from my face, even as he strapped me, what I felt most, along with the inevitable anger and fear, was pity—pity for him, pity for us both. In those moments when my tortured father beat into me the disowned vulnerable boy in him that he had learned to despise, I willingly received into my own blood his unacknowledged wound and cradled it there for most of the remainder of my life, mistakenly calling it my depression. Reading Bob's letter, and thinking of my own past, I recalled Bly's description—the shame of the father heading east through our body, the anguish of the mother heading west, fury and contempt passing each other, meeting somewhere in the chest. With characteristic male understatement, Bob describes his parents as "giving me more than a youngster should be called upon to carry." As a child Bob accepted his burdens; as a grown man, they weigh on him still. They threaten his peace of mind, his marriage, and stand a hairs-breadth away from being passed on to his own children. If he and I are to succeed in an emergency rescue, we must understand what it is that he carries—and why.

Here is the unholy triad: the mother's shame, fear, sadness, and rage; the father's shamelessness, buried sadness, and rage; the child's own fear, pain, and anger. Such are the filaments that make up the entangling knot threatening to pull Bob down. While his story may be extreme, is it anomalous?

James Baldwin writes of his childhood in *No Name in the Street*:

> My mother's strength was only to be called on in a desperate emergency. It did not take me long, nor did the children, as they came tumbling into the world, take long to discover that our mother paid an immense price for standing between us and our father. He had ways of making her suffer quite beyond our ken, and so we learned to depend on each other and became a kind of wordless conspiracy to protect her."

The most important word in Baldwin's description is "wordless." I did not speak to my father about his pain oozing into me. Bob does not speak to his mother, nor she to him, nor either of them to his father—despite so much that needed to be said. The burden Bob carries is the weight of the unspoken, which brings us to the final, and most chilling aspect of psychological patriarchy—the *conspiracy of silence.*

The first of the three rings is the division of a whole human's qualities into two halves. The second ring is a relationship between the two halves marked by the disowning, controlling, and despising of the "masculine" toward the "feminine." *The third ring is the imperative that this toxic relationship, this dynamic of domination, remain hidden, unaddressed. If those inhabiting the "masculine" side of the equation act out contempt, those inhabiting the "feminine" instinctively move to protect the other, even as they are being abused.*

Since Carol Gilligan's groundbreaking research, the idea that girls approaching adolescence "lose their voice," that they learn to back away from conflict and swallow the truth, has become virtually a cultural axiom. But it takes factoring male development back into the analysis, understanding the patriarchal cultural influences on both sexes, before it occurs to us to ask the next critical question: *When girls are inducted into womanhood, what is it exactly that they have to say that must be silenced? What is the truth women carry that cannot be spoken?* The answer is simple and chilling. Girls, women—and also young boys—all share this in common: None may speak the truth about men.

"It looked authentic," says Oliver, a thirty-three-year-old actor. We are approaching the seventh hour of a weekend men's group. Ten days before this encounter, Oliver had attempted suicide. "But that's really *all* that it was. It was about *looking* good. We all looked good, from the outside. My dad was a minister, highly respected, perfect family, the whole thing. But, underneath, it was about the performance, about him. He had no interest in me, really." Oliver pauses. For a moment, he lets his sadness break through, but quickly shrugs it off. "It was subtle," he claims.

"Sounds lonely," I counter.

"Yeah, well. It's a long way from broken bones, or screaming . . ."

"It's covert," I agree. "But sometimes that can just make it more lonely."

Oliver turns his face from us. Unacknowledged tears streak his cheeks. "There's a *lot* I could say to that man," he breathes.

"About how it was?" I inquire.

"About how it still is," Oliver answers.

"Your father's alive?" I perk up.

Oliver nods, facing us again. We look at one another for a moment.

"Why don't you tell him, then, Oliver?"

His head recoils slightly, as if encountering something surprising, distasteful. Then his eyes fill without restraint as he shakes his head. He opens his mouth but grief stops him.

"Go on and cry," I say, but he shakes me off.

"I *can't* tell him!" he whispers, looking past me to the other men, eyes sad, frightened. "It would *crush* him."

Not two weeks before our encounter Oliver lay in a local ER getting his stomach pumped. Yet his major concern remains his father's vulnerability. I tell Oliver I think his father is "fragile like a Mack truck," a truck headed in Oliver's direction. But I can tell Oliver doesn't "get" it. The bonds of silence and protection run deeper, for the moment, than his trust in me.

To understand fully why girls, boys, and women dare not tell the truth about men, we must describe what that truth is. *What is the open secret that everyone around the man sees but from which he himself must be protected? It is the dance of contempt itself, the dynamics of patriarchy as they play out, unacknowledged, inside the man's skin.*

A client of mine once shared an old Wampanoag saying with me: To discover your unique strength look deep into the heart of your worst enemy. As a young therapist, I was eager to treat all sorts of difficult conditions in people. Like many idealistic, hungry young clinicians, I first built my private practice by deliberately relieving more experienced therapists of their most challenging and unrewarding cases. The one type of client I could not treat, however, was

an angry, abusive man. I was still too unhealed in my own relationship to my raging father to be of much use to these men. I hated
them too much to help. As I grew to understand my father's pain
and violence, as he and I spoke to one another, quieting the tumult of
our past, I felt psychologically ready to take on such cases, but still
ill equipped professionally. I realized that it wasn't just my personal
history that made me wary of such men; it was also the fact that my
training had not prepared me to deal with them. As I listened to
hurt, angry men I felt torn asunder. Part of me wanted to cradle
these pained, injured boys in my arms, while another part wanted to
snap these shameless damaging offenders to attention and tell them
to knock off their outrageous behaviors. At the time, I felt that each
of those impulses was wrong. Looking back, I now realize both were
right. The problem was in neither position, but in their lack of integration.

I now see that I was experiencing the split in our culture's attitude
toward men, and the split, as well, in the therapeutic community.
Feminist-oriented therapy, including most batterer's programs, hold
men accountable for their offending behaviors, but often fail to
address the significant trauma underneath. Too often, the focus on
behavior leaves out the man. I doubt that it will seem shocking to
assert that feminism, thus far, has failed to capture the hearts of most
males. By contrast, much of the work on male psychology, and virtually all of the work coming out of the men's movement, is wonderfully sensitive to men's wounds but blind to the crucial work
coming out of the women's movement over the past forty years. An
interested reader can pass through whole shelves of work on men's
trauma, men's wounds, men in therapy, and not once encounter
the word *power,* or *sexism,* or even *violence.*

A woman client of mine recently informed me of a conference
that had taken place the previous weekend entitled "The Burden of
Masculinity."

"White, middle-class, heterosexual men," she'd sneered, "the
new minority."

"Well, don't you think there are burdens to being a man these
days?" I took her up.

"Sure." She smiled sweetly. "And next week let's have a conference on the burdens of being a Nazi commandant."

Sitting each day with men and their families, I was bathed in the raw emotion of both my male clients' terrible pain and also their often selfish behavior toward others. Feminism responded to men's wounding behavior. Men's work responded to their wounds. But as a clinician, I needed a way to bring them together, to hold men accountable and still hold them with love.

My breakthrough came in the application of a remarkable idea of a great friend and mentor, Pia Mellody. Pia observed that there wasn't one form of childhood abuse, but rather two. What Pia has called "*disempowering abuse*" is the one we can all readily identify. It is made up of transactions that shame a child, hurt him, physically or psychologically, make him feel unwanted, helpless, unworthy. What Pia has called "*false empowerment*," by contrast, is comprised of transactions that pump up a child's grandiosity, or at the least, that do not actively hold it in check. Pia's genius was in understanding that *falsely empowering* a child is also a form of abuse. Failure to supply appropriate guidance and limits does a grave disservice to a child, and represents a serious breach in parental responsibility. The combination of these two kinds of abuse lie at the core of the conspiracy of silence about men.

I must not have been more than ten or eleven when I first came home with failing grades. My father, whom I expected to erupt, to my surprise shrugged it off. "You're just too bright," he startled me by saying. "You're bored. Those assholes don't know what to do with you." Incorporating his attitude, I proceeded to defy "those assholes" until I graduated from high school. I didn't get my first good grade until I had wormed myself into college on the strength of test scores and my writing ability. Even in middle age, I find myself with gaping holes in the basic knowledge I was too busy rebelling to learn. My father's response was no favor to me.

Like any functioning parent, just as I help my kids lift themselves up from occasional feelings of shame, I often also find myself pushing back against their natural tropism toward the "one-up position." It is part of what I find taxing and wonderful in raising them.

When, at seven, my son Justin had a friend over for one of his first "overnight" play-dates, his encounter sounded something like this: "Hey," Justin suggested to his friend, "do ya wanna play hockey? How about hockey? Want to hit a puck around? Some hockey, maybe? A little hockey? How about it?" When the kid left Justin asked me if I thought he had had a good time.

"No," I informed my son.

"No?" Justin looked up at me, stunned.

"Honey," I said, "let me tell you something that's really important. Ready?" He nodded. "Justin, if you want to do exactly what you want to do—be alone." This seemed to come as shocking news. "If you want to be with other people, son, you have to at least ask them what they want to do, and then be willing to bend."

"I kinda went overboard on the hockey, Dad?" he looked up at me. I put my arms around him, gave him a squeeze.

"Kinda," I agreed.

Kit is a twenty-six-year-old salesman whose three-year marriage is teetering. Kit has just returned from the Bahamas, where he's taken Paula for a long, reparative weekend. According to Paula, the weekend sounded something like this: "Hey, Paula, do you wanna have sex? How about sex? A little closeness, maybe? Interested in some intimacy? Want to make out?" I ask Paula if she'd had a good time and she says, "No." Kit is devastated.

My therapeutic intervention with Kit is to tell him about Justin. "There is a name for what I did with Justin," I tell Kit. "It's called parenting. It's what you deserved. Did you get it?" As I'd inferred from his current behavior, Kit's answer was, "Not much."

Disempowering abuse leads to issues of shame, riding in the "one-down" position, feeling worthless. Disempowerment sets up a bad relationship to oneself, and it tends to pull one into the victim position. False empowerment leads to issues of grandiosity, riding in the "one-up" position, feeling superior and contemptuous. It sets people up to have difficulty, not with themselves, but with others. And it tends to result in offensive, or at the least, irresponsible, behaviors. Psychiatrist George Valliant once claimed that there were two kinds of people in the world, those who stepped into an elevator, got claustrophobic, and turned green, and those who stepped into an elevator, lit up a big fat stogie, and turned everyone around them green. That's the difference between disempowerment and false empowerment.

Now, girls in our culture are subject primarily to what form of abuse? Disempowerment. And boys in our culture are subject primarily to what form of abuse? It is a trick question. One is tempted to answer, false empowerment, but that is only partially correct. In fact, boys are routinely subjected to *alternations between the two*—exaltation and degradation; shame and grandiosity; being on the "masculine" side, or relegated to the "feminine" side, based upon their performance. The dance of contempt does not play itself out as simply as boys become grandiose, girls shame-filled. While it is true that girls and women struggle predominantly with shame, boys are subject to a two-step process of first, feeling shame, and then, fleeing from it into grandiosity. Repudiating the inner vulnerability that is made up of equal parts humanity and trauma, boys learn to punish in others what they dare not risk showing themselves. *It is this unacknowledged superimposition of grandiosity on shame, this burying of hurt boy inside hurting man, the sweet vulnerable self wrapped in the armor of denial, walled off behind business, work, drink, or rage, the hidden "feminine" inside the bluff "masculine," that is the truth about men which dare not be uttered.* And why must it remain unspoken? *Because women and children fear triggering either extreme grandiosity or shame in the men they have depended upon.* They fear that the very act of naming these states, of unmasking their effects, will escalate them. And their fears are far from groundless. And yet, while speaking may trigger explosion, the destructive power of silence works like a slow-moving poison, infecting not just the women who still themselves, but the sons and daughters who watch as well, passing on to the next generation, as Bob wrote in his letter, "burdens no youngster should be asked to carry." Bob's mother communicates explicitly what James Baldwin's mother—like most mothers living under the sway of *psychological patriarchy*—communicates tacitly: *Here is my loneliness and pain; keep it between us.* Herein lies one of the most potent and pernicious phrases in the lexicon of family life, rarely spoken aloud and yet ubiquitously intuited: *"Please don't tell your father."*

CHAPTER SIX

The Unspeakable Pain of Collusion

How complex it is, this voice that urges us not to speak, so fluid and quick to change, cajoling, denying, accusing, seducing. "Shh," my grandfather soothed his eleven-year-old son. "Shh," stroking his hair, cupping the boy's head onto his broad shoulders, comforting him to sleep, preparing to kill him. "Shh. Be still. Be quiet. All will be well."

"Don't speak," says the voice. "Don't name what you see. Not even to yourself."

Let not the eye, the receptive "feminine," record what the hand, the active "masculine," performs. In *Macbeth* usurper Macbeth prays for darkness; he knows he cannot bear to perform his crime while seeing it: "Stars, hide your fires! / Let not light see my black and deep desires / The eye wink at the hand; yet let that be, / Which the eye fears, when it is done, to see."

"Come, thick night," Lady Macbeth adds, "and pall thee in the dunnest smoke of hell / That my keen knife see not the wound it makes." And later, Macbeth pleads, "Come seeling night / Scarf up the tender eye of pitiful day."

For the masculine ritual of disowned domination to proceed, the eye in the doorway, the higher faculties, sensibilities, must be shut down. In Macbeth's words, we must "outrun that pauser, reason." In order for Agamemnon, the leader of the Greek armies, to launch the greatest of all recorded combats, the Trojan War, he must first sacrifice his own young daughter, Iphigenia, the voice of the adolescent girl who tells the truth, an innocent who loves her father, and yet knows that his endeavor is madness. It is her life the gods require before the ships sail. It is that part of my three-year-old son, Alexander, that wears a fairy dress and casts spells that must be abandoned before he can join the older boys at play with their swords and guns.

In Stanley Kubrick's film *Full Metal Jacket*, the first and most brutal fatality is Private Leonard "Gomer" Pyle, the "weak" platoon scapegoat, who finally snaps and blows his own head off in boot camp. He stands like a male Iphigenia, who sees too much, feels too deeply, who offers up his own blood sacrifice on the eve of his company's departure for war. "Good morning, ladies," the drill instructor greets his men with customary derision for their "softness," until even he is stilled by the spectacle of that derision's consequence splattered over bathroom tiles. In order to preserve the patriarch, the voice of connection—the feelings of the young boy, the truthfulness of the young girl—must be sacrificed.

In writing about his reasons for making public the "Pentagon Papers," Daniel Ellsberg recalls listening to a young draft resister, a bright, idealistic, sweet man about to be jailed. From that encounter, Ellsberg, then at the Rand Corporation, went straight to a staff briefing at the U.S. Defense Department where he was once again schooled in the deliberate misinformation and lies about the war in Vietnam that he, among others, were expected to propagate. "My God," Ellsberg remembers thinking, "we are eating our young." On the strength of that realization Ellsberg decided to blow the lid off the administration's manipulations, risking a possible jail term of "up to one hundred twenty-two years." That's a lot of prison for one man to contemplate. It shows us, if we didn't already realize, just how dangerous Iphigenia's voice can be. And the countervoice of patriarchy, whether it speaks in the State Department or the living room, does not suffer disobedience graciously.

Earlier, a moment from the film *Good Will Hunting* illustrated what can happen when some men are faced with the simplicity of love. We saw how the prospect of connection triggered in Will a visceral recall of his many traumatic disconnections, and how the young man, flooded with feelings of worthlessness, of shame, fled into grandiosity, mistrust, and rage. But what about his lover, Skylar? Bathed as she is in the intensity of both Will's aggression and his hidden wound, would any sane person advise her to keep speaking? Is she to continue asking Will what he is afraid of while he pounds his fist in the doorway? Skylar's offer of love triggers in Will a tremendous vulnerability. "What if I love her and she hurts or abandons me as all others have?" is the obvious question that rises up in him. Or as Skylar puts it with characteristic bluntness, "You're afraid you'll love me and I won't love you back." But Will avoids such feelings of vulnerability. He disowns the wounded boy inside, wrapping that small self in a large cloak of coldness and rage. Encountering such reactions, most women freeze. A further escalation of either state in the man bodes no good. If the man's grandiosity intensifies, so, too, will his irresponsible behaviors; in Will's case, his aggression. If the shame escalates, women fear that the man will "fall apart," that a lifetime's worth of suppressed pain will flood him, overwhelming him. *Grandiosity pushed to extremes ends in homicide, shame in suicide. Both states are potentially lethal. This double-edged threat stops the truth in a woman's mouth. Afraid of being hurt, afraid of hurting someone she loves, she backs down. Caretaking is, after all, her mandate, her primary training since birth.* Will Hunting, in effect, hands his disowned wounded boy (the "feminine") to Skylar, who forms the empathic connection to it that he himself does not. *The problem for women (or anyone inhabiting the caretaking side of the dynamic) is that while their empathic connection to the disowned "feminine," the vulnerable, in the other is exaggerated, the connection to their own vulnerability, to self-care, is attenuated. In this way, many women, caring more deeply about the little boy in the man than the man does himself, find themselves bathed in sympathy for that hidden boy even while being psychologically, and sometimes physically, harmed by the man.*

Robin had been in therapy for close to a year in her hometown of Atlanta when her therapist sent her to Boston for a "one-shot" consultation with me. Robin's husband, Ray, had stormed out of their house close to eighteen months earlier, engaged a tough divorce lawyer, been uncooperative, bullying, and injured-seeming throughout their separation, forgetting, apparently, that it was he who'd left her. Drink had not helped matters. Ray put aside "a good-sized tumbler or two full of vodka most evenings often followed by half a bottle of wine," Robin tells me.

"You mean your husband has a drinking problem," I clarify.

"Well, I guess you could say that," Robin demurs.

"Well, yes, if what you tell me is accurate I *would* say that. But who cares what I'd say? I'm not married to him. The question is what would *you* say."

"Sure, he's an alcoholic. Right," she agrees, preoccupied, dreamy. Even after traveling all the way to Boston, her presence in my office seems as translucent as rice paper. It feels as though, if I pushed too hard, I'd go right through her.

"Have you told him that?" I ask.

"Oh, sure." She nods.

I wait. Nothing happens. "And?" I finally prompt.

"He says I have a *meddling* problem," she answers, nonchalant, in her slow Southern drawl.

I contemplate her for a moment. Thick black hair, short skirt, mid-thirties, sexy, smart, says she wants kids, has done okay on her own as a real estate broker. I'm thinking, What does she need this guy for? Feeling frustrated, I decide to regroup.

"Say again," I ask her, "what you'd ideally wish for from our session together?"

"I just want to know if there's some way I can get through to him." She leans forward. "I *love* this man. We were *married*. I hate watching him bury himself like this."

I ask about the possibility of an AA-style intervention—assembling five, ten, twenty people in a room to confront Ray lovingly about his drinking problem with a plane ticket to The Meadows or Hazelden in someone's back pocket. But Robin says "No." She'd already explored that option with her therapist but nobody "bit." No one around the couple saw Ray's drinking as all that problematic. "You have to understand," Robin tells me. "Ray's a lot older than I am, fifty-seven now. I'm his third wife. He's started up, ran, and sold several companies by now . . ."

"And a few families," I interject.

"Ray gets his way, if you know what I mean. Not too many people take him on. But the thing is, in my work with Caroline, my therapist, in the things I've learned going to Al-Anon, I just feel like I have opened up to a whole different way to live. I don't think I'm being codependent, honestly. It's just, I *know* there's a dear man in there. I have seen it. If there's any way to teach him there's a better way to live in this world . . ." She drifts off for a moment, and returns with "It just feels so hard to *abandon* him."

What had at first struck me as flighty and unrealistic moves me now. "You're a faithful woman, Robin," I tell her. "But you keep forgetting, it isn't you who is abandoning him. It's Ray who's abandoning you."

"Abandoning himself is the thing that hurts me the most," she says.

"I can see that," I tell her. "I really can. But there's nothing you can do about it. It's like you're standing next to someone you love and they're starving, and you're just inches away with heaping plates full of food in your arms. And you're thinking, 'If I could just get this son of a bitch to eat some of this, it'll all be fine.' And, here's the heartbreaking thing; you're right. It would be fine. But, meanwhile, every time you hand him a plate he chucks it in your face and you're getting bloodier by the hour, and yet you keep acting like somehow it's going to be okay."

Robin yanks a tissue out of the box and pats down the edges of her eyes, contained, dignified. She looks out the window. "It's really over, isn't it?" she finally asks, defenseless.

"I hope so," I tell her.

One of the few observations about female psychology shared by both Freud and current feminist theorists is the understanding that disassociation is the central disorder plaguing troubled women, a disorder of knowing but not knowing. And both psychologies see disassociation as related to trauma. But when Freud heard his female clients' reports of their injuries, their abuses and molestations, he, by his own account, simply could not take it in. Surely, Freud reasoned, the daughters and wives of the civilized men of his own circle were distorting. The other possibility—that the men he knew and admired really were perpetrators—was simply unthinkable. His patients' reports of abuse must have been fantasies! In one of the grandest mistakes of the century, Freud chose not to believe his patients, and the core concepts of his great system—infantile sexuality, the Oedipus complex, unconscious symptom formation—were born. What needed to be repressed, according to Freud, were the patient's own sexual and aggressive impulses. A century later, writers like Carol Gilligan, Judith Herman, and Dana Crowley Jack have returned to the central issue of women's disassociation, choosing, this time, to credit the voices of the women to whom they have listened. The very essence of female development, according to these pioneers, is induction into the shadow world of knowing but not knowing, seeing but not speaking the truth one sees. But if women's common experience of disassociation does not stem from their own repressed impulses, as Freud maintained, from where does it arise? By focusing on the dynamics of psychological patriarchy, the covert dance of contempt, we can place women's silence in context, shifting their experience of disassociation from an intrapsychic to an *interpersonal* issue. Women disassociate not because they are split off from their unconscious fantasies, but because *there is no safe place for them to stand in the truth of their own experience.*

Robin, faced with her partner's unaccountability, has resorted to a kind of impotent pleading. Others, like Skylar, are eventually worn, or bullied, into paralysis. The first time Will tries to leave the room, Skylar blocks him. By the second time, she lets him go. What else could she do? There is no longer a spot in the relationship she can inhabit. Knowing what they know—that Will loves her, that Ray would be a good man if he would stop drinking—and yet having no ground upon which to stand upon their truth, both women disassociate. Women in Skylar's position often speak of feeling "confused," even crazy, while women in Robin's position tend to block out, in an almost deluded way, their own vulnerabilities and the reality of their mistreatment. Neither can bring their perception to men whose stability requires not hearing it.

Skylar is young enough, clear enough, rich enough to let go of a partner who denies loving her. With help from her therapist and Al-Anon, Robin is able to do the same. But what of the women who, out of fidelity or circumstance, chose to stay, and yet have no greater platform for authenticity than did Skylar or Robin? What is the cost, to them, and also to those around them, when the apparent security of managing a relationship substitutes for the passionate dangerousness of real intimacy?

"Mostly I took to my bed," Laurie tells us, eyes clear, back straight, ready, her posture suggests, to engage. The setting is the "family group" at The Meadows, an inpatient facility outside Phoenix whose program is based on the work of Pia Mellody. For years, Pia and I have collaborated. I have helped bring her thinking to a mainstream psychiatric community unfamiliar with it, and she has brought me to consult at The Meadows. Laurie—tall, athletic—looks calmly out at the circle surrounding her, members of her own family—son, daughter, and husband—as well as sixteen witness/participants from other families, thrown together for one of the most intense weeks of their lives. Laurie has asked me to work with her and her family.

"I suffered fairly severe depression for much of my marriage," she says. "I tried hiding it from the children, but . . . Low self-esteem for sure. I was on meds." She looks up at me through her blond bangs. "It was bouts, you know. Unipolar, no highs. Episodic." Internally, I note her use of medical jargon; she seems comfortable looking at herself like a clinician viewing a patient. "I tried everything." She leans forward, smiling, white teeth, beautiful eyes. It was easy to imagine doctors falling in love with her. "Therapy, medication, yoga . . ."

"Booze," interjects Michael, her twenty-seven-year-old son, and the reason for her visit.

"Booze?" I pick up on it, even though he's broken the format by interrupting. "How much, Michael? What are we talking about?"

"Not that much." Michael reddens, aware he has spoken out of turn. "Not too bad." And then he slips in the point. "Not like Dad."

I let that sit between us for a minute and return to Laurie. We go over her drinking in detail and Michael is right. While it wasn't wise for her to mix alcohol with medication, the drinking itself was fairly benign. Dad, on the other hand, had a problem. Dad had a problem with booze. Dad had a problem with anger. Dad had a problem with, as Laurie put it delicately, "the occasional extracurricular activity." Dad wasn't so easy to live with.

Randall Jeffries was my kind of patient. A closed-mouth scrapper who'd grown up along the back roads of Nevada, he'd pulled his way up through law school to become a powerful force in local politics. He was short, handsome, with sandy hair and huge forearms, an aging cowboy. He was the kind of guy who drove to his office with a six-hundred-dollar, hand-tooled briefcase on the seat of an old pickup, a gun rack behind him and an occasional flask of whiskey in the glove compartment. To his family, throughout most of their lives, he'd been a true bastard.

His daughter, Janie, thirty-two, now married, had figured out early that both of her parents were crazy, and she had put as much distance between her and them as she could. Janie was a classic "hero" child—straight A's, scholarship to Vassar, nice marriage, two kids, couldn't stand being vulnerable. Randall's son, Michael, moved into the scapegoat role. He acted out all the grief and rage no one else in the family dared speak. Unhappily married, Michael had been a boozer like his dad, though he had been sober and "in program" for six years. Michael's rage was untouched by sobriety and so was his depression and chronic underfunctioning. He had bounced from job to job, relying heavily on his father's money, alternating between hating himself and lashing out at his wife, Camille. A month before I saw him, a screaming bout directed at his eight-year-old daughter had been the straw that led Camille to pack up their kids and take off. Coming home to an empty house, Michael slipped into a drinking binge, took a handful of pills, wound up in a local ER, and, after a brief stay in their locked ward, he flew to Wickenburg, Arizona. He had worked hard at The Meadows, by all accounts, dealing with the twin horns of his contempt—for himself, his shame; and for others, his grandiosity. Michael's older sister, Janie, had walled off and moved on. But Michael, the "sensitive child," had been the family sponge. He had soaked up both his father's fury and his mother's despair. Learning to defend against his misery with rage, Michael would, sooner or later, make a mess of things at work, at home. The inevitable trouble with colleagues, bosses, and Camille only made him feel worse, which pushed him further into the anger that had caused his difficulties to begin with.

"It was a vicious cycle," Michael tells us. "I couldn't see a way out of it. My guess is if I hadn't stumbled into this program, I'd be dead by now, or heading toward it." I believe him. "It's all about my dad." Michael faces his father, exercising his hard-won new insights. "My whole life my father's love has been like a piñata to me. I keep hitting it this way, that way, trying to get the candy out. He's a lot better now." Michael speaks to me, glancing at his father. "Mom's dragged him off to some marital enrichment things, through their church. His drinking has slowed down considerably. He's softened up. But back then, Jesus . . ." He trails off.

I hold up a hand to still him and face Randall Jeffries. We sit for a minute watching each other, the eyes of twenty-some people on us, the silence between us thick.

"What do you want me to say?" He breaks it at last, though not angrily.

"I don't know," I reply. "What's it like to hear all this?"

"Well, it's hard." He shifts in his chair. "It's difficult."

"What's hard about it?" I ask.

"Well, Jesus," he answers, less challenging, more open, than I had imagined. He pauses, takes his time thinking about it, then looks me square in the eye. "Look, it's all true," he says, brusque, uncomfortable. "Everything he says. Everything they all say. It's utterly true." Hearing his father's words, Michael begins to cry. Seeing him, his mother and sister follow. I look at Randy carefully. He shows no sign of feeling but also no sign of backing down.

"What's true?" I ask him.

"All of it," he answers curtly. "The drinking, the women, my temper, that I'm different now. Everything."

"You're different now?" I ask.

"Trying to be," he answers. "I don't act those ways very much anymore."

"Drinking?"

"Down," Randy answers.

"Temper?"

"Hardly."

"Women?"

"No!" emphatic.

Silence for a moment. I turn to Randy's family. "Is this true?" I ask. An unconvincing nod from Mom, nothing from Janie.

"I think he's white-knuckling it," offers Michael.

"What's that?" Randy asks.

"I think you're in remission, Dad, but not real recovery," Michael explains.

"And what's *that?*" Randy challenges.

Michael looks up at me and I give him the floor.

"Dad," Michael begins. "I think you're a nice man. Even when . . . I think you've always meant to love us." I look at Randy, sitting stone-faced, listening. "It's just that . . ." Michael turns to me. "My father had a terrible childhood," he tells me.

"Talk to him," I direct.

"Dad, you know you went through a lot. I mean, I don't even know, really, because you never . . . But your mother died; your father gave you away. You were in and out of foster homes, institutions."

"There were some relatives for a time," Randy corrects.

"Yeah, right. And I know a little bit about how *that* went," Michael retorts. Randy's face darkens.

"Stay respectful," I coach Michael. "Stay on track."

"Dad, I know you've never dealt with any of it. Your whole life, there's been a . . ." Tears stop him. He stretches out his hand to his father. "You've been buried, Dad. I can feel your sadness, but I can't feel *you*. I've never been able to feel you. It's like you're not *there*." He bends his head. "All it is, is that I miss you. You keep acting like I want to take something from you, like I'm trying to put something over on you. But it's just . . . I just want . . ." He can't finish.

Randy sits facing his son, ramrod straight, no expression, brimming eyes.

"See those tears, Randy?" I point to Michael. "See them?" I ask.

Randy nods. "They're yours, you know. They belong to you."
Silence.

"You have to understand—" Laurie, Randy's wife, interjects from across the room.

"Leave him be, Laurie," I remind her softly, not taking my eyes off Michael. "He doesn't need your protection." I turn to Randy. "Do you?" Randy shakes his head. I put my hand on Michael's back and wait while his crying subsides. " You understand." I speak quietly to Randall, still holding Michael. "You understand this grief nearly killed him? Nearly cost him his family?"

Randy sits very still, answers slowly. "I believe I do," he says.

"Good," I answer. "Now, what, if anything, do you want to do about it?"

Randall thinks a long time, finally answers slowly and with grave simplicity. "Terry," he says, "I'll do anything. I'll do anything you say to. Anything I can." His eyes begin to tear.

"Why?" I push. "Why would you do anything, Randy?"

"He's my child," he answers, taking his son's hands. "He's my boy." Ignoring me, he turns to Michael. "Give it to me, son," so softly I can barely hear him. "Give it up. This pain. I don't need you to bear any weight for me. You understand? I'll deal with it, Michael. It's my grief, not yours." Michael nods. Randy can barely speak. "I don't want you to die, son," his voice frail. "Just don't die." Randy reaches out toward him timidly.

"Go ahead," I urge.

"Can I hold you?" he asks. Michael nods. Randy crosses, awkward but not caring, folding his son, twice his size, in his arms. Neither man speaks.

"Take a while," I tell them. "It's been a long time coming."

Michael recounts an episode. "I must not have been more than eight or nine," he tells us, when his mother and he sat cuddling on their living room couch, reading together. "Dad came in, and turned up the lights, glaring," Michael continues. "He had that funny look I knew even back then meant trouble. Now, I understand he must have been drinking, but then it just seemed like a bad mood or something. He looked at us like we'd been doing something wrong, like he caught us out being dirty or something. He said, 'What are *you* two doing?' " wrinkling up his face. 'You *two*.' " Michael laughs without mirth. "Jesus."

"Go on," I tell him.

"Mom says, 'We were just reading, honey.' She puts on that voice, that debutante voice. About now, I remember, I start getting scared. She stroked my hair, patted it down. It felt nice.

" 'Time for you to stop *petting* that boy, Laurie.' I hated the way he said that. I felt bad. He says to her, 'Bedtime's over. He can read to himself from now on.' "

"I looked at my mom as she looked at him, worried, mad, I knew, but she wouldn't show it. She looked at me and smiled, her bright-bright smile. That's how I used to think of it. There was her real smile, which I loved, and then there was her Southern smile, when there were people around. So she put on that public smile, and patted me one last time, and she just . . . She was gone. I guess she went upstairs with him or something. I remember I waited. Waited for her to come down. I just sat there not knowing quite what to do. And then, after a really long time, I guess I must have put myself to bed. I don't remember exactly. I mean, life went on."

"Without her," I interject.

"Pardon?" Michael asks.

"Life went on without her," I say.

Michael looks across the room at his mother, who leans forward, hand clutching hand, fighting tears.

"In some ways," he tells me.

As we hold that moment, the sweet, rueful smile that passed between mother and child, it begins to carry the weight of unspeakable sadness. A lot was packed into that smile. "She was telling me," Michael remembers, 'Let me go, darling,' " his voice slipping into a deeper Southern accent, 'Just let me go. *We* know that your father's a brute. *We* live together in a world of refined feeling he can *never* understand. But you see, darling. I am helpless, aren't I? What am I to do? You do forgive me, don't you? Of course you do. Nothing can break the bond between us, certainly not him. I'm so glad you understand. I *knew* you would.' And all the while I'm just sitting there. I don't know what the fuck's happening."

"Oh, but you do," I correct him. "You know exactly what's happening. You see it all."

He turns to Laurie across the room, hot tears, anger. "How could you do it to me, Mother? He was an animal. He was what he was. But you *knew*, you *knew* better!"

Laurie cries, spreads her hands, unable to speak.

"Is it true?" I ask her.

She turns on me, furious. "Of *course* it's true," she snaps at me. "Do you take me for an idiot? Don't you think I know what I did?"

But now sister Janie has had enough. "I'm tired of this," she fumes. "You seem to forget," turning to her mother, "what life was like when you crossed Daddy. You don't remember the yelling, Mother?" She is almost screaming herself. "You don't remember the fights?"

"That's no excuse, darling," Laurie answers.

"*You* didn't know." She turns on her brother, with venom. "You didn't know; you were little."

"Why are you so mad, Janie?" I ask her.

"I'm *sick* of her playing the martyr and I'm sick of her being blamed," she snaps back.

"But, Jane, I . . ." Michael starts.

"You didn't sit with her like I did," Janie throws at him. "You didn't hold her like I did. Do you remember that time he grabbed you," turning to Laurie, "grabbed your wrists? And you were going out to some party or something? Do you remember that?"

"Yes," Laurie answers, crying.

"And you put fucking makeup on over your wrists, and I caught you at it. I told you. I said to let everyone see, let the world know what a bastard he was. Remember that, Mother?"

"Yes, Janie." Defeated.

"What did you want her to do, Michael? Blow up the whole family? Blow us all to hell?"

"I'm sorry," Laurie says to no one in particular. "I'm sorry. I'm sorry. I'm sorry." Like breathing, like a mantra.

"I just wanted . . ." Michael turns to his mother, bent in her chair.

"Ma. I just wanted," his voice is small, like a child's, "I just wanted you not to leave me there."

"I'm sorry, darling." She turns to him. "I'm sorry, I'm so, so sorry." Michael turns his face away from her, unable to look, unwilling to give anymore.

"I'm used up, Mother," he tells her. "I just don't have it in me right now to comfort you any longer."

"I don't *need* your comfort," Laurie wails.

I turn to Janie. "Who's to blame here?" I ask her.

"It's not a question of . . ." she begins.

"Bullshit," I stop her. "Everyone's angry. How could you not be looking to blame? So, okay, let's do it. Who should we blame? Your father? Him more than anyone, I'd say. No one *made* him tyrannize the family."

"Yeah but . . ."

"Go ahead, Janie," I say.

"What did he know, right?" her tone ironic. "Isn't that what you're fishing for?"

"Yes, it is," I answer. "Who ever taught him what to do with his pain? Or your mother?"

"I *went* to a shrink," Laurie tells us. "For three years, twice a week. You know what he told me?" she asks, furious. "He told me I had issues with my femininity. He said I was uncomfortable in my womanhood. Fucking penis envy, for God's sake."

"Or shall we blame you, Janie?"

"Leave me alone." She seems to congeal in her chair, though she hasn't moved.

"Shall we blame you for not solving it for them?" I go on. "You were the one with all the answers. Shall we blame you for abandoning your brother?"

"We all abandoned Michael," she answers.

"If your mother wasn't strong enough to stop it, do you really think you should have been?" I ask.

"I *knew*," Janie spits at me.

"You were a child," I counter.

"I could have *told* him," she wails. "I could have said something. Been there for him."

"You were trying to save yourself, Janie."

Janie's face turns dark red as she screams at me, "Don't you understand that's what I feel so bad about?" She turns on her mother, vicious, spitting her words, "*You* left, Mother. You took to your bed, fucking Blanche DuBois . . ."

"Janie, please," Laurie begs.

"I watched. Do you know? Do you know what it was like? I watched Dad go to work on Michael. Do you have any idea the job he did on him?"

"Janie, stop," Laurie cries. But Janie is on a roll. Twenty years of silence breaks open like a torn dam; nothing will hold her back.

"'Sit up straight, Michael,'" Janie imitates her father's voice, hoarse, cruel. "'Don't talk with your mouth full of food, boy. You look like a sow. Is that what you want? You want to sleep out with the pigs tonight? Put you out in the barn with the other sows. What are you looking at? You need me to give you something to look at, son? I'll give you something to look at. You slack-jawed piece of—'"

"Stop it!" Michael yells at her, unable to stand it.

"No, don't stop her," Randy calls from his chair. Without raising his voice, he brings them all to attention. We turn to look at him. "Don't stop her." His voice trembling, looking at Michael, then Laurie. "My son," he begins. "My *son* tried to kill himself just a few weeks ago. What have we . . ." He cannot speak for a moment. "Tell me what we've got to lose."

"Janie." I lean toward her, riding in on the opening Randy gives me. "So, tell me, what was it like?"

"What was what like?"

"Watching him. Watching your father do Michael?"

"What do you *think* it was like?" she sneers.

"Say it," I tell her.

Now Janie leans forward, matching my posture. "But I didn't, did I?" still sneering. "I didn't stay and watch. I left, in every way, just as quick as I could."

"But you saw it," I push. "You felt it. You knew. How was that for you?"

She stops and thinks for a minute, collecting herself. "Did you ever read Orwell?" she answers finally. "*1984*?" I nod. "You know how they try to break him, what was his name, Winston? How they try to break Winston? They go every which way with him. And then, at the very end of the book, they discover his most secret fear, rats. He's mortally afraid of rats. So they clamp this cage on his face full of hungry rats. Do you remember what he screams, what finally breaks him?"

"No," I tell her.

"He says, 'Do it to her, don't do it to me.'" She turns away. "I felt *glad* it was him and not me, if you want the truth. That's how it was, really. I felt bad for him for being so stupid and playing into Dad's hands all the time. Mostly, I wanted him to shut up."

"When that guy says that in the book," I say softly, "you know, 'Do it to her,' he stops loving her, doesn't he? That's how they break him, isn't it? He stops loving her." Janie turns round to face me, lifting her chin.

"What are you saying?" she asks softly, delivering her whole gaze to me. I feel suddenly overwhelmed by her fragility, like I hold her in my hand. "I can love," she says.

"Go on," I tell her.

"I love my children," her voice small.

"And your husband?" I guess.

Janie looks at me for a while, eyes narrow, jaw firmly shut. "We understand one another," she answers at last, not bothering to rebut me.

"Thank you," I tell her.

"You think it's connected?" she bravely asks.

"Who am I, Janie? I'm just some guy in a room . . ."

"No, go on," she urges.

"Yes," I answer, feeling great fondness for her. "I think somewhere along the line you made a vow that you would never feel that helpless again."

"Which is?" she challenges.

"Costly," I answer. "Understandable. And costly."

Janie says nothing, leans back in her chair, folds her arms, lets it sink in.

We sit in silence for a while.

"I've done a lot of damage," Randy says at last.

"It didn't start with you," I tell him. "You were the spark plug, the carrier that brought it into the family." But, as I look up, the expression on Randy's face stops me. "Yes," I answer simply. "You did a lot of damage."

"And I let you," Laurie adds from across the room.

"Yes," I agree, not even trying to rationalize. "You let him."

"And in so doing," Laurie fearlessly goes on, looking squarely at her children, "I did my share of damage as well, didn't I?" looking at Michael. "Didn't I?" she insists.

"Yes, Mom." He looks at her with great tenderness. "I'm afraid you did."

What was the cost of silence in this family? Laurie, facing overwhelming despair, abandons her children to a brute. Janie turns her back on vulnerability, and along with it her own capacity for receptivity and love. Unable, unwilling, to face his pain, Randy rages, ruled by appetite and anger, rewarded by the world at large and despised by his own family. And Michael, the tyrannized boy, has grown up to fulfill the legacy. Fusing "feminine" sensitivity with "masculine" entitlement, he stands poised to transmit the virus to the next generation.

In my last book, I examined the pain of the "father wound," what I called the "toxic legacy of masculinity" passed on from father to son across generations. But for most boys and men, beneath the father wound—earlier, deeper, harder to talk about—lies a mother wound, crystallized in that shimmering moment when Laurie begs Michael's collusion in the sad drama of his own abandonment. Freud is correct in saying that the son's love for his mother is, in many ways, his prototypic romance. And he is also right in observing that this great love affair most often ends badly. *But Freud's explanation for the grief the boy carries is wrong. It is not, as Freud suggests, the tragedy of the son's inability to possess his mother. It is his broken-heartedness that they may no longer possess one another, as they once had. And, more sadly still, it is the burden that comes with the realization that his beloved mother does not stand in full possession of herself.*

The choreography of patriarchy, this unholy fusion of love, loss, and violence, spares no one. Not the man whose blind actions further his own alienation. Not the woman who betrays, *knowing,* unlike her husband, the cost, all the while wordlessly asking her children's forgiveness. Not the child who walls off and leaves, nor the child who absorbs and expresses. And while each may be culpable in his or her way, while each must weigh the cost of compliance or resistance, as a clinician my passion lies beyond the transformation of any single dancer.

I want to change the dance.

CHAPTER SEVEN

Narcissus Resigns:
An Unconventional Therapy

Psychological patriarchy—the devaluing of the "feminine" in oneself and others coupled with an instinct to protect the "masculine," even at great cost to oneself and others—has wrought incalculable damage to families across generations. In traditional marriages, like Laurie's and Randy's, the most tender part of sons has been offered up on the altar of masculinity, while daughters have been inducted into the feminine game of collusion. In more contemporary marriages, a woman may be less willing than Laurie to stand by in silence while her husband behaves irresponsibly. But an increased capacity to speak out on her part may not be met with increased willingness to listen on his. Most men understand, having bumped up against their partner's complaints at home and against new codes of behavior at work, that the rug has been pulled out beneath them. But rather than take it in, many men, in both their public and private lives, read women's chronic dissatisfaction simply as confirmation that they are an irrational and insatiable breed. The husbands I see in my office, when peeled away from their wives, often admit to feeling equal parts bewildered, resigned, and appalled. "Ah, yes," I reply. "I understand. But, then again, are you willing to change?"

Midday and the sky is too luminous to bear. Every particle of dust is infused with radiant heat from the sun. In the wind, the smell of the sea, and olive trees in the distance. The exquisite boy leans his thin frame over the well. I can see the bend of his heartbreakingly beautiful shoulders. I am afraid to look into his face. Beside me stands the girl, Echo, the naiad, wild eyes, hair, mouth like a river. I don't know why she took the hand I offered and came with me so easily, leaving her spot far behind him. Maybe she understands she can trust me, or, maybe she just hasn't much choice.

"Narcissus," I call, but he is far too absorbed in his meditations. Carefully, as gently as I can, I place myself between the boy and his reflection. I guide Echo to come stand beside me. With our backs to the well, our two shadows fall over his face, like a wall. "Narcissus," I call again, less gently this time, "can you hear me?"

He leans back on his heels, startled and angry, searching past us for the dear love with whom he had been communing. He cranes around us, tries looking through us. Small animal noises emit from him.

"Narcissus," I say sharply. "Listen." Then I turn to Echo. "Tell him," I say to her. She looks at me, nodding.

"Tell him," she says.

"Tell him what will happen to him if he does not leave this well," I continue.

"Tell him," she begins.

"Him," I say, pointing in her love's direction.

"Narcissus." She looks down at him, her voice, my words. "Can you hear me? Listen. What will happen to him if he does not leave the well . . ."

"Tell him, Echo," I say, "*him.*"

She crouches down. Ready to break Hera's curse, if that's what it takes to save his life, unwilling to stand by while he perishes. She takes the boy's face in her hands. At first he resists. She tries calming him with her eyes. "Narcissus," Echo begins, "what will happen . . . what will happen to . . . *you* . . . If you do not leave this well . . . what will happen to you . . . is that you will die. Please, listen!"

"Look at her." I add my voice to hers. "Look at her face." For a moment, his desperation quiets as he lets himself see her. She holds him with infinite tenderness. "She means you no harm," I tell him as he stills. "She means you no harm."

•   •   •

Conventional therapy has failed most couples. After thirty years of marital counseling, the divorce rate has decreased by not 1 percent. In a recent national survey, researcher John Gottman tested out one of therapy's most cherished assumptions—that teaching couples to listen to one another empathically, that improving their "communication skills," leads to longer-lived, happier unions. Gottman reports that he was as surprised as any other clinician to find that his data did not support this view. Empathic, or, as it is sometimes called, reflective listening, when tested empirically, did not correlate, over time, with either happiness or longevity. Scrambling to find a reliable predictor of satisfaction, Gottman's team rounded up the usual therapeutic suspects. Fighting, or its lack, proved to predict neither happiness nor longevity. Some hard-fighting, hard-loving couples did quite well over time, as did their more restrained brethren. A good sex life seemed important to many, though definitions of what that entailed varied so dramatically it proved to be of small use as a variable. After sifting through reams of data, Gottman found that the most reliable predictor of long-term marital success was a pattern in which the wives, in nonoffensive, clear ways, communicated their needs, and husbands willingly altered their behaviors to meet them. Women, it turns out, want more than to be understood by their men; they want men to change. Derisively dubbed by journalists the "Yes, dear," study, Gottman's findings appeared in most major newspapers throughout the West, often accompanied by snide commentary. What the press and general public found interesting, amusing, and difficult was the unidirectionality of needed change. A study finding that both men and women needed one another to listen and change would not have made the headlines. It was empirical data supporting "henpecking" that captured and repelled us. The thinly veiled subtext of the jokes was that ball-less men make for good husbands. But does a man's willingness to listen to the woman he loves and change his own behavior constitute a form of castration? A great many men, while too well informed to say it aloud, certainly act like it. Women, fearing their partners' reactions, withdraw their real needs, scream them out ineffectively, or vacillate between the two. In families like

Laurie and Randy's no one tells the whole truth, everyone suffers, and traditional therapy comes along for the ride. In much the same way that many women have been willing, albeit with great agony, to offer up their children to the maw of psychological patriarchy, when women turn to therapy for help, they are themselves quite often turned over and betrayed, and for much the same reasons.

"After years of patient, understanding therapy with my husband," a wife confided to me one session, "Dr. Ridley has built up enormous psychological credit. My only problem is that the good doctor seems disinclined to ever spend it."

My therapeutic strategy is quite simple. I take Echo by the hand and bid her to speak. The "return of the repressed" is the reemergence of her lost voice. Together, we place ourselves between Narcissus and his addiction/entitlement, the false god of his solace that stands in—poorly—for self-esteem and connection. Why do I throw my weight behind Echo? Because, by and large, I trust her to tell us the truth. In crediting what she says, I break one of therapy's cardinal rules. I take sides.

I first trained as a family therapist over twenty years ago. Then, as now, one learned quickly that forming a "coalition" with one partner against the other was tantamount to "blowing" the case. "Ah, you have been *inducted* into the family system!" our supervisors nodded sagely, in such instances, setting the fledgling therapist back on the course of wise "neutrality." From the moment of its inception as a distinct field, couple's therapy has rested upon a foundation of "even-handedness."

The unique contribution of family therapy lay in the shift from the purely intrapsychic to the interpersonal, a shift from thinking about character to analyzing the interactive choreography of several players. In an early prototypical anecdote, one of family therapy's founders, Carl Whitaker, was called upon to consult to a severely depressed, hospitalized woman. Whitaker, an M.D., psychiatrist, and psychoanalyst, conducted the kind of individual interview his conventional training directed him to. But he also met with the patient's husband, and observed the couple together. The spouse was an inveterate cheerleader, and Whitaker noticed that the more the man reassured his wife, the more glum she became. In one of family therapy's most quoted remarks, Whitaker observed to his students that "Everyone has noticed the pathology of this woman's too-much crying. But who here has observed her husband's too-much smiling?" Whitaker and his generation had stumbled upon what would later be called "the system," the "fit" between individual moves. As a young family therapist, I learned to be facile in describing such patterns of interaction. "The more he reassures, the more despairing she becomes," I would have said of Whitaker's couple, or, of others: "The more irresponsible and boyishly he behaves the more she acts like a controlling mother," or "The more he withdraws, the more she pursues." We trainees learned to "punctuate" the "sequence" in odd ways, deliberately shifting the angle of our perception. "One can say," wrote the anthropologist Gregory Bateson, "that the swung bat causes the baseball to be hit out of the park. But one might equally say that the pitched baseball causes the bat to be swung."

Surveying interpersonal transactions, godlike, from an aerial view, has become an essential component of all couple's therapy, whether the practitioner is aware of it or not. Useful as it may be as a tool, the paradigm of the family as system, with its implication that all members are equal participants, has raised some thorny ethical questions. Can we properly speak of a *dance* of spousal abuse, or incest? If the ball "causes" the bat to be swung, does the wife "cause" the fist to be swung? The good news about thinking systemically is that it pushes us beyond the level of individual character out into the transactional field, and it gives us a powerful lens with which to see and describe. The bad news is that it flattens out issues of power.

The problem with treating heterosexual couples even-handedly is that it assumes men and women in therapy are on an even playing field, when after twenty-plus years of clinical experience I can unequivocally say that most are not. Let's start with who initiates therapy. Are men as likely as women to pick up the telephone to call a couples therapist? I like to tease my students by saying that if I had a nickel for every guy who dragged his wife into therapy complaining of their lack of intimacy I would not be able to retire. Men do not bring women into therapy. Some men may volunteer, but most are brought; they are what I call "wife-mandated referrals." Once in the door, do most couples approach therapy as a gender-neutral endeavor? Think about it a moment. Talking about the relationship? Getting in touch with your feelings? Learning to better communicate? It doesn't take a rocket scientist to figure out that therapy is coded as "feminine," with "feminine" goals, "feminine" skills, and "feminine" values. As I train therapists around the country, women clinicians often ask if they, as females, can do the work I demonstrate. The answer is complex, but one aspect of it is this: all therapists, under patriarchal mores, are coded as female, and as such they are subject to the same devaluing and intimidation as are traditional wives.

In her classic article "Feminism and Family Therapy," Virginia Goldner advises therapists to heed historical context. If you remember only one thing when sitting with a man and a woman, Goldner tells us, remember that historically, woman's participation in domestic life, both logistical and psychological, has been mandatory; men's has been discretionary. This is not a criticism; it is a simple statement of fact. When women needed their partners to do something they would plead, reason, seduce, or threaten, have a tantrum, grow coy—anything but put their foot down—for the simple reason that they had no basis for doing otherwise. The unspoken secret about therapy is that men bring into the clinical setting the same privilege they bring to the living room and bedroom—the privilege to flee. A client, enamored of the book *Women Who Run with the Wolves*, once suggested that I name my new work *Men Who Flee with the Ferrets*. The open secret is that both the woman and the therapist, whether male or female, tacitly agree that if the man is "pushed too hard," he will exercise his options and vote with his feet.

"I can't *believe* it," exclaims Julie, a woman I have never spoken to before, calling from Chicago. "Jim and I go to see Dr. Kastenbaum. He tells me, 'Julie. I see everything you're saying about Jim. He's locked up, angry, has little insight. I'm going to shut down the couple's therapy and go to work on him. I'm on your side. But,' here's the part that kills me," she confides, " 'But,' he tells me, 'we're gonna have to go slow. If I push him, he won't come back to me. Trust me,' he tells me. 'Give it time.' And so what do I get in return for my patience? While I'm waiting around for the therapy to take hold, Jim, meanwhile, has found himself a nice little apartment and has retained a lawyer! Thanks a bunch!"

Under the rubric of "forming a relationship" or "winning the man's trust," or forging a "narcissistic alliance," therapists are taught to, in essence, replicate the traditional wife's role. First they are to form a trusting relationship, and only then do they dare confront the difficult truths. In relational recovery, we stand that formula on its head. I teach my students to form a trusting relationship with their male clients *by* dealing with the difficult truths—right out of the starting gate.

Two core assumptions underlie conventional therapy, or as I have come to call it, *collusive therapy*. The first is that once a trusting relationship has been established, the man will be better able to deal with tough confrontation. This sunny idea has not been borne out by my experience. Over the last twenty years I have noticed that the trusting relationship with men, particularly those struggling with issues of grandiosity, lasts up to the minute I seriously cross them, whether that be in the first weeks of therapy or after several years. The second assumption is that men won't be able to "take" the truth about themselves, that being direct with them will blow them out of the office. Most often, I have found just the opposite. Many of the men I treat express enormous gratitude and relief that I am square with them, that I make it clear, for example, why it would be worth their while to come back to see me. Like conventional therapy, relational recovery also has a few underlying assumptions. One of them is that men, by and large, are not stupid.

Treading lightly on their male clients' issues, therapists, like many wives, work to finesse over time the needed increase in their patient's insight and accountability. To be fair, I have seen that tack work upon occasion, and I have known my more direct approach to blow up. But I am convinced that for the vast majority of cases, handling men's reactions with kid gloves is not the best option. When encountering a client with one foot out the door, one logical strategy is to reel him in, over time, through understanding and nurture. Another tack I call *leverage*. "Mr. Jones, you are free to leave. You may continue your drinking (or raging, or withdrawal) if you like. You may choose never to see me, or any other therapist, again. That is your choice . . . and *these*, as I see it, will be the consequences."

I sometimes say to my clients, "I'm in service, not sales." Far be it for me to presume to tell you what you should do with your life. I practice Al-Anon's core idea of "detachment from outcome." It is your life. But, since you're here and you've paid for my time, I will tell you what I see as the probable result of your choices. Do with my thoughts as you wish. "If you go out into the pouring rain without an umbrella," I might say, "you will get wet. It's a law of nature. Don't blame me. I didn't make the rules; I'm just the reporter." "If you continue to work eighty hours a week," I might say, or "If you continue to 'yes' her to death but not follow through," or "If you continue subtly to put her down every time she tries opening up to you, you will get left, or if not left, then at the least, lovelessly treated. Is that what you want? What you *really* want?" Rather than playing the men like fish, I engage them by looking them in the eye and daring to tell them the truth. I do not know how to teach men to be authentically related without being authentic with them.

Cort comes from a terrible childhood. His father was a sadist, a man who took actual pleasure in torturing others who were vulnerable. Listening to tales of his own abuse, and even more painfully, of his inability to protect his younger sister, I marvel that Cort has been able to walk and talk and move about in the world, let alone have a wife and children of his own. Although Cort has managed to create a family, it is one far from healthy. Cort's daughter is obese and depressed, his son is ADHD, his wife is unable to set limits on anyone in the family, and Cort's rage is out of control. Over months of treatment, piece by piece, the family begins to settle down. The rage subsides; the children get treatment; mother begins to speak out. It is exactly at this juncture—when the myriad distracting crises still—that the predictable marital collision occurs.

"Underneath it all," Cort tells me one session, "Maryanne thinks

I just don't have it in me to love her, not in any normal way." I look inquiringly at Maryanne.

"I've been reading," she begins. "I've been reading about abuse."

"Go on," I encourage.

"You see," she warms, "it's fine as long as I respond to Cort in just the way he needs me to. If I'm there when he wants, not there when he doesn't want. No real complaints. No needs of my own. But if none of that happens. If I'm, say, on the phone, or having to deal with one of the kids or even in a bad mood, he'll either crash and get all depressed or he'll get mad and go after me, or maybe the children." Even now, Maryanne cannot stop herself from nervously glancing at him to see how he's taking it. "It's about *him*," she tells me. "It's hard to explain, but I know it's true. It's all about him. What *he* needs. What *he's* scared of. I love Cort and I think he means well. But I live with him. I know what I know. I don't think Cort knows how to love me for me, independent of what I do for him. I don't think he can do that with anyone."

"So what do you think?" I ask Cort.

"I don't know," he ponders, upset, confused. "I don't know."

I lean forward, hands draped over my knees. "So, do I get to say?" I ask him. "You want to hear it?"

"Yes," he looks up at me, sad eyes, straight shoulders. "Yeah, sure."

"Take a breath, Cort." He does. I go on. "She's right," I tell him, and let it sit for a moment between us, gathering weight, let him take it in. "You mean well, Cort," I tell him. "You're a good guy. And there's no reason why we can't fix this. But, as things now stand, you don't know much about love. It's about need, just like she says it is. It's what we call love addiction. I think you're still too traumatized to love."

"How do you know?" he asks, softly, not challenging.

"I'm not sure," I tell him. "And I could be wrong, but, I've been in this business a long time. When she speaks it has the ring of truth in it. I've watched you in these sessions. I see you do it. If I didn't think so, I'd tell you."

"No, I know you would," he murmurs, his thoughts elsewhere. "So you think this is why I'm so angry all the time?"

The sweetness of his trust profoundly moves me. My son Alexander, when he was small, would walk down the street beside me, nattering away, and, when we encountered a street corner, without breaking stride, he would raise his small hand in the air for me to seize hold of, not even bothering to look, knowing my hand would be there. That's how Cort feels to me now.

"It's partly why you're so angry," I say.

"I love my kids, I think," he mulls.

"They're easier," I tell him.

He looks up at his wife and smiles, so much sadness in his face. "Maryanne says she feels sometimes like a walking blow job—you don't care if I say that, do ya?" She smiles and shakes her head. "Like I'm one of three kids. I mean, I know women say that, but this is deeper. I really *am* like a kid. I mean, I trail around after her like a puppy dog."

"Yeah," I say. "Only you get a whole lot less cute when she doesn't respond."

"I guess I didn't . . ." looking at her, brushing me off, "I didn't have much of a mother, you know, when I should have." They look at one another for a while. "Will you help me?" he asks me, still looking at her. "Will you?"

"Yes," I say. "Count on it."

While I may be willing to crawl out on a limb with a man like Cort, I am not willing to go there alone. If I supply the direction, the woman's ability to set limits provides the steam driving the engine of therapy. Remember, by and large the reason why the man was not the partner to pick up the phone to call me is because he is not fundamentally unhappy with their arrangement. Having been raised to be stoic most contemporary men don't ask much more of their marriages than their fathers had. But the winds of change have swept over a generation of women. Having been raised to be self-abnegating peace-makers, many women find themselves rethinking the way they were raised—and demanding more, from themselves and from their relationships. *There is a fundamental asymmetry in their agenda for therapy. She is there because she is unhappy with him, and he is there because she is unhappy with him. Pretending that both partners are equally troubled, equally skilled, and equally motivated is simply a charade.* I do not mean to suggest that she is devoid of issues about intimacy, nor do I mean that I will not in time address both of them. What I mean is simple: he goes first.

In an early session Maryanne reports that at a recent family dinner Cort grew so angry with his daughter that he slammed a bottle of salad dressing down on the table hard enough to make the liquid shoot up to the ceiling where it left a permanent stain. When Maryanne got upset about it, Cort turned on her. "What's wrong?" he had sneered. "Did I mess up your perfect ceiling?" While Cort acknowledges that he really shouldn't behave so badly, he thinks the incident's kind of funny, just one of those moments in rollicking family life. I emphatically disagree, as does his wife. We all circle around the issue several times and no one backs off.

"Look, I admit that I have a problem with my temper," Cort tells me. "But I feel like you just focus on all the bad things sometimes, Terry. I have to say often in these sessions I feel a little ganged up on."

"Just a little?" I tease.

"Well, you're not ripping my toenails off or anything, but . . ." He misses my humor.

"Listen, Cort," I tell him. "You're right. Let me confirm your perception. You are being ganged-up on right now."

"I don't mean . . ." Cort begins back-pedaling.

"No, it's all right," I stop him. "Let's be clear. I am saying that your anger, your impatience, control, and put-downs, are every bit as bad as Maryanne says they are—whether you are aware of it or not. And I am also dead certain that if this behavior doesn't stop your marriage is close to a crisis, maybe even close to over. Have I got that wrong?" I turn to Maryanne.

"No," she says. "You're on the money."

"Do you not believe her?" I ask Cort.

"Well . . ." he equivocates.

"You think she's all bark but no bite?" I press. "She's threatened before but nothing has come of it?"

"I'm not sure." He squirms in his chair.

"He doesn't believe you." I lean back, folding my arms.

"Well, I . . ." Maryanne begins, then turns to me. "What doesn't he believe?" she asks.

"I don't know," I answer. "That you'll leave him. That his behavior really is as bad for you as you say it is. That this isn't just histrionics. I don't know. Ask him."

"Listen," she turns to her husband. "I would do anything, anything to make it all happen for us. I'd crawl through the snow naked. I don't want to threaten our family."

"But . . ." I interject.

"But?" she asks.

"I'm waiting for the other shoe to drop."

"Right," she mutters, turns, looks imploringly into his eyes. "But . . ."

"Go on," I urge.

Maryanne takes a breath. "This has to stop, honey," she tells him. "One way or another, it is *going* to stop."

When I am faced with a woman in trouble, my first move is to empower the woman. And when I am faced with a man in trouble, my first move is also most often to empower the woman. Why? There are a number of reasons. Once we divest of the fairy tale that both Cort and Maryanne arrive in my office equally lucid and equally motivated, the question becomes, where is the impetus for change in this system? Cort does not come into therapy passionately committed to ending his put-downs of his wife. Cort, were he to be perfectly frank, doesn't really see what all the fuss is about.

"You don't get it, Cort," I tell him later on in this session. "That's not a criticism. It's a simple observation. You're like all of us who have been raised in dysfunctional families. Look, you're sitting there, having survived the extraordinary violence that was leveled against you, and you're thinking, 'You think *this* is a put-down? Honey, you have no idea . . .' And she's sitting there thinking, 'I can't live with this guy much longer.' Which of you is right?"

"We both are?" he ventures, timidly.

"Actually, no." I smile at him. "Sorry, Cort. She is. You see, when you've been brought up in a dysfunctional home it's like your thermostat is busted. You don't 'get' what a normal temperature feels like. For the first few years of my marriage, Belinda was on me for yelling all the time. Now, if she'd spent a week in my childhood with my family she would know what real yelling sounded like. See, you grow up in a family where the volume on some issue—like putting people down, or raising your voice, or being controlling, anything—is cranked up to level ten. With tremendous effort, over years, you manage to turn the volume down in your life to, say, level four. So, now, you're sitting there thinking, 'God, I've really licked that problem.' And meanwhile everyone else sitting around you has got their ears covered, going 'Could you *please* turn that thing down?' Do you understand what I'm saying, Cort?"

"Yes," he answers sincerely.

"But, you don't get it," I go on. "If anything, you feel unappreciated for all the hard work you are, indeed, doing."

"Sounds bad," Cort allows.

"Well, it is bad," I agree, "only in the sense that it's hard to fix what you don't see."

"So what do you do?" he asks.

"Listen, it's important for us guys to realize that strength is not the absence of vulnerability. Strength is knowing what your weaknesses are and working with them. The first thing to do about an issue like this is sit in the knowledge of having it. Know that you have a blind spot because of your history, and then let yourself rely on others, even your wife, to give you feedback. Here, may I tell you another story from my life, one that's not far from this point, actually?"

"Of course," he says.

"In my family, under the guise of humor, we all indulged in a lot of cutting remarks, a lot of put-downs, like you, Cort." He nods. "Because they were cloaked in humor, we could deny them, if anyone called us on it. You know, 'Hey, it was only a joke!' Anyway, for years when I first started teaching family therapy I would get at least a few students who would write on their evaluations, or complain to someone, that my humor had felt hurtful to them. 'Unsafe' was the buzzword back then. I *loathed* that word. 'Terry was smart, but his class felt unsafe.' Yuck! So I used to think, Jesus, here I am in Cambridge, Mass., like the Athens of political correctness, ground zero, and these wimps can't take a joke. Until one day a couple of colleagues, people I really respected, sat me down and put it to me. They said, 'Listen, we really care about you. You are a wonderful teacher and we think this is getting in your way and it would be good if you'd stop blowing off the feedback and take it seriously.' And it was really hard for me to blow *them* off because I respected them . . . so I came up with this idea of the volume thing. Compared to what I'd grown up with, what I was putting out was a love tap. But to my students, it was a major shot. So I stopped. I even sometimes tell my classes about my deficit in this area and invite them to tell me if anyone feels I've gone overboard. It's okay. I'm human. We'll all deal with it."

"Well, I can see that in some circumstances." Cort tries it on. "But Maryanne is hardly objective in her own right."

"Yeah?" I say.

"I mean, she's a vested interest if ever there was one."

"So what?" I challenge.

"Well, you're asking me to trust what she says." Cort winds up for the argument.

"Look, Cort," I head him off. "Maryanne is not some dominatrix, at least as far as I know. She's your wife. She loves you. She's not here to grind you under her heel. She just wants to live with you, that's all."

"Oh, so she has no issues on her end, it's all me," he begins.

"Listen. What are you afraid of? That some Tuesday afternoon she'll tell you she feels put down and in that one instance she's got it wrong? You'll both learn how to deal with that later, but even so, what does it matter? Isn't it more important to you that she feels that way? I mean, you have to live with her, I don't. Even if it's not true, don't you think it's in your best interests to deal with it if she feels it? Why be so stubborn? Why not just figure your thermostat's busted on this point and if your wife feels put down, take it as a working hypothesis that you've been a jerk?" Cort covers his eyes with the back of his forearm and groans, but I can tell he's enjoying himself, at least a little.

"Why is this all so *hard?*" he complains.

I can't help smiling at him. I notice Maryanne is as well. Cort really can be cute.

"They say maturity is doing even what your mama wants you to do." I shrug.

"Excuse me, but I do feel a bit cornered," he pouts.

"Here, take this old Buick," I agree with him, still smiling. "Kick the tires. Try the horn. Beep. Beep."

"Yeah, *right,*" Cort goes on. "I'm just not sure what you're selling me exactly."

"*Her,*" I answer exuberantly, putting my hands out toward Maryanne. "I'm offering—if you don't mind my using that language, Maryanne—a happier, warmer, more loving, appreciative, sexier *her*. Is that okay?" I ask Maryanne.

"I'm *there,*" she grins.

"Don't you want those things?" I ask Cort.

"Uh-huh," he nods, mock-whining, like this is all over his dead body.

"Wouldn't you say they're worth fighting for?"

"Uh-huh." Same enthusiasm.

"Come on, Cort," I play along. "Don't be such a big baby. Can't we get a little *commitment* going here?"

He sits up straight in his chair. "Uh-*huh,*" with maybe a decibel's worth more emphasis.

I clap him on the shoulder and glad-hand him, almost making him blush. "That's the *spirit,*" I tell him, in my deepest voice. "By *God,* we've got a winner here!"

I enjoyed teasing Cort out of his usual assumptions. But underneath the humor was a serious question—what *about* Maryanne? It wasn't really that I'd forgotten her so much as that it wasn't her turn.

"A friend of mine," I told Cort in a subsequent session, "used to say that everyone's either blatant or latent." I never doubted that Maryanne had her share of difficult behaviors, psychological luggage imported from unfinished family business, like a trousseau. The issue was, as I explained to Cort, that I couldn't really "get at" Maryanne's relatively subtle issues while she was able to hide behind his flagrant ones. When confronted with the ways she held back affection, Maryanne had simply to lean back, fold her arms, and say, "Well, who would you expect to remain affectionate after so many years of *his* treatment?" And the problem for me, as Cort's advocate, would be that she would be right.

"I have no doubt, " I told Cort, "that you have a detailed list of exactly what's screwed up about Maryanne, what she needs to change. We'll get to it. I promise. I also imagine, " I continue, "that at least a part of you is sitting there thinking that even if you do effect all these wonderful changes, it still won't really matter. That you already have changed a lot and it hasn't made a dent as far as your wife is concerned. No matter what you say or do Maryanne will never be fully satisfied because she's basically a champion complainer who doesn't accept you or know when to shut up and be happy."

"Well, that's a bit overdone, but . . ." He crosses his legs, glances over at the neutral face of his wife. "I guess the question for me is what happens if I go through all this and it just doesn't matter?"

"Right," I acknowledge. "I think we both just said the same thing. So here's the deal. If in fact you do this work, and Maryanne, as you fear, still dances to the same old beat even though the music has changed, I give you my word that I will deal with her with the same directness I am showing to you right now. How is that?"

Cort thinks it over for a minute. "Sounds okay," he begins. "But I still have to go first?"

"Yes," I concede.

He shakes his head. "It doesn't seem fair," he says.

"It isn't, particularly," I agree.

"But I'll do it anyway?"

"Yes."

"Because?"

"Because you're a nice guy," I say. "Because someone has to move or we'll never get out of the starting gate. Because you need to do this work anyway, no matter what happens with Maryanne. And mostly you'll do it to call her bluff."

Cort looks at me for a while, at his wife. "All right," he says evenly. "I'll give it a shot." Maryanne, who has been sitting, ankles folded, hand holding hand, leaning forward toward her husband, relaxes and smiles.

"Why?" I ask Cort.

He grins. "This is the part where I tell you I love my wife?"

"No," I answer, "this is the part where you tell *her.*"

"But you know that," he protests.

"It wouldn't kill you to come right out and say it," I tell him.

He smiles at her, sheepish, dimples showing. "I do love you, Maryanne. Always."

She leans in toward her husband. "I just want to say . . ."

Her tone frightens me. "Now, Maryanne . . ." I warn, but she holds her palm out to me, firmly, like a traffic cop, and I stop.

"I just want to say . . ." Her lip trembles, stuck out like a child's; tears splash down her cheeks. I can tell Cort wants to put his arms around her and I don't blame him. "I just want to tell you," she regains her voice, "that I am very proud of you, the work you did today." She nods her head, as if agreeing with herself. "Thanks," she says.

Cort smiles at her, takes her hand, and presses the back of it against his lips. Suddenly, they look like lovers.

"See," I tell Cort, rising from my chair, signaling the end of the session. "It's working already."

What I said to Cort wasn't anything new. Maryanne and their children had been trying to get through to him for a long time. This early stage of the therapy had little to do with novel insights and everything to do with helping Cort listen. A difficult issue in treating hurt men, like Cort, who retreat to the one-up position, is that grandiosity, like intoxication, impairs judgment. *If you're in the one-down, shame state—which is where most women are, overtly—at least you know it. It feels uncomfortable and you have a natural impulse to get out of it. But one of the insidious things about the flight from shame into grandiosity—which is where many men go—is that it doesn't feel bad. In fact, it often feels pretty good.* Manic-depression offers a clear illustration of this clinical challenge. While medication can transform the life of someone suffering from a bipolar disorder, many clients routinely take themselves off their regime because the grandiose state of mania, triggered by their illness, though it wreaks utter havoc, can, nonetheless, be enormously seductive.

While it can be argued that conventional therapy is reasonably effective in treating issues related to shame, my experience with men has convinced me that most therapy utterly misses the boat when it comes to issues of grandiosity. Shame states represent a kind of empathy deficiency toward oneself; what is missing is the capacity to cherish the self. And a nurturing therapist can model a more loving relationship toward the client that the client can eventually incorporate. *Grandiose states, by contrast, represent a kind of empathy deficiency toward others; what is missing is a capacity to sufficiently cherish those around us. In such instances, supplying empathy toward the client, while necessary, is not sufficient. More to the point is helping the client regain sensitivity to his impact on others.*

A central concept in Alcoholics Anonymous is the notion of "bottoming out." An addict or alcoholic *bottoms out* in that moment when the pain of continuing the addiction outweighs the considerable pain of recovery. It is a simple matter of psychological physics. Until the scale tips in such a way that persisting in the dysfunctional behavior becomes more difficult than cleaning up, treatment will not succeed. Cort does not enter therapy in a state of distress about his behavior. He is far from "bottoming out." And, until very recently, Maryanne had been accepting enough that Cort's poor treatment of her brought few obvious consequences.

While we can't "make" someone change, in relational recovery we can help tip the scale—not, as conventional therapy teaches, by "motivating" the man (whatever that means)—but rather by *amplifying the consequences,* the pain he faces were he to continue his hurtful conduct. *Conventional therapy tries to entice the man into recovery by somehow rendering treatment more appealing. In relational recovery, we invite change by rendering the man's difficult behavior less appealing.* If Cort undertakes the considerable effort of learning how to relate in dramatically new ways, he has to have a good reason. And for now, fair or unfair, if Maryanne wants the relationship to move, it will be up to her to supply it.

In this early phase of therapy, my effectiveness as a change agent comes from my willingness to amplify the woman's dissatisfaction and then use that as leverage with the man. A therapist of either sex can do this. In my work with Cort, I happily take advantage of any trust I might garner by virtue of my being male. But this isn't about a hero thundering over the hill, shoving the woman aside, and straightening out her guy, "man to man." Framing it that way strikes me as patronizing to both partners. A new therapeutic system is formed when a clinician of either sex demonstrates with authority a willingness to back up the *latent* and address the *blatant*'s difficult conduct. As a male therapist, I have the advantage of side-stepping some of the discounting a woman clinician might encounter. But many of the women therapists I work with are not shy about dealing with that impulse when it comes up in their clients. And women therapists bring a different set of advantages to the process. Many men more readily confide in women, accept women as knowledgeable about relationships, and avoid with them some of the "power struggles" they would fall prey to with a man. The three consultants I turn to when I feel stuck with a difficult male client all happen to be women—my wife, Belinda, and my two closest colleagues, Pia Melody and Carol Gilligan. Each of these three, though with radically different styles, brilliantly manages whatever devaluing messages may come her way to form a profoundly truthful connection in order to help the man through his impasse.

No matter the therapist's sex, and no matter their style, the asymmetries between men and women's relational skills must be put on the table. Men must be brought in from the cold, and often brought down from a perch of bewildered grandiosity. If intimacy is the conjunction of truth and love, then for couples to reclaim passion, connection, they must first reinhabit full honesty and then warm the starkness of truth's landscape with their hearts. But the play of shame and grandiosity blunts many men's sensitivity to the impact of their behavior on others, while women withhold the missing information—and for good reason. As any woman knows, a man may have achieved great things in the world, may be acclaimed, enjoy the wealth of a king, but the one thing most men do not to possess is a stable sense of self-worth. Like naked emperors, many men parade their disowned vulnerability even as they cloak themselves in the vestments of grandiosity. Damaged as boys, men often combine a boy's vulnerability toward being wounded with a man's entitlement to withdraw or lash out. Such an arrangement renders many men at best frustrating, and at worst dangerous. I often remind my students that if women had a platform from which to work this out, they would have done so. This is where therapists, educators, activists come in. *Women need help establishing a space in which their truth is voiced openly and not met with reprisals. And men need help holding fast, without recourse to the age-old responses of discounting, retaliating, or running away.*

As a young man, I remember being shocked to learn that in old China the saying "May you live in interesting times" was considered a curse. To the ancients, periods of boring stability, not change, yielded prosperity and safety. Like it or not, as men and women, we now find ourselves living in interesting times. The old roles are gone, and carnage lies in their wake—in the violence of boys, in their endemic restlessness. Sociologists and family-values conservatives alike bewail the break-up of the traditional family, the epidemic of "fatherlessness" in the West. But no one asks *why* so many men find themselves extruded from their marriage beds, what has rendered them so unlivable, unlovable. The voice of a generation of feminists, which so galvanized women, falls shrilly on the ears of most men. Psychologists and couples therapists, constrained by theory, sit on their hands for fear of losing precious neutrality. Meanwhile, an army of gender conservatives wage a mean-spirited war against anything vaguely smelling of difference.

Family therapy teaches that relationships must be held from without. Now more than ever, in this uneasy time of transition, men and women in our society must be encircled by a third force, larger than partisanship to either sex, a vision beyond blame, nostalgia, or platitudes about immutable differences, a vision beyond the lie of grandiosity or shame. This is not feminist work, any more than it is "masculinist." It is the next step for all of us.

CHAPTER EIGHT

Small Murders:
How We Lose Passion

Once the woman has become empowered enough to speak and the man has become connected enough to listen, the first phase of therapy is over. Now that true dialogue between them has been reestablished—or, in some instances, established for the first time—the work of restoring intimacy can begin. The couple has passed through the first phase of relational recovery, *bringing the couple back into connection,* and has moved on to the second phase: *reclaiming real passion.* After addressing what has been missing or skewed in each of the partners as individuals, the next treatment phase begins by diagnosing what is absent or distorted in their relationship.

"Somewhere along the line the feeling between us just went away." Judy looks at her husband, Dan, and smiles, full-lipped, sensuous. A mop of blond hair, big glasses, big eyes. Dan thinks Judy, closing in on fifty-five, has never looked better. Plump by any account, "a victim," as she once put it, "of gravity," Judy wears her age like a comfortable suit. She seems physically luxuriant, settled inside her own skin. Dan listens to his wife, eyes down on his shoes, arms drawn into his lap. Without moving, he manages somehow to seem like he's dangling his legs off a dock. Short hair crowns his large round head. With his egg-shaped body, thick glasses, and emphatically nerdy clothes, Dan appears all at once doughy, hurt, and wickedly intelligent. He looks, as I tell him in our first session, like a fiendish Baby Huey.

"Baby Huey dot com," he had ventured.

"Don't we wish." Judy had shot him down.

Judy was brimming over with sarcasm back then, barely contained disgust. Dan had been withdrawn from her for years, enormously passive. They had no real sex life—he stayed up late, woke her up when he climbed into bed and kept her up snoring. While they had remained good parents together, by the time I first met them they were barely a couple. Adding insult to injury, Dan had topped off years of withdrawal, of burying himself in his work, his computer, by getting in over his head with someone he supervised at work, an affair that though it was "mostly fantasy" was nevertheless realistic enough to warrant a complaint by the woman to Human Services, which is how Judy had first found out about it.

"If it weren't for the kids," Judy announces in an early session, "I would have been out of there so fast your head would spin." But there were kids, two of them, and Dan's bumbling adventure was "mostly harmless" and so the whole mess served as a wake-up call reminding them that they had both been, as Judy put it, "maritally brain dead" for years.

Dan recommitted to his marriage. With my insistence, he got himself a personal trainer and a new wardrobe. He trimmed down, put some energy into his appearance and into courting his wife. Judy, for her part, had to let go of her abiding revulsion, park her talons at the door, and let herself heal. Neither job came easily. Like most of the couples I see, by the time they reached me, they had ample reason to mistrust one another. But way back in the hoary mists of pre-kid history Judy and Dan had once loved each other, not just tolerably, but passionately.

"You wouldn't think to see us now," Judy tells me one session, "but when we first met we could hardly keep our hands off each other."

"Nice to know you have it in you," I comment.

"Seepage," Dan interjects, characteristically oblique.

"Pardon?" I ask.

"It's been a long, slow process of seepage. Nothing dramatic. Drip, drip, drip."

"What a tasteful image," Judy remarks.

"Drip, drip, drip." Dan can't help himself from needling her.

"Let's see if we can't turn it around," I say, ever optimistic.

Like most couples, Judy and Dan began their journey in that pro-found state of recognition and joy we call falling in love. And like most of us, they were initially full of passion for one another, passion of all kinds—emotional, intellectual, sexual. Each found in the other an unknown terrain at once fascinating in newness and yet somehow deeply familiar, less a discovery than a rediscovery.

"I called my best girlfriend, Cleo, after my first date with Dan and I told her, 'I'm gonna marry this guy.'" Judy smiles. "I *knew*. I just knew."

"I was slower on the uptake," admits Dan, "as usual." He smiles wanly, apologetic, stabbing his glasses back up on the bridge of his nose. "I was more like . . . 'Hey, I'm not ready for anything too com-mitted, you know.' Then one day, about three weeks into the whole thing, I remember standing in my kitchen, with absolutely nothing to do, but holding myself back from being with her. You know, don't want to go too fast, give her the wrong idea or anything. And then I thought, 'This is so stupid.' The truth was that the *only* place I wanted to be was with her. I called her up. She was in. I drove over. I remember it was really late. It was like, a salmon going upstream, you know, moth to a flame, sperm to an egg . . ."

"So charming, dear," cuts in Judy.

"I mean the proverbial wild horses couldn't—"

"I think we get the picture," I say, but he will not be dissuaded. This egg-shaped, fringe-topped, bespectacled man gazes at his aging wife and grins. "We were *seriously* overheated," he confides.

Dan stayed that night with Judy and pretty much every night thereafter.

"After about eleven months he calls me up at work," Judy tells me, "and he says, 'Listen, let's go out tonight, I've got something I want to ask you.' So I go, 'Oh sure, honey.' Right? Cool as a cuke. So, of course I call Cleo and we get all excited. So he takes me to this place in the North End, very romantic, fancy dinner and the whole thing, and he goes, 'Well, I've been thinking, and, you know, it's been so great and everything and well, anyway . . . *Would you move in with me?*' Jesus, God Almighty! It was all I could do not to break a breadstick over his fat little head. Move in?" she sneers. "Joe Romance. But of course I do. Six months I give him—either all the way in or out by that time. So, five months and twenty-eight days later he finally gets around to it, and there we are." She stops, kind of breathless. Suddenly no one can think of anything to say. "There we are," she repeats lamely.

Two kids and twenty years later, I think to myself in the pause of their silence. There we are. Drip. Drip. Drip.

"The thing that just kills me," says Judy one session, "is that we're so *normal.* I mean if you look at us *then* and look at us *now,* the difference could just make you sick, but it's maddeningly unclear how we wound up here. We know other couples with real problems, you know, he drinks, or she's had affairs, or, God forbid, they have a sick kid, or money troubles, you know what I mean? But we . . . we never yelled and screamed, threw things, we never went for days not speaking to one another. We're *nice* people."

Listening to Judy, I recall an article by journalist John Taylor reflecting about his own impending divorce. "My wife . . . and I didn't hate each other; we simply got on each other's nerves. We had just, over the years, each accumulated a store of minor unresolved grievances. Our marriage was a mechanism so encrusted with small disappointments and petty grudges that its parts no longer fit together." In the film version of the heartbreaking, deadly quiet climax of one of John Updike's many reflections on the unjoining of marriage, a couple on the brink of divorce drop off their daughter at college and find themselves in separate twin beds in a strange motel room. "It's a long way between beds," John Maple muses aloud, staring up at the ceiling. "Oh, honey," answers his wife. "You could come over." After a silence John sighs. "I'm sorry," he says. "It's just too far to walk."

Drip. Drip. Drip. Here's how it went for Dan and Judy.

"We're driving off to some *thing*," Dan explains. "Some kid thing. I don't remember."

"It was Julie's class dinner from school," Judy helps.

"Whatever," says Dan, dismissive. "Anyway, this is not my cup of tea to begin with, but I'm cool. It's okay. Judy's late, as always, and fussing with everyone, getting the kids in the car and everything."

"I'm late," Judy winds up, "*because* I'm trying to get both myself and the kids ready. First, you don't help and *then* you get impatient when I—"

"Anyway," Dan bravely plows on, "as you can see we get tense. But we're used to it. We don't do great in transitions, but we're handling it. I'm talking and she's talking. And then she starts backseat driving."

"I hate that phrase," argues Judy.

"Well, *what* would you like me to call it, dear?" asks Dan, patience fraying.

"I just think I have the right . . ." she begins. "Look, Dan, your eyesight isn't that good—"

"Jesus Christ," Dan mutters.

"You're not that attentive. I get nervous. Even the kids notice that—"

"The kids 'notice . . .'" Dan lifts his fingers to surround the imaginary word with quotation signs, an abhorrent gesture from a grown man his size, "because you have 'taught . . .'" the fingers again, "the kids to 'notice.'"

I can't stand it. "What are you feeling right now?" I ask Dan. He shrugs. I repeat the question.

"I just think if she asks me to—"

"That's what you think," I stop him. "What do you feel?"

Dan looks down at his shoes, suddenly bashful.

"Dan?" I go after him.

"It's just that . . ."

"Angry?" I help out.

"I just . . ." he peters out.

I look at him for a while and change tack. "So, what's he do at home?" I ask Judy. "What did he do in the car?"

"You're looking at it," she answers.

I glance at her husband, arms folded, eyes down on the floor, jaw clamped shut.

"He pouts," I venture.

"That's one way of describing it," she answers.

"Well, what would you . . ."

"He just goes away." She looks up at me. "He leaves. He picks up his marbles and retires deep into the center of himself, and I mean that's all she wrote."

I look back at Dan. It's clear he's not about to offer anything to anyone at this point.

"And you?" I ask. "You go after him?"

"Yeah, *right*," she snorts.

"It was a serious question." I hold fast.

"Like, what?" She puts on a Donna Reed voice, fifties sitcom, '*Honey*, what's wrong? You seem so quiet'. Or, 'Sweetheart, let's not fight. I'm sorry.' That what you mean?"

"Well, yeah," I say, weakly.

"Good luck," she answers, disgusted.

"So, instead you—"

"Turn on the radio, talk to the kids, look out the window—"

"Hate his guts," I finish for her. She doesn't answer. We sit for a minute together in uncomfortable silence. "Does anybody actually come out and *say*, 'I'm angry'?" I ask. More silence. "Or, 'I'm sorry'?" I continue. No response. "So then let me guess." I jump into the breach. "You go on like that for however long and then eventually one of the kids says something, or you get to the dinner and interact with others, or some sort of break-set occurs and then it's like—"

"Like nothing happened," finishes Judy. "We warm up slowly and tacitly agree to forget it."

"Until next time," Dan cuts in.

"More or less," Judy answers.

Dan sighs, like a bog exhalation issuing from his heavy frame. He looks out my window. "What this marriage needs," he mutters, "is more more and less less."

"What's that supposed to mean?" Judy bristles.

"I don't know," he abdicates, but I don't believe him.

"I think you just said exactly what you meant," I tell him.

Judy and Dan let go of each other, let their passion dissipate. Not, as they said, in any large, dramatic way, but rather in hundreds, thousands of tiny transactions like the one they described in the car. Faced with disjuncture, one or both, out of anger, despair, self-protection, simply gave up.

"You're in the car, Dan," I tell them at the end of our first session, "and you feel, I don't know, whatever you feel. Controlled, probably, disrespected, hurt beneath that, I imagine. But you don't tell her . . ."

"I've already told her a million times I don't like—"

"Let me finish," I stop him. "I'm sure you both have your reasons for everything, but, at this point in the story, for whatever reason, you don't tell her." He shakes his head. "Instead, you withdraw."

"I . . ." he begins, but I am not interested.

"You pull back into angry withdrawal," I confront him.

"I'm just trying to protect myself," he protests.

"That may be what you say to yourself," I answer. "You may even think that's what you mean. But I'm here to tell you it just isn't so. Your silence isn't neutral, Dan. You're pissed. And you let her know it."

"Well, I . . ." he begins.

"And you." I turn to Judy.

"I know where you're heading," she answers, contrite.

"Then go ahead and say it," I yield.

"I answer in kind," she allows.

"Am I wrong?" I ask.

"I don't do this in any other relationship." She squirms.

"I'm not talking about your other relationships," I reply. "Am I wrong about this one?"

"No," she admits.

I cast a cool eye on the two of them. "And this has been going on for . . . ?" I ask.

"Years," they each answer, thoroughly chastened, kids before the principal.

"Now, listen." I lean forward, trying to engage their adult-selves. "Here's the missing ingredient. Where's the repair?" They look at me. "Where," I repeat, "is there room in this dance for correction?"

"We were like a leaky crankcase," Dan once philosophized, resorting to his usual romantic imagery. "No one meant any harm. We didn't even notice, really, that the lubricant was going. But things just got progressively more abrasive until one day, riding down the highway of life, bang, the whole thing freezes up on us, paralyzed."

"Highway of life?" Judy teases. But Dan was right.

"Here's the leak," I tell them, "the missing ingredient. There is little room in your repertoire for correctability. Angry withdrawal evokes angry withdrawal. You guys are fine as long as everything's okay. It's like found money. If things happen to run smoothly, you're great. You really do love one another at base. But when something goes wrong, as a couple you don't have the wherewithal to correct it."

"I used to try," Judy winds up.

"Let's not point fingers," I head her off. "It's not a contest. I'm just saying that now, without much stimulus, first you retreat, Dan, and then you follow suit. So, how does anything ever get fixed? When things go off track there needs to be some mechanism for bringing it back. Like a thermostat. The way a thermostat works is that you set a temperature, seventy-one, and every time it gets warmer than that the air-conditioning kicks in to bring it back down. In the winter, when it gets colder, the heat kicks in. When things veer off track, move out of range, an action is triggered that corrects for it. But you two literally have had no effective means for pulling things back. If they're on track, great, and if not, you just feel bad. Nothing gets efficiently addressed. You get pissed that she's telling you what to do, and you're pissed that he's pissed and then . . . There you are, twenty years' worth of pile-up." I turn to Dan. "How did things get fixed in your family growing up?" I ask.

"Fixed?" Dan muses.

"I'm trying to figure out where you learned this from, this reflex to withdraw."

"So," he answers, "you mean did my parents, in their marriage, share their thoughts and feelings, hash out their differences, put it all on the table, and then, after a clear, fair process of resolution, go on with their lives? Is that the question?" I nod. "You're joking, right?" he answers. "Listen, compared to my dad, I'm Errol Flynn. I mean, I'm hanging from ropes here, boarding enemy vessels. I'm charging the marital Light Brigade."

"A bit passive, your father?" I pick up his subtle hints.

"My father said four words in his lifetime. 'I'm fine,' followed by, 'I'm dying.' "

"Was he?" I ask.

"Dying?"

"Fine."

Dan takes a minute to think about it. "No," he answers solemnly. "My father was a beaten-down, absent, bitter man. But you'd never get him to admit that to you."

"And your mother," I ask. "Where was she in all this?"

"My mother," Dan looks out the window, "was a selfish pig." His hatred blasts over me like a wave of heat.

"*That's* strong," I observe.

"Is it?" he asks, ready to fight.

"She wasn't much of a wife?" I try steering back into their marriage.

"There wasn't anyone to be a wife to." Dan dismisses my question. "But that didn't matter. She had an all-consuming preoccupation that kept her quite busy."

"Which was?" I ask, fearing I already know his answer.

"Her 'disturbed' son." The quotation fingers, stretched smile over hard, shiny eyes. "Me."

This is the most passionate demonstration of feeling I've experienced with Dan and I log it, but deliberately choose not to steer my little boat of inquiry into those churning waters for the time being. "So their marriage was . . . ?" I ask.

"Utterly bankrupt," he replies. "Though it all looked good enough from the outside. Pillars of the community. Et cetera, et cetera, blah, blah, blah."

I contemplate him for a moment, his bitterness. "So, anyone teach you much about how to set things to rights in a relationship?" I ask.

He laughs, though it doesn't look like he finds it very funny.

"And you?" I turn to Judy.

"My father died when I was eleven. I acquired a stepfather at fifteen who was a pleasant enough man, I guess, though he was always awkward around me, budding young woman that I was. He had a lot of money and drank too much. My mother was delighted to have nabbed him, though I'm not sure she actually liked him very much. My mother was a truly nice person who couldn't stand conflict, or even acknowledge its existence."

"You would fight?" I ask.

"With my mother?" Judy smiles. "We would have *discussions*. And if ever I dared raise my voice, or speak out of turn, or do anything other than act like the forty-seven-year-old I was expected to be I was—politely—asked to retire to my room until I 'regained my composure.'"

"So neither of you came into the marriage with any of the skills one needs to duke it out," I observe.

"*Duke it out?*" Judy comically cocks a supercilious eyebrow, suddenly the quintessential garden-lady. "*Duke it out?* I was raised to believe that in a good marriage the skills of 'duking it out,' as you put it, would be really *quite* unnecessary."

The vicious cycle works like this: you can start from either side, but let's start off with him. Things are running along smoothly enough, and then Judy disappoints him somehow. She might be overly aggressive, as with his driving, or she might be underresponsive to some difficulty he is having at work. Dan might experience her as either too bossy or as abandoning, or both. But, none of this is said, and none of it is dealt with. Dan gives Judy no opportunity to correct or apologize. He withdraws. Judy might guess at what has happened; she might go after him for a bit. But her staying power isn't great and he doesn't help very much, and so, in short order, she also withdraws. Not overtly, and by no means dramatically—these are not red gaping gashes; they are small punctures, little nicks, everyday hurts. But the next time Judy is called upon to be giving to Dan—to silence the sharp remark on the tip of her tongue, or come forth with the kind word he needs—that nick holds Judy back, just a teeny bit, from her previous unstinting generosity. And Dan feels it, feels this new reserve in her. Although he may not articulate it, perhaps, even to himself, it hurts, hurts deeply. It creates, in fact, the next injury that Dan now carries, causing him to hold himself back, which in turn causes her . . . In the feedback language of family therapy, diagnosing their choreography is elementary: the more Dan withdraws, the more critical and less loving Judy becomes; the colder and angrier Judy becomes, the more Dan withdraws. Wind up the machine and let it self-reinforce for twenty years and what you have at the end looks like two decent people trapped inside a dying relationship.

So go love's small murders, tiny, everyday escalations of injury reacted to by disconnection, causing more injury, until one fast-forwards to a couple whose initial passion has become so "encrusted" with disappointment that they barely function as a couple any longer. While conventional therapists are trained to keep an ear open for particular stressors—his father dies, she loses her job, a child is born with a medical problem—in relational recovery we are drawn to the cumulative effect of such everyday lesions. As Dan talks about work, Judy turns her back. Instead of telling Judy to turn back around, Dan stops talking. A few years later, without much notice, Dan has stopped sharing his work life at all. Or this—angry at his perceived lack of participation in the family, Judy finds herself less interested in sex. The whole thing starts to feel like more bother than pleasure. Judy hears from her girlfriends that at her age, women just lose interest, and so she writes it off to menopause. But she's playing a shell game with herself. Down deep, Judy doesn't really want to give Dan pleasure, or, if she were honest, give him the satisfaction of giving her pleasure. She doesn't want to give in to him at all; she's too angry. With the couples I see there are always obvious issues to be dealt with. But, while these must be taken seriously in their own right, they are also the media through which the couple's unique downward spiral plays itself out. *The degeneration of connection that spans years is made up of thousands of tiny incidents of disconnection that span mere moments.* In the absence of closeness, other feelings rush in to fill up the vacated space—anger, bitterness, despair. Metaphors of choking come to mind, unruly growths—weeds, rust, cancer. It's not that anything dreadfully bad happens to people like Judy and Dan so much as that there comes to be less and less good.

Some couples manage well enough, dragging their carapace of unacknowledged hurts, crablike, through their lives, buoyed up by tradition, religion, good manners. The world calls these unions successful and in a way I suppose they are, though I wouldn't wish their lives on anyone I cared for. Others, like Dan, less stable and more ambitious, find some way to blow up the stultifying structure containing them, often irresponsibly and at great cost. One partner goes into menopause or therapy, someone has a "midlife crisis," rages at a child, has an affair. Often, when women wake up to their thirst for more passion they lean on their husbands, throwing the marriage into crisis, while a great many men find their lost passion in the arms of someone new, also throwing their marriage into crisis. However the job gets done, in a clean way or bloodily, few couples enter my office feeling as though the vital connection that once bound them together still holds. Passion has fled. And one if not both partners have decided, whether or not they have had the clarity or courage to voice it, that life is not worth living without it.

"My name is Lester Burnham," a disembodied voice informs us. "I am forty-two. In less than a year I'll be dead. Of course, I don't know that yet. And in way, I'm dead already." Such are the opening lines of the Academy Award–winning film *American Beauty,* a meditation on passion lost, gone awry, and, finally, recovered. The image on the screen shifts. "Here I am jerking off in the shower," the voice-over explains. "It's the high point of my day."

If Judy and Dan face a slow leaching of their life's blood, dazed Lester has suffered a massive internal hemorrhage.

The scene shifts to a lawn where a perky, attractive woman

crisply snips a long-stemmed rose. "That's my wife, Carolyn." The forlorn man watches from the window, and then nails her character in a two-sentence summary. "See how the handle of her pruning shears matches the color of her gardening clogs?" asks the voice. "That's *not* an accident."

We see a close-up of Lester's face as he rides in the backseat of the family car, depressed and vacant. "My wife and daughter both think I'm a gigantic loser," says the dreamy voice. "And they're *right*. I *have* lost something. I'm not exactly sure what it is, but I know I didn't always feel this . . . sedated. But you know what?" the dead voice suddenly quickens. "It's never too late to get it back!"

If patriarchy were conceived of as a psychiatric illness, it would best be classified under the heading: disordered desire. *American Beauty* depicts each member of this dark, prototypically modern family as struggling with desire—uncovering it, maturing it, discovering it for the first time. What Lester has lost, we instantly grasp, is vitality itself, his capacity for deep feeling. He is an ordinary man stranded in that stock ironic setting, the suburban wasteland. "This is the dead land," writes T. S. Eliot. "This is the cactus land / Here the stone images / Are raised, here they receive / The supplication of a dead man's hand." Bullied by his wife, alienated from his daughter, stuck in a meaningless job, Lester's "lifestyle" has eaten his life.

The luxurious, vibrant, catalytic agent of Lester's recovery is his daughter's vixen girlfriend. Lester Burnham is rescued by lust. At Janie's high school, Dad becomes violently smitten. The camera cuts ludicrously between Lester's near-drooling face and the imagined striptease of the girl, who opens her blouse to unleash a cascade of blood-red rose petals. "I felt like I'd been in a coma for the last twenty years and I was just now waking up." In subsequent scenes we find the girl, Angela, fantasized in lush Technicolor, nude and alluring, bathed in, buried in, rose petals. In his mind, Lester kisses her, extracting a petal from his mouth. All of these sprouting buds are a Hollywood update of ancient vegetation symbolism, the return of life to the desiccated terrain: ". . . breeding / Lilacs out of the dead land, mixing / Memory and desire, stirring / Dull roots with spring rain."

"I think he's sweet," Lester overhears Angela telling his daughter. "I'd fuck him if he worked out a little." Clownish Lester dashes to the garage, where he scrambles madly to retrieve some old dumb-bells and has at it. His transformation has begun. In short order, he quits his job and takes up pot, rock and roll, and a sports car. He begins, in Joseph Campbell's famous phrase, to follow his bliss.

We do not track one love relationship in this tale, however, but three—Lester's, his wife's, and his daughter's. While Lester's dull root is being stirred, his family is not standing still. If Lester has been a disaster at following the masculine agenda—first failing at it and then blowing it up—his wife, Carolyn, can't get enough of it. Feed-ing on motivational tapes, frantically ambitious in her real-estate career, she rules herself and everyone else, a tightly clenched over-achiever on steroids.

"I will sell this house today," Carolyn repeats her affirmation, rub-ber-gloved, furiously scrubbing a rundown property. "I *will* sell this house today!" While Lester wants desperately to resign from the madness of "power over," Carolyn would love to drown in it. She meets her match in Buddy Kane, "King of Real Estate," whose wife left him over the trifle that he was never home, and who relieves his stress over her loss with a handgun. "Nothing quite like that kick in your hand to help you relax!" We soon see Carolyn, wearing a sprightly smile, blasting the face off a silhouette in a shooting gallery. "How does it feel to be nailed by the king?" Buddy asks, in their slap-stick sex scene. He energetically pounds away at Carolyn, her legs flung open wide to receive him.

"I love it!" she screams. "I *love* it! *Fuck me, Your Majesty!*"

Whether on her own, or through association with Buddy, Carolyn adores power. If the sheer thrill of dominance could be sold in a pill, she would be first in the purchasing line. While Lester's natural desire has grown dead, Carolyn's has gone terribly wrong. From the first frames, we are meant to see her as Lester does, as that male night-mare—the frigid, controlling wife. In the film's only scene in which they touch, Lester reaches out for her sexually and she begins to respond—until she notices the bottle of beer in his hand. "Lester," she warns, "you'll spill beer on the couch." Ignoring her, he kisses her neck. "*Lester,*" she emphasizes, alarmed, "the *couch.*" Rather than enshrining the furniture, however, Lester would prefer using it with her. "It's just a couch," he murmurs, growing edgy. Carolyn sits bolt upright, offended. "This is a four-thousand dollar sofa upholstered in Italian silk," she sputters, indignant. "It is *not* just a couch!" Her anger invokes his. "We used to have *fun,*" he protests, impotent and enraged. "When did you become so *joyless?*"

The film means for us to side with Lester, seeing Carolyn as that abomination—the Housewife, she who worships dead gods like Lysol, Sub-Zero refrigerators, real estate. Left to her own resourses, the film suggests, she would burry them all in Astroturf. But Lester is no prize in his own right. Middle-class Carolyn worked hard for that couch; it wouldn't have killed him to put down his beer. Irresponsible, rebellious boy-husband meets overly responsible, angry mother-wife—the Burnhams offer a broadly drawn rendering of contemporary American marriage. Both partners long for passion, but they are both too hurt by the other—his selfishness, her shrewishness—to sustain it inside their marriage. Real passion requires surrender. And the last person either Lester or Carolyn wants to surrender to at this juncture is one another.

Presented as a postmodern farce, the Burnham's story reveals a great deal about the deformation of desire under patriarchy. We first meet the couple in a state so devoid of passion that it approximates death. Is this merely the natural degenerative course of erotic intensity in any long-term relationship? Is passionate monogamy an oxymoron? It is, frankly, difficult to say with authority what healthy long-term sexuality looks like because the patriarchal context in which we all live is so profoundly inimical to health. Patriarchy's damage goes beyond pulling men and women away from the fulfillment of their desires. For couples like Lester and Carolyn, Judy and Dan, patriarchy erodes the capacity to desire at all.

While women appear to be overly dependent, and men appear antidependent, actually both genders are taught to renounce their wants and needs. Traditionally, a good woman's defining characteristic is her willingness to subordinate her wishes to those she loves. And for the heroic man, one who "serves and protects," who "does his job," his own wants and needs are supposed to hold such little importance that he is barely to take note of them. Women learn service and men, stoicism. The transition from childhood into these adult roles is a journey toward what psychiatry calls "anhedonia," the relinquishment of pleasure. This is each sex's official story, and it is a script followed in real life by a surprising number of couples.

"When I learned of Dan's affair," says Judy in a later, reflective session, "it was first a bomb, and then later a wake-up call. I don't condone the affair, or even forgive it. But I can't in all honesty claim not to understand it. We drifted apart, went our separate ways, slowly over decades. In the last couple of years, there's been hardly anything left between us other than life's little details and our kids."

"Why did you put up with that?" I ask her. "Why didn't you push for more?"

"I thought all that time that it was enough," she says. "I knew it wasn't great, but there always seemed to be a reason. Someone in the family was ill, or there was stress at his job."

The third ring of psychological patriarchy, the collusion of silence, eats at partners' desire like a slow disease. Women like Judy swallow their wants and needs, consciously minimizing their sacrifice, but all the while pulling away from the abundance of pleasure—their own and their partner's. Fulfilled desire restores us; it reminds us of the joy we take in one another. But for "giving" women, and "hardworking" men, sacrifice, not joy, becomes the preeminent value.

While most realms of desire—our minds, our hearts—can be corralled into renunciation, sexual longing, the realm of our most purely animal selves, is the last domain to comply. But in those instances when sexual passion does break through the constraints of patriarchy, as it did for Dan and for the Burnhams—what surfaces is often wildly immature. Dan's erotic longings for one of his staff amounted to little more than a leering puppy-love, "icky enough," as Dan described it, to trigger a complaint against him. Developmentally "arrested," each gender's longings, when they reemerge, often carry the flavor of the age the person was when passion was first put behind bars.

In *American Beauty*, Carolyn's bedazzled worship of Ron looks suspiciously like a preadolescent's adoration for her horse, her teacher, or a soap-opera doctor. They are a young girl's dreams of a tamed brute animal, Beauty's "Beast" filled with wild masculine power dampened down and made mild. Many common female fantasies align with the inchoate yearnings of a ten-, eleven-, twelve-year-old girl. While anorexic waifs may grace fashion runways, well-endowed heroines swoon in the arms of pectorally spectacular heroes on covers of the eternally popular romance novel. When women speak frankly about their sexual fantasies, they are often shockingly "incorrect." To be swept away by Prince Charming, Clara's handsome Nutcracker, someone both soft enough to be unthreatening and yet at the same time omniscient and omnipotent, this is a longing for the perfect father, youthful, powerful, and benevolent.

Men's fantasies tend to be even younger and, consequently, more troubling. If romance is the great seller among women, the insatiable market for men is porn. What many women find offensive in the male sexual marketplace is not erotic explicitness per se but pornography's characteristic lack of mutuality, or even real personhood. Even when not overtly aggressive, pornography posits women as existing for men's use. But as the pioneer sex therapist David Snarch once observed, people tend to do in the bedroom what they do in every other room. To be of use is the essence of women's traditional, if increasingly archaic, job description, so why would we expect it to be different sexually? One recalls the famous Victorian journal entry of Lady Alice Hillingdon: "I am happy now that Charles calls on my bedchamber less frequently than of old. As it is, I endure but two calls a week, and when I hear his steps outside my door I lie down on my bed, close my eyes, open my legs, and think of England."

It is no accident that middle-aged, flagging Lester should exploit for his rejuvenation a girl literally his daughter's age. If Carolyn longs to be overwhelmed by a vulnerability-denying motivational tape with a penis, Lester urgently requires resuscitation—to be inspired (breathed into) by the freshness of Angela's youth, her flesh. This is not love; it's ingestion. And yet, when Lester envisions Angela sexually, there is nothing girlish about her; she is lush, knowing, abundant, and all-giving—a sexual goddess, a porno queen. The essence of porn is a fantasy in which everything the man does is perfect, and the woman's sexual pleasure lies in the giving of pleasure. This archetype of male desire resonates with another. Who else in our culture is pictured as deriving pleasure in the giving of it? What Lester most yearns for, as do most of the men in my practice, indeed, in my life, is the unstinting limitless nurturer, she who was untimely ripped from his arms as a little boy. I call this voluptuous pleasure-bestower the *sexual mother,* the caregiver boys did not get enough of, now transposed to manhood and eroticised.

What is common to Dan, Lester, and Carolyn's erotic yearnings, in their immaturity, is how cut off they are from a real relationship. Carolyn's benevolent brute, Lester's idealized slave—these are children's fantasies with grown-up consequences. And yet one can also see in such longings a sexualized version of patriarchy's essential quid pro quo: "Serve me and I will take care of you perfectly," says the man. "Perform for me, and I will answer all of your needs," says the woman. These are difficult promises to fulfill in real life. And Lester and Carolyn show us what Dan and Judy have already, bitterly learned—we don't.

CHAPTER NINE

A New Model of Love

A woman can be proud and stiff
When on love intent;
But Love has pitched his mansion in
The place of excrement;
For nothing can be sole or whole
That has not been rent.
—W. B. YEATS,
"Crazy Jane Talks with the Bishop"

The first phase of relational recovery, *bringing the couple back into connection,* requires the partners, as individuals, to move beyond gender roles that were imposed upon them, with or without their consent, as children. Relational recovery supports women in reclaiming their full authority and men in reclaiming connectedness. Once the partners can speak and listen, once they are reconnected enough to function as a real couple, we can work on their relationship. The second phase of therapy aims to retrieve the passion the partners once had and have lost. Like most of the couples I see, the marriages of Judy and Dan, and Lester and Carolyn, degenerated over time because their capacity as partners to hold on in the face of difficulties simply wasn't up to the task. Overwhelmed by dozens of instances of disconnection, both large and small, each of them, in different ways, turned his or her back on their bond, and harbored, instead, a growing sense of disappointment and loneliness. The cost of letting go may have seemed insignificant at first, but it steadily grew to the point of threatening their marriage's survival. In the first phase of treatment, women move back into intimacy by daring to tell the truth, and men move back into intimacy by stepping down from "privileged obliviousness" and coming in from the cold of disconnection. Each partner is asked to move beyond patriarchy's version of what constitutes being a good woman or man. In the second phase, *reclaiming real passion,* each partner is asked to move beyond his or her compelling, understandable, but ultimately childish fantasies, to move beyond patriarchy's version of love.

The love story that Judy and Dan, and Lester and Carolyn, have been raised with ill equips them for real love's challenges. In order to begin the work of recovering passion, we must understand both what has been lost and also what has come to replace it. What has been lost is the state of authentic connection that we are primed for at birth, a state that is intrinsically ardent, vital, and, despite its ups and downs, pleasurable. The model that takes its place posits love as both exalted and unattainable. Connection is usurped by romance.

> *I'll go write a poem*
> *and then take a nap.*
> *Or stand for a while in the sun.*
> *Some ladies are cruel to their knights.*
> *I know which ones.*

Thus begins Europe's earliest secular verse, William of Aquitaine's "L'Amour Lointain," "Distant Love," the first known modern love poem. The poem contains many of the characteristics that will become stock features of the tradition known as courtly love. In Aquitaine's poem, the valorous, faithful knight suffers piteously at the hands of a "cruel lady," who keeps her distance, not delivering unto the hero the sweet relief he so craves. This poem, as were many that followed, is essentially an extraordinarily well-wrought come-on, a three-part fugue sung by the lover, the coy maiden, and her resistance. (O gather ye rosebuds while ye may!) If courtly love had remained nothing more than a lighthearted seduction romp our lives might all be less complicated. Instead, it became nothing less than our culture's template for love. Lancelot and Guinevere, Tristan and Isolde—Europe's first great lovers spilled their amorous exploits onto the pages of the "romances," popular literature written in the vernacular tongue—the burgeoning "romance languages"—which set them apart from "serious" works written in Latin. The characters, themes, dramas of these romances became the foundation for romance itself, the cultural embodiment of our deepest feelings of connection. What are those elements and why did they so readily gain such a powerful grip on our collective psyches? The gift and the burden of romantic love is captured in the two-word title of its first known iteration: "Distant Love." The operative word is *distant*. Sir William's lover would undoubtedly have been some other man's wife. Courtly love, our prototype for romance, was adulterous. Any thoughts that these doughty knights were burning themselves to a crisp slaying fire-breathing dragons, cutting themselves to ribbons crossing sword bridges with bare hands and feet, humiliating themselves by submitting to public pillory, all for the sake of their *wives*, should be immediately banished. Whether it was Guinevere, Isolde, Dante's Beatrice, Anna Karenina, Helen of Troy, or Katharine of *The English Patient*, throughout Western literature, the women who seem to inspire men's greatest passions are those belonging to other men, or at the least star-crossed beauties who do not, and cannot, belong to them. I challenge any reader to find in the whole of modern Western literature a list of more than three scintillating, enraptured, heat-drenched . . . marriages.

The romantic love story is a paradoxical fusion of two extraordinarily potent messages. The first is that love, deep connection, is the most important, indeed the only truly important matter in the world. And the second is that true love cannot exist in this world. Romeo and Juliet in sweltering Verona; Jack and young Rose aboard the *Titanic*, Katharine and Almásy, the English patient, in the Saharan sands, even the prince and his enchanted swan princess—in our culture what great lovers have always done best is die, heartrendingly and gloriously. There is even a term for this apotheosis of passion—*liebestod* in German, "love death," the ultimate climax.

The poet Goethe once said that tragedy ends in death, comedy in marriage. But the romance story fuses the two; it portrays love's union as a kind of suicide pact. What's going on here? There are many ways one might answer that question, but the one germane to our discussion is this: what's going on here is patriarchy.

In the great divide of psychological patriarchy, intimacy and love are coded as feminine, and, within that value system, being feminine means being devalued. How do we get from love devalued to love romanticized? Through some complex and revealing twists and turns. An essential element of patriarchal culture is the predominant value of production, or, if you prefer, of heroism. In the beginning, says Goethe's Faust, is the deed. Love and connection are well and good so long as they do not interfere with the real work at hand. Aeneas must turn away from the sensuality of Dido and march off to found Rome. Odysseus must break free of love's enchantment, Circe, to return to his adventures and earn his way home. Even in the courtly romances themselves, love is supposed to *drive* great deeds, not *replace* them. Sir Gawain rides from King Arthur's court to visit the great hero, Yvain, who has fallen in love and has lived for a year in peace and harmony with a beautiful country woman and her children. This is all fine for a while, Gawain reminds his friend, but you are Yvain, a knight of the Round Table. You have lingered here long enough. And then, the clincher: "Think of your reputation!" Yvain is saddled and gone within the hour. The most famous ancient who put love over valor was Paris of Troy, and look at the chaos he unleashed!

It isn't that the patriarchal system teaches us to hold love in outright contempt, as it does vulnerability. Craving love is such a powerful, essential force in human nature that any cultural scheme holding it in explicit disdain would eventually evoke rebellion. Rather, the code of masculinity invites us to keep love corralled, relegated, like women and all things feminine, to its (second) place.

It is important to remember that while boys may live in "boy culture," and girls in "girl culture"—in other words, while each sex may have a subculture of its own—all of us, boy and girl, man and woman, live within the larger context of patriarchy. And patriarchy glorifies the values and attitudes of masculinity. Patriarchy is "boy culture" writ large, and performance-based esteem is the name of the game. What you *do*, not how you feel, or even who you are, is the paramount value. Patriarchal culture can easily absorb a generation of women learning to do more, women who act more "like men." Women's newfound assertiveness and public competence produce turf battles, certainly, but no fundamental threat to the masculine values of our society. But a man, or even a boy, who rejects those same masculine values, who deliberately chooses to become more "like a woman," represents an elemental challenge to the importance of heroism—performance, production—over relationship. And such a man, even more deeply, poses a challenge to the *dance of contempt*, patriarchy's central organizing principle; its core value of privileging half of our humanity while disowning the other. For men to deliberately cross over into the despised realm of the "feminine" defies the structure of patriarchy itself. When women cross the line into the "masculine" domain, they reappropriate qualities the world holds in high regard. But for a man, crossing the line represents a decision to reject those values in favor of qualities that are at best deemed second-rate and at worst explicitly reviled. It doesn't require tremendous subtlety to understand why moving into a despised domain is more difficult than moving into an exalted one. Ambitious women may threaten particular groups of privileged men, through the force of sheer competition. But relational men reject, and thereby threaten, the core values of patriarchy itself. This is one reason why men— many of whom long to be released from the confines of their traditional roles—still find change so difficult, both collectively and individually. Remembering this asymmetry of value, the dance of contempt, helps us understand the singular ugliness leveled against boys deemed "too feminine." It is why a collective men's movement paralleling the enormously effective women's movement has not, and most likely will not, form and take hold. Our society is organized around production and consumption, not connection and relatedness.

As far back as 1978, pioneer sociologist Joseph Pleck conducted a national survey asking men about their job satisfaction. Pleck found that over 80 percent of the male respondents did not like going to

work and, if given the choice, would prefer not to. What kind of
socialization pressure, Pleck wondered, does it take to keep a man at
a job most of his waking day, year after year, despite, often deep and
articulate, dissatisfaction? I have joked that if every man in the
West woke up tomorrow in full relational recovery, our economy
would quickly collapse. It is alluring, I must admit, this vision of
millions of men simultaneously calling in "sick," struck with the
sudden realization that they'd rather talk with their kids, make love
to their wives, or play with their dogs.

Our need for love and connection cannot be forgone, and yet society demands that we, particularly men, subordinate that need to the
exigencies of work and competition. When it comes to love, patriarchy truly can't live with it and can't live without it. The cultural
task then becomes how to induct both sexes into a vision of love that
honors humans' profound need for it while at the same time ensur-
ing that it won't get in the way of the "serious" agenda of production,
consumption, business, and war—the "real" matters of the world.

One way of protecting masculine values and pursuits from things
deemed feminine is denigration. When patriarchal values seek to
assert their predominance over "feminine" values, one basic move is
suppression. But as most woman are acutely aware, another common
tack is one in which the speaker is not combated at all, but merely
disqualified.

A few years into my private practice I had to hospitalize a client for
a severe manic episode. I wished to keep him safe and have him sta-
bilized on medication. The ward staff implored me to attend their
"rounds" and contribute what I could to their treatment of my
patient. I cleared a morning of clinical work and joined a team meeting lead by an older psychiatrist. After forty-five minutes of listening to this doctor's theories on a client I'd seen for years and he'd seen
only once, with five minutes left to the conference, I was asked my
thoughts. But, in the mental-health pecking order, as a young psychiatric social worker I was ranked "feminine" to the "masculine"
authority of this older physician, and for some reason he felt a need
to pull rank. Halfway through my third sentence, he leaned forward

and asked solicitously, "Where did you train?" I recall being stunned by the question. "Excuse me?" I said. "Where did you go to school?" he pressed. Flustered, I told him. He smiled. "I hear that's an excellent program," he remarked and then summarily closed the meeting.

While women on the job may encounter more of this kind of treatment than their male counterparts, it is also true that few men have evaded being on the receiving end of such behavior. In the dominance rituals of patriarchy, such condescension may be as effective as outright intimidation in dismissing the "feminine" in someone of either sex.

This sort of disdain can be overtly demeaning, as it was here, but it can also nest covertly within a cloud of apparent benevolence. When the voice of the patriarch dismisses "feminine" values it often becomes "patronizing." *One way to discredit people or traits is to position them as beneath concern; another is to place them above it.* Women, and "womanish" values, may be seen as too weak, flighty, irrational to be taken seriously. But they might just as effectively be excluded for being "too good"—too sensitive, too refined, too spiritual—for the vulgar realities of our world. "There, there, dear. Don't worry your pretty little head about it. We'll see to it." Romanticized versions of women's "higher natures," Goethe's "Eternal Feminine forever drawing us up!" have always been closely associated with romanticism, since the days of the troubadours. The impulse here is one I call *marginalization through idealization.* Some "feminine" traits are not invited to the negotiation table because they belong under it; others, because they belong over it. But in either case, they don't belong. What has all this to do with romantic love? *The patriarchal tale of love does to intimacy what it does to many things deemed feminine—it idealizes it in principle and devalues it in fact.* From the twelfth century to the present, romantic love, for all its sexuality, is primarily spiritual; love's drama follows the rhythm of doom and resurrection. Unable to exist "in this world," lovers die but are never defeated. Their great love remains, eternally set free from the fetters of earthly life.

This vision's debt to the transcendentalism of Christianity could hardly be more patent. For the Roman Stoics the word "passion" connoted a diseased state, an aberration that threatened their ideal of psychological equilibrium. The new religion imbued passion with positive connotations. Christ's willingness to die for mankind stems from his passion for us, and the sacred drama of his crucifixion and resurrection become known as Christ's Passion. From its earliest use in the Christian West, passionate love has always been associated with feelings too refined for the world.

When we as a culture take human passion, idealize it, and place it outside the realm of real life, we do two things at once. At one level we succeed in honoring intimacy while yet making sure that it doesn't impede the "real" work of the world. And yet, at another level, we also acknowledge that love, indeed, does not fit into patriarchal order. *By simultaneously idealizing love and placing it out of reach, the romance story offers a compromise between human instinct and patriarchal order.* It serves us collectively in much the same way Freud described neurotic symptoms as serving individuals.

Arguably the most fundamental aspect of Freud's system is his analysis of intrapsychic conflict—the endless struggle between the two titans, instinct and civilization embodied within each of us as the unconscious and the superego. Freud's prototypic disease, hysteria, serves as a good illustration. A typical case would sound something like this: A young patient falls onto the floor, in a hysterical fit, writhing and shaking convulsively. Hypnosis—later, free association—uncovers a secret forbidden attraction to her own cousin. Repelled by her incestuous impulse, she banishes it from her mind, only to have it resurface in her body. The fit—which always occurs in her cousin's presence—with its savage shaking and gyrations at once disguises and yet also partially gratifies her wish for sexual "discharge," and for her cousin's attention. Like all neurotic symptoms, it represents a compromise solution to the equal, and contradictory, pulls of instinct and propriety.

I would suggest that the etherealization of love represents just such a compromise; it is the collective cultural symptom we have employed for centuries in order to live with the contradictory demands of patriarchal order and our own hearts. *Like a compromise symptom, the phrase "distant love" is self-contradicting, an oxymoron. Love means closeness. As a prescription, the paradoxical injunction that we must keep closeness distant, at a remove from our real lives, is enormously conservative; it serves the status quo. As a description, however, the insight that true love is fundamentally inimical to patriarchal values is highly radical. All great lovers are anarchists, insurrectionists.* They are killed, like Christ himself, because their message deeply threatens patriarchal order. Romeo and Juliet are defeated by that quintessentially masculine value—honor. Katharine and Almásy in *The English Patient* are defeated by war. Jack and Rose aboard the *Titanic,* by class. *Like a patient reenacting trauma, the romantic love story endlessly replays the plight of "feminine" lovers who come up against and are ultimately crushed by the "masculine" world of politics, class, war. It is the drama of deep connection overpowered by the forces of disconnection, the recapitulation of our own forced exile at age three, four, ten, thirteen.* We once loved this wholeheartedly. Before the curtain of gender taught us to dampen and lie, we knew what this passion felt like. And we know, whether we consciously remember or not, what grief at its loss feels like as well.

The patriarchal vision of love at once memorializes the passion we once had while teaching us that it is "unrealistic" to want it any longer. It is about love *over there,* far away, unattainable. But what if we were to tell another story? What if we rejected patriarchy's invitation to marginalize intimacy by enshrining it, resisted the spiritual tale of distant love in favor of an earthly tale of love right here in front of us—everyday passion, with all its travails and tumult?

The new paradigm is captured in this moment: the infant and mother are in a state of such tender closeness that one can truly speak of it as bliss. Cuddled close, you can see how the tiny child has "molded," allowed its body to relax and conform to the contours of the mother. Skin against skin, the two have literally shaped themselves into a physical union. And then something happens. First, in the baby's face—its cheeks scrunch up, quickly turn red, muscles tense. The baby suddenly stiffens, a log of wood in the mother's arms, and emits an ear-splitting scream. The mother's face first shows startle, then alarm; she scans her child and in quick succession relief flits over her face, followed by annoyance. She jostles the baby, cooing to it, smiling. To no avail. She puts a finger in her child's mouth, begins walking. Mother runs through a quick repertoire of movements, sounds, gestures. "She's hungry," she says, smiling apologetically to someone off-camera. She gives her daughter her breast. The infant turns away, stiffer, angrier, louder. More walking, jostling, more noise. Mother looks down at her daughter, only not smiling this time. Frustrated, her face is dark with anger and agitation. The infant throws up her arms, shielding her face as if to protect herself from the beam of her mother's wrath. Her hands are balled into tiny fists, a primordial gesture of protection, protest, her piercing wail now a scream of "NO!" And then, as suddenly as it came, like some hot summer storm, it stops. The nipple is accepted, milk flows, looks of relief flood both mother and child. The baby cries a few more times even as she suckles. And then she begins to relax. Muscles release, molding resumes, and . . . bliss.

This scene is one of thousands captured and closely analyzed by Dr. Edward Tronick and his team at Children's Hospital in Boston. Tronick and other infant observational researchers are revolutionizing our understanding of early human relationships. In turning to infant research as a portal to a greater understanding of love relationships, I am not unusual. Since Freud gave birth to modern psychology, our understanding of development has meant understanding our first relationships. Questions about the nature of human attachment, connection, love inexorably lead to the primordial bond between mother and child. Since Freud, psychology has told one story about that bond, one developmental love story, as it were. And it may come as no great shock to learn that conventional psychology's developmental love story replicates many of the same values and impulses found in the romantic love story, or, in other words, in patriarchy.

Freud's tale begins with mother and child wrapped in a state of "oceanic bliss," a primordial union. The infant possesses no boundaries, nor even a clear recognition that he and his mother are separate entities. In our first, prototypic relationship we are the passive recipients of milk, warmth, comfort; we flourish in a state of pure ecstatic pleasure. And we, most particularly males, spend the rest of our childhoods getting over it—as well we should, Freud might have added. In order to get on with the business of growth, of becoming human, our development is comprised of successive stages of leave-taking. As our nervous systems and psyches grow, we peel away from Mother, piece by piece and bit by bit. We move from passivity to activity. We begin to "self-regulate." Where once *She* was the sole source of comfort, we begin to "self-soothe." Where once *She* mediated all feelings, we begin to identify and have our own. Where once *She* was the source of flowing milk, we learn to pop a frozen pizza into the microwave and get a ride with Joey to the mall. On the "feminine" left side of this great developmental divide resides Mother, union, connection, regression, and on the "masculine" right side resides the world, growth, autonomy, competence. Maturation means crossing from the left to the right. Health is a synonym for passing from the world of attachment, and moving off into the world of "individuation," "separation," or, as one evangelical theorist phrased it, "psychological birth." Connection versus competence, relatedness versus strength—does this dichotomy sound familiar? *The traditional story of human development recapitulates the essential polarities embedded in the romance story and in psychological patriarchy. Our development is a path leading away from our idealized, marginalized mothers—and all things "feminine"—toward the worldly heroism called "autonomy."*

In *I Don't Want to Talk About It*, I recounted in some detail the hundreds of hero stories strewn with the bodies of dead or abandoning mothers—from Moses to *Star Wars*, even Bambi. What good mothers do, age-old stories inform us, is get the hell out of the way. My personal favorite is Perceval, from the medieval Holy Grail story. The tale opens with the hero's mother, whose husband has been killed in war, desperately trying to protect her young son from the wages of manly battle. She spirits him off to an enchanted grotto where he is so naive he doesn't even know what a horse looks like. But can the regressive suck of mother prevail against the exploits that are his destiny? Are you kidding? One day, knights on horseback shudder through this idyllic dream. Young Perceval gazes up at these creatures—which he sees as some undistinguished amalgam of horse-man-and-armor. He takes them for gods and begs to join them. Off he is whisked, without breaking stride, and Mom, help-

lessly watching her son vanish into the horizon wordlessly, immediately drops dead on the road—never to be mentioned again. Now,
that's a good woman. Mothers, like many things feminine, like love
itself, are too good for this world—and evidently need to be shoved
aside for the work of the world to proceed.

A generation ago, women researchers and theorists across the
West challenged the predominant developmental love story. Jean
Baker Miller, Carol Gilligan, and the theorists of the Stone Center all
claimed that while boys may grow, as we have been told, through
separation and autonomy, girls speak in a different voice—living and
developing throughout their whole lives embedded in relationships.
The terms of growth *versus* connection were junked in favor of a
brand-new idea; *growth-in-connection*—and *relational psychology* was
born. I am pleased to have added my work to that revolution. Not
only girls, I and a host of others now say, live and grow in the
matrix of relationship, but so, too, do boys. The story of boys'
retreat from connection into autonomy is not how real boys develop.
It is our culture's story about how boys are supposed to develop. In
fact, boys no less than girls breathe and grow in relational context. *It
isn't, as I tell the parents I work with, that development requires us to "separate" from relationships in order to grow, but rather that we must transform
immature relationships into mature ones.* As children develop, the family must accommodate their increased mastery over themselves and
the world. The parents must *change*, not "let go." The idea that
children must "leave" in order to "strike out" or, conversely, that parents, particularly mothers, must "back off' to give children, particularly boys, their "space" has no basis in truth or science. After
dozens and dozens of studies, not one shred of empirical data supports this century-old paradigm of development. The language of
"autonomy," "separation," "individuation," the idyll of an idealized
mother making way for the "real" work of the world, the positing of
growth and connection as opposites, all reveal our culture's antirelational bias. The development story is simply the age-old idea of
heroism versus connection dressed up in a lab coat and clipboard.
But if we begin to recognize that humans mature in relationship, we
must ask ourselves what, exactly, do we mean by *relationship?*

A few beats behind the advent of relational psychology a generation of researchers did don lab coats and clipboards—or at least video
cameras and banks of graduate students armed with the skills of
"close analysis." Daniel Stern, Ed Tronick, and others replaced the
usual armchair philosophizing about our earliest relationship with
actual rigorous observation. Until that time, most of what we "knew"
about infant relations were "inferred" from the analysis of adults.
What the new field of infant observational research found challenged most of psychology's sacred cows. Gone was the regressive,
all-giving mother. Gone was the passive, recipient infant, and gone,
sorry to say, was that state of original bliss. In its stead was this: a
dance, a stormy, gorgeous, ever-changing mosaic in which, from the
first weeks of life, mother and infant both actively collaborate. Yes,
the mother gives and the mother regulates, but so, too, it turns out,
does the child. The child stiffens or softens, reaches out or turns
away, coos or screams. Love, from its inception, is not a one-way
street. Neither is it some idyll of harmony. *The pattern, recorded and
repeated endlessly, is the rhythm of harmony, disharmony, and restoration.* As
in the scene I related, mother and child begin in bliss, move into
fraught, intensely disturbing disequilibrium, and, after frantic, often
angry, attempts on both sides, find their way back to equilibrium
once more. This is the rhythm of real relationships—not some air-
brushed, sentimental greeting card of ever-giving mothers and ever-
smiling cherubs. The most striking thing, in reviewing this research,
is how abundantly obvious it all seems once it is named—all we really
needed was to ask a few mothers about their real-life experience and
take their descriptions seriously. Fulfilling, perhaps, they might have
said, but I have yet to hear a mother describe her challenging and
rewarding dance with an infant as "uninterrupted bliss." The essential quality of real relationships, from our earliest days on this earth,
is the dynamic of change itself, the flow of balance, imbalance, and
balance again. Holding fast to one another in the midst of this flux—
that is our most critical task. Infant observational research teaches us
that our prototypic bond is not characterized *by the absence of disconnection, but the experience of its survival,* in a dozen small ways. It is love
holding firm against the waves—what I have come to call: *connection*

in the face of disconnection. The essential ingredient in all relationships turns out to be precisely the one Dan and Judy, Lester and Carolyn, were never taught: repair.

Why did Dan and Judy let go of one another over the years? Because no one showed them how not to, no one even addressed the need. The official love story posits a state, like the idealized infant and mother, of uninterrupted bliss, while the "real" love story taught Judy that a good wife doesn't push too hard, and taught Dan that he needn't bother pushing at all. Their marriage was a near casualty to society's impulse toward idealizing connection in principle all the while teaching men and women, in complementary ways, to turn from it in their real lives.

The shift from dreaming of passion to living our passion, the work of reembodying love, requires of us nothing less than restructuring most of the terms we have always lived by; it throws us deep into our most frightening internal domains, and it breaks the spine of an order that has determined our world for centuries. Hercules and his labors, Theseus and his Minotaur, Perseus and snake-headed Medusa—would these heroes have possessed the strength required to break that spell, the courage needed to hurl themselves heedlessly into such *terra nova?* In the seconds before we begin our session, Dan nervously slides his glasses up the bridge of his nose, absently fingers the color-coded pens that despite Judy's protests nestle in the breast pocket of the crisp Ralph Lauren shirt Judy bought for him. Looking both warm and harried, Judy contemplates her round husband with the bemused frustration of a resigned mother before turning her face expectantly to me.

You're the ones, I think to myself. If anyone can do it, you can.

CHAPTER TEN

Recovering Real Passion

I visualize the obscure process of mate selection . . . as largely based on unconscious signals or cues by which the partners recognize . . . [opportunities] for joint working-through . . . of still unresolved splits or conflicts inside each other's personalities, while at the same time, paradoxically, also sensing a guarantee that with that person they will not be worked-through.

—H. V. DICKS

When I speak of the journey back to real passion I do not mean a return to that state of uninterrupted erotic bliss the promise of which screams out at us from the headlines of women's magazines and the shelves of the self-help section of bookstores.

Sorry.

When I talk to couples like Judy and Dan about the return of passion, I mean a rekindling of passionate engagement with *all* of the seasons of their lives together, all the nuance, the multitude of feeling, that comes with being fully present to one another. The state of passionate connection they once knew as children, and found again, briefly, in the first flush of love, must be reintroduced into their everyday lives.

The utter joy Judy and Dan describe in their initial months together is one of the great human experiences. Few things thrill us as much as that deep recognition of the early stage of a relationship.

The problem for couples like Judy and Dan is that the patriarchal romance story freezes this early phase and turns it into a static ideal for the whole of the relationship. In much the same way that we have come to hold only one standard of physical beauty and health—a lithe, strong, and above all *youthful* body—we have only one standard of a good relationship—erotic, intoxicated, and, again, *youthful.* Our ideal of relationship is youthful in two senses of the word: youthful in that our standard captures a loving relationship in its earliest stages, the youth of the relationship, as it were, and youthful in the sense that our picture of romance fits the life-stage of a young person—innocent, inexperienced, eager to surrender all of herself in ways more mature people are not. These lovely images capture a beautiful time in our lives, but they exert a monopoly on our thinking that marginalizes the rest of our experience. No real relationship rests in a state of uninterrupted bliss, nor would I wish that for anyone I cared for, even though a part of me yearns for it as much as everyone else does. Real intimacy is a deep engagement with the whole dance, the endless dialectic of harmony, disharmony, and repair. By holding up only the first of these three states as desirable, we cripple couples like Judy and Dan in their capacity to negotiate the rest.

I speak to couples about three phases of healthy relationship—the *promise* (harmony) *disillusionment* (disharmony), and *deep love* (repair). While I call them phases, in fact each facet of a relationship can occur over years, but could equally occur over a single dinner conversation. A couple can move from *promise* through *disillusionment* to *deep love* in the space of several decades, but they could also move back and forth between the three domains, in a dozen small ways, in one evening.

Psychoanalyst Ethel Person once claimed that when a couple dines out together it is normal for them to experience the same kind of mini-fluctuations in their perceptions of their partner's worth that we feel all the time toward ourselves. Over the course of a dinner, your partner may seem to you handsome, oafish, charming, stiff, interesting, tedious—just as, glancing in the mirror, one moment you may think of yourself as quite attractive, the next as singularly ugly. A healthy individual leaves such a dinner and thinks, "That was a nice evening." An immature individual, Person maintains, finishes the evening and thinks, "If only I were with the *right* partner, none of these feelings would be with me." The first person has moved through *disillusionment* to *deep love*, the second has gotten stuck. All in the space of a few hours.

The first phase, the *promise*, is the state of falling in love that has been celebrated for centuries in story and song. I describe it as *love without knowledge*, because even though there may be a deep and real soul recognition, the couple is first coming to know one another in their actual lives. The clearest description I have encountered of this phase comes from Plato's *Symposium*. In it, Socrates claims that long ago, in some primordial past, we were all spheroid, perfect, and bisexual. As we enter our human form, we are divided into two beings, male and female. A chief characteristic of our lives on earth is the great yearning we carry for the state of completion we once enjoyed. If we are lucky, fate brings us into the presence of our split-off half, whom we immediately recognize and with whom we feel compelled to unite.

Contemplating Socrates' tale, two things command attention. First, how closely this simple archetype of love parallels our actual development under patriarchy. Our "halving" into "masculine" and "feminine" parts does not occur in some primordial past, but as we are enrolled into traditional gender—at three to five for boys, ten to thirteen for girls. The second deeply resonant aspect of the tale is the sense of completion, of profound spiritual recognition, that most of us feel when we first fall in love—the conviction that this is literally my other half, my soul mate. It has been fashionable lately in therapeutic and recovery circles to denigrate this youthful experience of soul-recognition. Falling in love is held as suspect. Psychoanalysts speak of it as "idealization," as "giving in to unconscious fantasies," and Twelve-Step counselors call it "love addiction." Let me be clear where I stand on this issue. Not only do I believe that the experience of falling in love is real, I think it one of the most truly real experiences of our lives. Pitting maturity against raw passion strikes me as wrongheaded and churlish, a kind of therapeutic Puritanism. We need to fall in love more deeply, surrender more fully, engage more passionately, not less. I am not blind to concerns about some people's addictive relationship to falling in love. But we shouldn't blame the gun for the murder. It isn't that the experience of falling in love should be held as suspect but rather the ways that we as a culture, and, consequently, many of us as individuals, have ripped the exhilaration of that experience out of its relational context, like a super-refined food, or a drug we get hooked on.

Right or wrong, suspect or trustworthy, the chief characteristic of the promise stage of relationship is, just as Socrates informs us, a visceral sense of completion. Whether we are too sophisticated to admit it aloud or naive enough to come right out and say it, many of us fall in love with the promise that in surrendering to the beloved, all of our unhealed places, all of the old wounds we carry from childhood, will be rectified, or at the least, permanently avoided. We will, at long last, be delivered from the churning caldron of our unfinished business. Were you a blue-collar scrapper? Here, walk down the aisle with a blond goddess from Wellesley. Was your family cold and disengaged? Why not hook up with a warm Italian who spends hours playing with his little nieces and nephews and who thinks sex should mean a full morning of giving you pleasure? Were you a crazed enfant terrible, on the edge of self-destruction? This stolid, domestic soul of stability may be just the gal you're looking for. When we gaze deep into our lover's eyes we often peer through a window at those parts of ourselves we needed and never quite had.

The image of gazing into one another's eyes, as if in a mirror, epitomizes the tone of this early phase of a relationship. It is a time of healthy narcissism, a time when the couple has as its main interest . . . itself. I call this a time of *"nose to nose"* energy, when partners of whatever age find themselves acting like teenagers, when it seems natural to stay up until three in the morning, talking, touching, making love, when nothing feels as compelling, as thoroughly fascinating, as the beloved. It is a wonderfully rich, alive, self-involved period. As one journalist remarked, "Friends in love are why God made call waiting."

Sooner or later, certainly by the time the couple has children if not before, the bubble bursts, the golden bowl cracks. The couple moves from "nose to nose" energy to *"side by side"* energy. They are no longer faced inward toward one another basking in their mutual gaze, but face out, shoulder to shoulder, unified toward a set of common goals—raising their children, paying the mortgage, getting ahead. Just as the exalted, self-reflective time of falling in love is normal, so, too, is this emergence from that marvelous cocoon. Each of these two facets of relationship is necessary and healthy. *Think of intimacy as comprised of two intersecting lines, a cross. The vertical line represents that "nose to nose" energy; it is the capacity to be fully present in the moment, the capacity to face one another. Really looking at one another in relationship is intense; it is sexy, nourishing, stimulating, "romantic." The horizontal line represents "shoulder to shoulder" energy; it is the capacity to sustain connection over time, to be thoughtful, responsible, to build trust. Living a good life together, sharing values, goals, remembering birthdays, paying the bills, these small acts of care are also nourishing, in a different way, and no less essential. There is a cozy comfortableness that comes from a strongly established horizontal line, a sense of domesticity.*

Some partners are the soul of stability—stalwart, steadfast, and tedious. Other partners are all vertical line—charming, intense, and maddeningly irresponsible. A healthy relationship needs to be able to shift back and forth between both aspects of intimacy. Couples often need to get out of the house and away from the kids to remember that they are lovers, and they also must learn how to work together to accomplish their goals.

The shift out of the early, intense, erotic phase to a more settled, domestic phase is natural and necessary, and yet, somewhere in the process of that transition—whether it takes months or years—something dreadful happens to most couples. The shadow, the underbelly, the incomplete past that each thought they had healed, or at least outwitted, reappears in their lives with a vengeance. They have entered the realm of *disillusionment*.

"I feel like such an *idiot*." Judy contemplates Dan, smiling ruefully. "Dan's moods. Dan's *insecurities,* Dan's *sensitivity.*" She glares at him balefully, her tone mocking. "Sensitivity, my . . ." she drifts. "What we really mean by Dan's sensitivity is don't piss him off."

"Or he'll . . ." I help her along. Dan crosses his legs, restive, in the chair across from her.

"Rage," she confides. "But nothing you'd ever hear out loud. A silent implosion, like a bomb going off in a box." She smiles, pleased with her turn of phrase. "That's what my marriage has been," she pronounces, "a bomb in a box."

"And what would you do?" I ask. She looks up at me. "Faced with his silent, angry, withdrawal—how would you react?"

Her lips purse, her face wrinkles. "Oh," she sighs, "I'd go after him maybe . . . once or twice . . ."

"Once or twice?" I ask. Judy just sighs. "So, Judy," I go on, "if that sigh could talk, what would it say right now?"

"That I'm *tired*," she offers, and laughs. "I've *had* it."

"And the emotion?" I ask.

"How about disgust?" Dan pipes in, uncharacteristically. My ears perk up; I turn to him.

"Disgusted?" I ask. He looks at her for a moment; she makes no contact back. "Judy?" I press, but she's not playing.

"Oh, leave me alone," she blurts out, like a girl. I can't tell if she's teasing or serious. "Just . . . go pick on somebody else for awhile. Work with *him*." She waves me off.

"Disgusted," Dan reiterates.

"Like now?" I ask, nodding toward Judy.

"Oh, this is easy," Dan asserts. "This is the light stuff. She's like, you know the joke—a ship leaving a sinking rat? She's like . . . if I'm gone, she's *way* gone. 'Hey, if you don't need me, honey, I *really* don't need you!'" Judy giggles. Dan's pleased to have made her laugh. "'Eat my dust,'" he continues, getting no reaction this time.

"Is this true?" I ask Judy. She nods, suddenly silent herself. I haven't seen this side of her before. "So, how long does he get the Ice Queen treatment?" I ask.

"'Bout as long as he gives me the speedbump treatment," she answers, her voice low, seeming fatigued and mildly revolted. Her abrupt show of indifference intrigues me. I try catching her eye but she turns from me.

"What are you so mad about?" I ask her. She looks down at the floor, doesn't answer. "Why are you so angry with him?"

"Because." Ignoring me, she wheels on him, pointing her finger as she speaks. "Because *you* let me down."

"Say it, then," I encourage her.

"Do you think it was always like this?" she asks me, still facing him. "That he was always this *dead?* That's not who I married. You were the wild one, Danny. I was the straight one. You have to realize," she reminds me, "we've known each other since we were kids. Remember the time . . ." She begins to crack up. "Remember when you swung out of that tree?" Laughing full throttle now. "On a dare . . . who was that kid? Never mind, on a dare." She laughs again. "He swings out of this tree. Totally naked except for his shorts. Screaming like a jerk. He's supposed to scare us or impress or . . ." They're both laughing. "He lands in this . . ." She can't finish the sentence.

I wait a moment. "So, your anger?" I try again.

"He was crazy!" she says. "Sure, okay, he was a bit of a nerd, but he was this big *crazy* nerd. He would do *anything*. That's what I loved about you," she tells him.

"People were wild and spontaneous in your family?" I prompt.

"Yeah, *right*," she snorts. "My family was a fucking museum. No one even *moved*. My family was pithed."

"Is that why you're so pithed at me?" Dan tries.

"Was he ever actually funny?" I go along with it.

She mock-purses her lips. "I wouldn't go that far," she says. "But he was fun." She's quiet a while. "You *were* fun," almost to herself. "You were a *lot* of fun. I don't know when you shut down, shut down from me, from the kids." She looks at him and I think she might start to cry again. "You were supposed to be my *savior*, Dan. You were supposed to rescue me from all that deadness, not throw me back into it! Shit." She turns away, exasperated with everything. "I just feel *cheated*, that's all," she says, looking at no one. "This isn't what I signed up for." Judy falls silent. We just sit for a while, the three of us. "If I knew that *this* was how it was going to be . . ." she begins, but can't find the wherewithal to finish. A thick, paralyzing quiet descends on all three of us.

In intimacy, as in most other things, we tend to re-create what we know. Today's drama isn't necessarily a direct reenactment of yesterday's. Roles change; there are variations. But the dynamic of the relationship, the interpersonal themes we contend with, have most often been brought with us into the marriage. Partners almost always play out a *template for relationships* they first "learned" growing up. In your first marriage you may be the pursuer, in your second the distancer. But, if we look at your family during your childhood, it will be a fair bet that someone pursued someone. Whenever a client is stuck in a dysfunctional quality—avoidance, disgust, fits of immaturity—I ask the questions I began to ask Judy: *Who did you see behave like this? Or, who did it to you? Or, who let you do it to them?*

Psychoanalytically oriented therapists look for the causes of such traits within the individual's character. But relational recovery views "character" as little more than a compendium of internalized relationships. *Along with our biological constitution, our personality is an internal troupe of players, our perennial repertory company, ready to reenact the core transactional themes we were imbued with as youngsters. We are the relational matrix we grew up in—until we do the hard, deliberate work of transforming.* Watching, it's not hard to see that the pattern eating away at Judy and Dan's marriage is one in which angry withdrawal evokes a response in kind. That pattern is like a thumbprint, and part of our work is identifying the thumb.

"Well." I break the quiet at last, looking at a dispirited Judy. "At least you're trying to shake it up now," I offer. The words sound weak in my ears even as I say them.

"Cold comfort," Judy pushes back. "Cold comfort. Twelve years of this, this *numbness.* All the damage it's done to me, to the children. They know how unhappy we are. I mean, we do our best, but . . ."

"So who taught you?" I ask. "Who taught you to be so disgusted, to answer withdrawal with withdrawal?"

"Well, they *both* did," she offers and then smiles, bitter. "But I have to say, between the two of them, Mother did it better. She was untouchable, just untouchable. Dad wasn't there; it was straight-forward. He had his friends, his social things. But Mother, with her it was a point of pride."

"What?"

"That no one could ever get at her."

"We call that being behind a wall," I say.

"Whatever." She brushes me off, showing some of the apathy she speaks of.

"A wall of indifference." I plow on. She doesn't bother to respond. "It's funny," I say, looking at her. "On the surface you seem so different."

"From?" she perks up a bit.

"From your mother as you describe her. You seem warm, open, casual . . ."

"Hate-filled, exhausted, miserable," she completes the sentence for me.

"So, you've turned into your mother." I stop fighting her.

She smiles, looking at Dan. "Different style," she pronounces, "same marriage."

Here is a story. A prideful king, impatient, imperious, given to bouts of anger, hears from a soothsayer that his son will one day grow up to murder him. I'll take care of *that*, thinks the king, and calls for a huntsman to bring the infant out into the woods and slay him. But the huntsman, a wonderful archetype of masculinity, cannot bring himself to do the deed; instead he gives the boy to another family. Years pass. The infant has now grown up to be a strong young man, in fact, a prince. One day a soothsayer tells the prince that he will murder his father. "I'll take care of *that*," thinks the prince, and runs away from those whom he, mistakenly, thinks of as his parents. He runs smack into a querulous old man at a crossroads. Desperate in his flight, the young prince verbally assails the old man, who, in retaliation, refuses to let him pass. Neither man—mirrors of one another—backs down. Tempers flare. Blows are exchanged. And, in the end, old King Laius, the father of Oedipus, lies slain.

The tragedy of Oedipus is not, as Freud would have it, primarily about sex. As in all Greek tragedy, the play's principal concern is fate, and our relationship to it. The irony of the tale is that each man—so like the other—responds to his destiny with *hubris*, the core patriarchal delusion that we are above nature and in control of it, rather than within nature as one humble component. The fulfillment of each man's fate is driven precisely by his arrogant attempt to escape.

While I do not agree with Freud's interpretation of the Oedipus myth, I do agree that it is a powerful meditation on paradox and relationship. As the great psychoanalyst H. V. Dicks remarked, when we fall in love, we attempt to outwit our fates, and escape the family wounds that hound us. Falling in love means believing that with *this* person those wounds will be healed. And yet somehow, after a time, we find out, like Judy, that we have been betrayed. James Framo, the father of couple's therapy, once said: "The day you wake up, turn to your spouse and realize that you've been *had.* That the person you fell in love with is not the person you are in bed with, that this is all some dreadful mistake. That is the first day of your marriage."

Life with the partner we chose, it turns out, precisely replicates the very dramas from which we sought refuge. *In love, we all desperately run from, feel ourselves delivered from—and ultimately, surrealistically, find ourselves transported back into—the dreamscape of our families, our own childhoods, the prototypic templates for connection with which we were raised.* This is what psychotherapist Charles Verge has called marriage's "exquisite design." The *promise* phase of relationship offers the deep recognition that with this person, all will be healed. *Disillusionment* hurls us into the realization that the very person to whom we have committed will stick the burning spear of past grievances right into our eye, over and over again. If the *promise* phase can be described as *love without knowledge,* the *disillusionment* phase brings us *knowledge without love.* You gain more knowledge about your partner than you ever wished for. Was your father a cheat? Imagine your panic the day you find your stalwart mate in some salacious chatroom. Was your mother overbearing? Contemplate the horror that comes as you stand, years deep in your marriage, watching your heretofore sweet-natured wife transform into a relentless shrew with your eldest son.

Yea, thou I walk through the Valley of Death . . .
Disillusionment is relationship's mortality.

And yet . . .

I turn to Dan and ask him if he wants to argue with the report Judy has given me. "It's substantially true," he replies. I ask if there was withdrawal in his background. "Are you kidding?" he answers. "Ask me if there was anything else."

"Your father?"

"Both of them," he tells me. "Totally shut down. My father was among the walking dead and my mother was obsessed with me."

"So, their marriage?" I ask.

"It was a desert. I was mortified to be there."

"So, how does it feel to find yourself reenacting it?" I ask.

"Let's not go there," he turns away. "I can't bear it. Just tell me what to do."

I look at him for a moment. "You'll do anything?" I ask. "Whatever I tell you?"

"Through broken glass barefoot."

"Because you love her that much?" I ask.

"No," he answers, blunt. "I do love her. I want to pull this thing out of the fire. For sure. But that's not the main thing, The main thing is that it sickens me to be here, just sickens me."

We look at each other a moment. "Good," I say quietly. "I believe you. Let's pull you out of this mess." And we begin.

Now here's the extraordinary thing. Dan, it turns out, is not quite Judy's mother. And neither is Judy Dan's passive father. They can each behave like their models; they can, indeed, must re-create the old drama. But finding themselves in the center of the familiar, bloody play, each moves toward a different ending. Judy stands up to the pull of withdrawal in ways her parents would not, and Dan hears her, ultimately takes responsibility for his actions, and offers to change, in ways his parents could not. Their marriage combines both the fruit of the past *and also* the seeds of something new. I tell them this, point out the replay but also the discrepancies.

"There is a name for this," I tell them, "this dropping into the old wounds but then having the capacity for difference, for healing. It's called hope."

It isn't, as the patriarchal vision promises, that intimacy either makes up for or helps us avoid our deepest injuries, quite the opposite. Every day we meet individuals whose character traits fail to activate us, whose personalities don't push our buttons. What is fascinating, challenging, and ultimately mystical about real passion is that, by and large, such people routinely fail to compel us. Part of that feeling of finding our "soul mate"—though we are scarcely aware of it at the time—is a visceral "click," an intuitive recognition that we have found "a player," someone with whom the old world we come from can be resurrected, *and yet also*, if we are brave enough and fortunate, someone with whom that familiar world might transform. We all fall in love with our mothers and fathers. We are all drawn, quite beyond our conscious intent, to those who pick up the unfinished conversation, the unanswered question. For the unfortunate, it is a straight replay of what they once lived through, a lifetime of repetition misnamed experience, re-creating what feels like home—despite pain or even danger. The romantic idyll, by contrast, promises to restore and complete all that was damaged or missing. Real passion is comprised of neither extreme—trapped replay or magic fix—although it contains a little of both. Men and women who sustain real love do not find themselves blissfully devoid of their old issues. They find themselves, just like the unfortunate ones, thrown back into wounds they'd rather not face. *But, unlike the unfortunate ones, they face them. Same drama, different outcome.* I call this last possibility *repair.* If the *promise* phase offered *love without knowledge,* and *disillusionment* brings us *knowledge without love, repair* offers the possibility of *knowing love,* mature love, the conjunction of truth and affection. Seeing, and feeling acutely, our partner's flaws and limitations, we nonetheless choose not to withdraw from them. We succeed in navigating the vagaries of harmony, disharmony, and restoration—the essential rhythm of relationship.

And it is precisely at this critical juncture that patriarchy betrays us. Traditional socialization teaches women to manage, smooth over, minimize the stain—albeit with allowance for occasional eruptions of histrionics. And it teaches men that they are entitled to run, wall off, deny—relational responsiveness has not been a part of men's job description. Neither sex has been given the encouragement or the tools with which to stay the course. And both wind up feeling hopelessly overwhelmed by the other. "No matter what I say, he won't listen." "No matter what I do, she won't be satisfied." Like Judy and Dan, by and large these are not horrible people, but good people trying to preserve love within a bad framework. The terms must change. They need to learn how to hold on.

CHAPTER ELEVEN

Love's Assassins:
Control, Revenge, and Resignation

Between the idea
And the reality
Between the motion
And the act
Falls the shadow
— T. S. ELIOT

With ruffled black hair over a round Slavic face, Rachel looks more like a harried suburban mom than an accomplished historian and scholar. Her husband, Steve, a short, square block of a man, projects a tough, blunt presence, a sheer wall. Neither of them appears very remarkable, until I notice their eyes, which appraise me and my surroundings with a precision I find unsettling.

"You've been to Africa?" Rachel asks.

I nod.

"East Africa," Steve murmurs, taking in an ebony figurine on my desk.

"What a *terrific* chair!" Rachel notes the ergonomic behemoth in which I cradle my often stiff spine.

"Want to try it?" I offer, but she shakes her head.

"Does it come with operating instructions?" Steve teases.

"Actually . . . ," I begin, but let it drop. "Well." I fold my hands in my lap, knowing full well that they are in the process of sizing me up as crisply as they'd ingested my furnishings. "I think we've done the decor. How about your marriage?"

Rachel and Steve have had an "interesting marriage." College sweethearts, together almost twenty-five years, though only in their mid-forties, they have passionately loved each other. They are true soul mates. They are terrific parents, with wonderful, if demanding, children. They stimulate one another's creativity, couldn't imagine being apart. And yet somehow, they have managed to spend the bulk of their days, not just currently but throughout the past decade, energetically, and with alarming openness, bickering with one another.

"We don't behave well," Rachel smiles charmingly. "In fact, I'd have to say, we're horrible to each other."

I cock an eyebrow toward Steve. "No contest." He smiles affably.

Their report is at odds with their effervescent presence. I like being with them. "Jeeze." I scratch my head. "Sitting with you, even in these few moments, there's something very attractive about you, a nice warmth. It's like, you strike me as one of those 'fun couples,'" I observe.

"It's true." Rachel laughs. "That's how people see us, and, it's not an act, we *are*."

"It's just that . . ." I try helping them along.

"It's just that, over the years," Steve says, smiling. "I think one could justifiably say Rachel has grown to hate me."

"Well . . ." She stretches the word. I wait for her to correct him, like, "I don't really hate *you*, darling, it's just . . ." But after that teased-out "well," Rachel just sits there.

"Oh, dear," I remark, facing Steve, his gentle, bright eyes. "What did you do?"

"As in, 'What did I do to deserve all this?' " he asks, almost laughing. "I'm a card."

"Pardon?" I say.

"I'm a cut-up."

"That's why your wife hates you?" I ask.

"Steve thinks," Rachel breaks in, "that he has the right to dispense with normal human civility."

"You wear your underwear on your head?" I ask him.

"Just about, " she answers for him. "For instance, we're out with friends at a really nice Indian restaurant and Steve starts speaking to the waiter with an Indian accent."

"He says what to the waiter with the Indian accent?" I try clarifying.

"No, no." She smiles, equal parts amused and annoyed. "It's Steve. *Steve* adopts a fake Indian accent. He sounds like an Indian." She nods at me. "From India."

At this Steve cocks his head and holds out a hand, placing his thumb and finger together in a delicate circle. "Prawns, if you please, cooked without butter, thank you. I would be very much appreciating also the spicy paratha, with mango lassi." A well-rendered send-up of a middle-aged New Delhi gentleman.

I contemplate him for a moment in silence.

"At this your friends are amused?" I ask her.

"Not particularly," she quickly returns.

"And the waiter?" I inquire.

"What do *you* think?" she answers.

I train my attention on her husband, who shrugs.

"The guy pissed me off," he confides. "He'd been really obnoxious to us."

"So you decided to mock him?" I ask.

"Sometimes I just step outside the box," Steve tells me.

"But you don't invite anyone to step outside with you," I reflect.

"That's *it*," Rachel interjects from the sidelines. "I've been *trying* to articulate it. But that's not the main thing," she goes on. "The main thing . . ." She falters.

"Go on," I tell her.

"Look. When *normal* people get out of bed in the morning it's, you know, 'Hello. How are ya?' Steve is shot right out of a cannon. Boom. We're *on*. It's the *Steve* show. You know that dreadful feeling when your alarm radio is tuned into some horrible, head-banging, loud-mouthed announcer?" Inwardly, I wince at her description, but affable Steve just smiles. "Here's *Steve*," Rachel mock-announces, "twenty-four/seven. *All Steve all the time.* Look," she leans forward. "I don't mean to . . . this isn't affected, but, I'm an academic, you know? That's what I do, how I'm wired. I like *books.* I like *quiet.* An afternoon alone with no students, no kids, that's bliss to me. Living with Steven . . ." She shakes her head. "I feel pinned to the wall. I am living my life *trapped* inside my husband's variety act."

"You two sound wholly incompatible," I agree, thinking that only a fool would attempt to counter her fervor. "Whatever did you see in him," I ask, "when you first fell for him?"

She slaps her hand vehemently on the chair, a surprising loud thud, her avid eyes amused and infuriated. "What did I fall for? His *liveliness,*" she answers. "His *wit,* his *irreverence,*" glancing back at him, petulant. "Everything I've grown to despise!"

If the healthy rhythm of relationship is one of harmony, disharmony, and repair, if *disillusionment* is a kind of relational purgatory leading back to resolution, even transformation, most of the couples that contact me have not found the means to push all the way through. Devoid of the skills necessary to hold on, incapable of connection in the face of disconnection, instead of the healing phase of repair, these couples deteriorate. If relational recovery is medicine, such stalled intimacy, the inability to push through disillusionment to repair, is the disease. As we head toward restoration, it is necessary to understand the process of decline. Couples who don't make it through disillusionment tend to get snared by one or all of three phases of intimacy's erosion—*control, retaliation,* and *resignation.*

"I know I'm supposed to *accept* my husband," Rachel complains, "but the truth is that I don't. I don't like how Steven chooses to behave. I don't like how intimidating he becomes when I try to talk to him about it. In essence, to be blunt, I don't like *him.*"

"And the payback is?" I ask her.

"*My* payback? Ask *him.*" She dismisses me. I turn to Steven, who imperceptibly nods.

"I bet I could just about do it for you," I tell him.

"Please," he waves me on.

I give it a shot. "She nags, micromanages; she's enormously dis-approving. Often angry, short fused. Long stretches of no patience, little affection, and your sex life is in the crapper."

Steve laughs. "Well, not in the crapper altogether," he corrects.

"I have an eighty-twenty, no quibble rule," I tell him. "If it's eighty percent correct, it's good enough."

"Fine," he agrees amiably. "Close enough, then."

"And your response?" I ask.

"Oh," he pauses, airily. "Sometimes I bark back, sometimes I go away."

"Sometimes you crank up whatever it is I'm objecting to just so that you can *really* dig in and torture me," Rachel offers.

Steven looks at her darkly. "I don't like being controlled," he says.

"Is that how you see it?" I ask. "Being controlled?" And for the first time in the session, he turns his dark look my way. Suddenly, I feel foolish and small.

"And how *am* I to see it?" he mocks.

"That's just where we're headed," I assure him. "Hold tight."

Although I was about to help Steve think about Rachel's behavior in a new way, his description of it was not essentially wrong. Like most of us who do not have the skills to navigate *disillusionment*, Rachel had moved into *control*. Facing the discrepancy between the promise we hope for and the woefully imperfect reality we find, most of us instinctively try to restore the old love by "getting" our partners back into shape, back to the qualities we once saw in them. "If *only* you could be less selfish," we might say, only to hear, "If only *you* could be more giving." Our partner's willful lack of conformity to our dreams seems particularly galling when, in fact, he *was* less selfish and she *was* more giving, back in the old courtship days of their good behav-ior. "Before," as Rachel once put it to Steve, "you got 'comfortable.' "

Like many of my female clients, Rachel's attempts to control Steve are overt but ineffective, shrewish, complaining. Sometimes, Steve replies with equal abrasiveness, but just as often his repertoire is what psychiatry calls "passive aggressive."

"I simply cannot sit still and watch him tramp all over people," Rachel proclaims indignantly in one session.

"Like you, for instance," I venture.

"Like me, for certain," she replies. "But also like our children, his own family, our friends."

The problem with Rachel's attempts at control goes back to the relational asymmetry between them, the disparity in their intimacy skills that traditional therapy cautions us never to mention. Just as she says, Rachel *does* see Steve shoot himself in the foot, not just in his personal relations but equally in his career, which has been seriously hampered by his lack of "people skills." There is no reason for me to search under or over Rachel's pronouncement looking for evidence of her pathology. Rachel is a smart, savvy woman. And she lives with Steve, after all; she watches him interact every day. Why would I begin their therapy by doubting her word? Watching Steve move through the world with relational immaturity and feeling the brunt of many of its consequences, Rachel feels sad, but also angry. "Why can't he just listen to what I, and others, have tried to tell him? Why doesn't he just *shape up?*"

Steve rarely complains about Rachel this way. She, not he, is the overtly controlling one. But Rachel will say, if encouraged to throw "fairness" to the winds, that Steve has less to complain about. *She* doesn't walk around treating people the way he does.

Rachel, like many wives, tries to "get" her husband to change, never realizing that no one ever has the power to "get" anyone to do anything in this world, short of outright coercion—least of all women in relationship to men. In her day, Rachel has reasoned, pleaded, threatened, and cajoled. She has spoken rationally and with wild desperation. Steve's basic take on all this, although he is far too political to speak it, is that Rachel is a controlling witch. And he reacts by letting her know, mostly between the lines, that she can go out and bray at the moon for all he cares. He will not be bent to her will.

"Do you read the cartoon strip 'Broom Hilda?' " he asks me one session. "There's this character, a troll, not too bright. And he asks this other character, a sort of pretentious, pontificating vulture—"

"Obviously, a culture vulture," Rachel interjects.

"The troll says something like, 'Hey, so what happens when two people fall in love and get married?' Okay? So, the vulture puffs all up and says, 'Marriage, my dear troll, is when two people become one.' And the troll thinks for a minute, puzzled, and asks, 'Well . . . *which?*' " Steve leans back, satisfied.

It takes Rachel a few seconds less to digest this than it does me. "So, what is this?" She warms to the attack. "Flag of Texas. 'Don't Tread on Me'? 'Live Free or Die'? Is our marriage reduced to license-plate slogans?"

The bottom line is that people don't like to be controlled. Sooner or later it becomes evident that efforts to restore that first blush of happiness through control are doomed, at which point the frustrated partner often moves from *control* into the next phase of the downward spiral, *revenge*.

Everyone knows what revenge is about and, unless we have lived as a saint or a hermit, most of us have been on both sides of it. "Keep it up," Rachel warns her husband one session. "Go on like this and you'll be passed over for your next promotion like you were last time. People don't like you, Steven. Don't you get it? You're a *loser.*"

That's revenge.

Failing in our attempt to "make the person better," we then lose all patience and just want to hurt them. Maybe *this* will get through, we might think, if we were reflecting at all at such times.

I owe to my wife, Belinda, the insight that, beneath the impulse to hurt the other lies a deeper impulse to heal. *Revenge is really a perverse form of communication, a twisted attempt at repair.* We want to "make the person feel" what they made us feel. Why? Though we rarely admit it, it is so that they might understand. So that they might "get" what they've done and feel remorse. Unaccountability evokes punitive impulses in most of us. We want to bring the shameless one to her knees, see her humbled. But we also want her to open her heart, so that there might be some resolution. The punch line of most revenge fantasies comes when the hurtful one falls to the floor sobbing and begs for forgiveness.

Don't hold your breath.

While it may be a natural impulse to want the person who dished it out to feel *your* pain, retaliation seldom achieves that end. You rarely increase someone's capacity for empathy and responsibility by being cruel to them. People don't work that way. In real life, revenge breeds a symmetrical response, or else wholesale withdrawal.

"At one point, early on," says Rachel, "things got so crazy between us Steve took himself off to a motel room and I followed him, *insisting* that he talk to me, banging on the door, calling him God only knows what. And he called the police. I mean we were both loaded; we were kids. But I will always remember that moment. The look on those cops' faces." She smiles, shakes her head. "Not one of my fonder memories."

As is true for all of these "phases," *revenge* can be writ large over years, as in Edward Albee's battling couple in *Who's Afraid of Virginia Woolf?* or the more pedestrian pair in the film *War of the Roses.* Revenge can also be doled out in small bits, over the course of a few sentences. Getting dressed to go out to a party, Belinda makes note of my incipient potbelly. "You really need to be careful about what you eat," she offers, unsolicited. A few minutes later she swirls before me in a new dress. "How is it?" she asks. "Great," I answer. "Do you wonder, though, if it's a little too *young?*" (Take *that!*) I recall a *New Yorker* cartoon in which a middle-aged couple sags in two overstuffed armchairs resting upon one of those black-and-white checkerboard floors that were fashionable some time ago. "Your move!" the husband calls to his wife.

At some point, usually short of the police being called, one or both partners realize that the escalation of *revenge* is getting out of hand, that the impulse is simply too destructive. The plutonium rods get pulled. At that moment, the critical mass often begins to shift from *revenge* to the final stage of intimacy's deterioration, *resignation.*

Research informs us that the state of worn-out disengagement is the surest predictor of eventual divorce. Even couples who fight bitterly stand a chance at recovery, but once the relationship has slid into chronic defeat most couples will not sustain themselves. Resignation—whether in the domain of sex, finances, kids, or the relationship entire—often masks itself as mature acceptance. "Well, after fighting about it and getting nowhere, I just figured Steve was always going to put work first. There are some battles you're not going to win." Or, as Steve confesses in an individual session, "To be honest, I never had the same passion with Rachel that I've felt with other women. I think I felt early on that she was held back. I tried talking to her about it—it's a pretty delicate issue. She got so hurt and defensive, after a while I let go. Sex isn't the only aspect of a good relationship." But did Rachel really come to terms with Steve's unwillingness to change his priorities? Did Steve truly, as he put it, "let go"?

The difference between real acceptance and just backing away from an issue, or away from the whole relationship, is resentment. "If you really can let go," I counsel partners like Steve and Rachel, "then go ahead and do it. But then don't mope around feeling like a victim. If there is one shred of resentment in your decision, then go back to the negotiating table, even if it means kicking up a fuss."

"But what if my partner won't come to the negotiation table?" you might ask. That's a fair question. I believe that two people operating in good faith can negotiate just about anything. The one thing that cannot be negotiated is getting to the table to begin with. One partner cannot "get" the other to communicate responsibly. If your spouse refuses to enter into a good faith process with you, that is one clear signal that you, as a pair, need professional help. Then you have to find the rare couples therapist who will not be shy about holding your unaccountable partner to the fire. And even then, there are no guarantees that the therapist will be more successful in helping your partner listen than you have been.

Rachel and Steve, like many younger couples, vacillated between all but the final phase, *resignation.* They moved fluidly from moments of *promise* to bitter *disillusionment,* then a flurry of *control* and *revenge* would ensue. Somehow peace would be restored, they'd recall that they really did love one another, and they'd enjoy a brief return to the relief of the *promise.* Irene and Billy, a couple in their late sixties, had blown through decades of fighting like Rachel and Steve had. Like tired boxers resting in one another's arms, their life together hovered almost exclusively between *revenge* and *resignation.*

"I used to be totally out of control," Irene tells me. "But medication has helped. Years of therapy." She looks over at Billy, weary, concerned. "I think we've got those kinds of wild blow-ups behind us," she asserts.

"It's behind us," Billy mutters when I press him to respond, "because I dare not cross her on anything. I simply do not resist anymore. It's a thorough rout."

The problem is that after thirty-some years of battle, there is barely enough vitality left between Irene and Billy to keep them alive.

"We've finished the hard stuff," Irene complains. "The kids are all grown. We're not without resources. I want to get out, travel, *do* things. See the world! But Billy's locked up with his books most of the time, or television. Asleep in his chair. We're only in our sixties. He's become an old man!"

"Perhaps he's depressed," I venture.

"What's *he* got to be depressed about?" she huffs.

I look at her, gathering my strength, about to launch into one of those "make it or break it" therapy moments. "You," I tell her.

Irene and Bill reversed the usual roles. In my clinical practice over the years about one out of every four couples presents with the woman as the flagrant offender and the man in the subservient position. When I claim that women in our culture tend to be raised with more relational skill than men, I do not mean to gloss over nuance and variation between different couples, nor to whitewash women's immaturity. There is no shortage of abrasive women in our society. In marriages like Billy and Irene's the dynamic of contempt remains essentially unchanged, while the sex of the actors reverse. The women in such pairs ride in the one-up position, often railing against the same "feminine" qualities in their mates that are despised by the culture at large. Their husbands are "too weak," "too nice," "can't stand up for themselves." And the men in these couples tend to manage and enable, just like traditional wives.

It became clear as I listened that Billy responded to Irene's volatility by retreating into a state of withdrawal so severe as to be virtually indistinguishable from a clinical depression, for which he was being treated. The bind for the couple was that Irene claimed desperately to want more intimacy from her husband, while Billy was convinced that speaking out to Irene would only provoke her wrath. Billy's "charcoal story" crystallized, for me, the feeling of life under the sway of *resignation*.

"We were having guests over for a summer barbecue and Irene calls me at about four-thirty to put up coals for the grill. Now, our guests aren't due to arrive until five-thirty, six. But there it is. In a former time I would have told Irene this and the amount of stress that would follow my refusal to do as I was told would be so enormous it might well dominate, if not ruin, our whole evening."

"So, this time . . ." I prompt.

"I have no interest in . . ." He harrumphs. "I put on the coals, man. I put on the damned coals!"

Four bags of coals, it turns out. Their guests arrived late, lingered over cocktails and hors d'oeuvres. It was well past seven by the time Billy grilled, and he'd burned through four bags of charcoal by that time.

"How can you sit there and spread such nonsense!" Irene moves into action. "I *told* you it was just my suggestion."

"I've failed to follow your 'suggestions' before, Irene," he returns. She explodes.

"I am really offended by this," she warns. "If you have an issue with me, Billy, I do *not* want to hear about it in some professional's office. How dare you humiliate me like this!" She begins to cry, and then snaps her head up, staring at him fiercely. "If you think life with me is so goddamned *awful*, if you aren't *man* enough to face me with a modicum of spine . . ."

"Irene," I interject, mildly.

"What? What do you want?" she snaps.

"What's happened to your recovery?" I ask. "I thought your rage was behind you."

"Rage?" she says, incredulous. "This isn't rage. I am *offended*, absolutely offended that he—"

"You understand that this is just the kind of self-righteous indignation he anticipated from you?" I press. "I can teach you another way to be angry that—" But she's having none of it.

"Self-righteous!" She just about jumps out of her chair. "Self-righteous!" Then, she suddenly bursts into tears. "I can't take this. I really can't take this. I did not come here to be *abused* by you."

"And I'm not abusing you," I persist. "I am telling you that there is another way of expressing your hurt and anger that—"

"Billy." She turns to him, her eyes darting around the room, desperate. "Billy, let's get out of here. I just . . . I can't . . ." But Billy sits firm, letting me play my hand.

"This is what you're afraid of?" I ask. He nods. "You'd better tell her yourself," I prompt. "Tell her what you see going on and how it's affected you over the years."

With great reluctance, moving at glacial speed, Billy angles himself to face his wife. "Irene," he begins, but she's way beyond him.

"The *two* of you!" she declares, rising out of her chair. "I can't," weeping. "Forgive me, Billy, but I simply can't!" She heads for the door.

"Irene," I say. "That's fine. Take a break for a few minutes. Walk around the block if you like and cool off and then come back and—" Slam!

Billy and I silently reverberate in the shock waves for a few minutes. He looks totally dispirited.

"So that's how it is?" I finally venture.

"That's how it is," he concurs. More silence. Neither of us can think of much more to say.

In the next few days Irene sent me long e-mail missives about how "near-suicidal" she'd been after having been "beaten up" by me. Like many women offenders, when confronted she moved into the victim role. Most male offenders, when hurt, jump to an emphatic one up position, attempting to disguise their shame. Women like Irene, when crossed, often dive for an overt victim role; they play at being one-down as a disguise for their grandiosity. "Maybe you're right," Irene exclaimed in one letter, "but it will do me no good if I cannot hear it." Well, perhaps, I thought. Perhaps someone less direct might put it more gently. I suggested such a referral in what proved to be our final meeting, but Billy wasn't interested.

"Been there, done that," he said. "Several times already. No," he said, sighing, "you're the only one who tried addressing what was really going on. If Irene doesn't want it, she doesn't. It was *her* idea to come here, not mine. But I won't go through another sham." It was the most animated thing I had ever heard him say, and, it turned out, one of the last.

In a follow-up visit about two months later, Billy, coming alone, told me with heartbreaking lucidity that he had returned to his muffled world of books, and naps, and monosyllabic responses. Irene blamed me for their short-lived disruption and brooked no more discussion of the matter. *Resignation* had reasserted its rule.

"We can talk about why you choose to stay," I offer Billy. "Why you ask for so little." But Billy raises his large frame heavily from the chair and only smiles.

"I'm old," he tells me. "Just like she says I am."

"But you needn't be," I counter.

He smiles warmly, offers his hand. "Could be true," he says. "Could well be. Thank you. Thank you sincerely." I've never seen him again.

Like a supernova that has exploded and grown cold, a dust cloud inexorably shrinking in on itself, *resignation* is the last stop in the degenerative process leading away from passion and connection. It is a place where truth is no longer possible and love is a matter of habit and form.

Irene and Billy were worn-out veterans of *resignation*. They'd been at it too long, felt too used up to disrupt their accustomed equilibrium. The choice for more hopeful couples like Rachel and Steve, those not yet lost in the quagmire, seems starkly clear. I am reminded of the old biblical story of Moses descending Mount Sinai, telling his people that there are two paths, at any given moment, in any given lifetime—a path toward life and a path toward death. Chose life, the ancients tell us. And so it is still. Faced with *disillusionment*, we too have the choice of following the course of *control*, *revenge*, and, ultimately, *resignation*, the path of degeneration. Or we can choose *repair* and healing, the difficult journey toward restoration. That choice sometimes looms large, but more often this extraordinary challenge

presents itself to us in perfectly ordinary moments, in our decisions *right now.*

And so we come to the third phase of relational recovery. Initially, the
couple was *brought back into connection* as the woman felt empowered
to speak and the man was empowered to listen and change. In the
second phase, the couple began to *reclaim real passion* by moving
beyond patriarchy's idealized, and limited, template for love. A
radical new vision, both richer and more realistic, was forged. In the
third phase, the *practice of intimacy,* the couple must learn how to create a path—a way not just to see the new vision but to live it, inhabit
it. In this phase, partners must develop the tools they need to carve
a living settlement of connection in this disembodied rock desert we
live in. This is the time for learning that intimacy is a skill-set. Not
a static capacity so much as a daily practice. Not something one *has*
but something one *does.* After the woman opens her throat, the man
opens his heart, and both have opened their eyes, it is time to bring
artfulness to their hands.

CHAPTER TWELVE

Intimacy as a Daily Practice

Pale sunlight
Pale the wall.

Love moves away
The light changes.

I need more grace
Than I thought.
—RUMI

The majority of men and women come into their marriages ill equipped to face the continuing challenge of pushing through disillusionment. Some version of the unhappy course of control, revenge, and resignation seems virtually inevitable. In those critical moments when connection in the face of disconnection is most required, each sex, following the mandates of traditional socialization, gives up. Faced with disillusionment, a woman might nag or complain, but after a flurry of control moves proves ineffective, she will most likely learn to retreat from expressing her truth and draw back from the brink of her insistence—fearing that her relationship (meaning her man) will not be able to take it. While women's criticisms might at times be vociferous, their control moves tend toward the covert, as does their revenge, except for episodic explosions. *For many wives, love's deterioration reads like this: you begin to push less, you begin to fight less, you begin to give less, you begin to feel less.* To be a "good woman" means

197

sacrificing your needs for the sake of the relationship. What you're not told is that along with your needs, pleasure, generosity, and feeling eventually diminish as well.

At the same time, the traditional gender arrangement fails to acknowledge that men, at their core, are just as dependent, just as emotional, just as wired for connection, as women are. After all, half of humanity—women—has been socialized for the job of caretaking them. When faced with the psychological challenge of dealing with disillusionment, a traditionally socialized man finds himself relatively incapable, and mostly unwilling, to sit down with his own feelings, bring them to his wife in a thoughtful, constructive manner, and straightforwardly negotiate his wants and needs. Such skills of introspection and communication in personal relationships are as foreign to conventional masculinity as direct assertion has been to femininity. Encountering disillusionment, many men, rather than accessing these needed abilities, feel instead a deep, inchoate sense of betrayal. They've done their job, after all. They've been reasonably civilized. Each day, without much fuss or complaint, they've picked up their briefcases or lunch pails and headed off to work. So where is the loving caretaker they were promised? Where's the payoff? As the old roles slip, many men still find themselves "following the program," even though the program no longer delivers. They feel cheated. They feel, to use journalist Susan Faludi's term, *stiffed.* While far too many men lash out in frustration, the vast majority manages to remain decent enough. With a disgruntled sigh, they retreat further from a relationship they come to find less and less gratifying, and more and more bewildering. They shoulder disappointment about their marriage in the same way they've learned to shoulder most everything else—silently. Their women will out-feel them, out negotiate them, out talk them anyway—they're *good* at this game. Most men don't work their relationships very well because working a relationship is a foreign concept; the prospect seems daunting, and the odds of success slim.

The vast majority of the men I've treated over the years have been good people, trying their best to accommodate to a confusing new world. They show up at their kids' baseball games, the dance recitals, and teacher conferences. They sincerely mean to be more involved than their own fathers were—and most are. But the demanding emotional work of identifying, expressing, and negotiating feelings—either theirs or their partner's—is a tall order for someone who learned, often against his will, to turn his back on the world of emotion and vulnerability sometime around kindergarten.

Of course, some couples enter into the task of intimacy blessed—by constitution, grace, the good fortune of a healthy family background—with an instinct for authentic repair. But most of us have to cultivate it. Some women seem to be born strong, not easily backed off from their needs, and some men willingly, even enthusiastically, enter into the fray of emotional negotiation. But these are our culture's exceptions, people who either enjoy a natural gift for relationships, or who, on their own, have done the hard work of rethinking their roles. The rest of us need help. For us, particularly us men, the first step lies in understanding that we need skills at all, that while falling in love is primarily about spontaneity, staying in love demands craftsmanship. And craftsmanship must be learned.

Before a couple can even begin to learn the new craft of intimacy, however, the partners must establish a safe, sober space to be intimate in. Attending to the *preconditions for intimacy* is a critical component to recovery that is frequently overlooked in therapy, with unfortunate, at times even devastating, consequences. I find it shocking how many clinicians skip over this concern, acting as though all parties were "on board," when, in fact, the application of intimacy skills doesn't stand a chance of succeeding in the couple's current circumstances. Is one or both partners drinking excessively? Is there an ongoing affair, sexual acting out, or aggressive acting out? Is there a threat of physical, emotional, or financial danger? Are either or both partners suffering from an untreated psychiatric disorder—anxiety, depression? Is there an eating disorder? Does someone need medication? Does someone need a job? Are finances spinning out of control?

Most often, a chronically unhappy couple "stabilizes," that is, renders its misery tolerable, by recourse to a "third leg of a triangle"—

booze, work, affairs, overinvolvement with a child. So long as a partner can easily take the position of being "fed up," turning for solace to his or her favored comfort, that person's willingness to stay engaged during instances of disillusionment will be compromised. It is, for example, quite difficult to remain present and artful after your third martini. *Clinicians must address three domains before work on the couple's relationship is appropriate: addiction, violence, and psychiatric disorders. If one or both partners are self-medicating, physically or psychologically threatening, or subject to a serious emotional disorder, the marital system is out of control, and no amount of coaching or good intentions on anyone's part will yield results.*

Even if a pattern of self-medication is not pronounced enough to qualify as a bona fide addiction, relational recovery takes careful note of its effects on the partnership, scanning for a host of "exits" that rarely blip on the screen of conventionally trained therapists. Over-involvement with work is perhaps the most common medium (read, excuse) for chronic avoidance; TV is another, as is spending too much time on the Internet, or exercise. Is someone's flirting, or sexual fantasy life, more alive to him than his actual erotic relationship? These self-soothing devices, though not necessarily objectionable in themselves, become problematic when they are used to stabilize a bad situation. I see them as "outriggers" designed to maintain the very equilibrium the couple needs to shake up. And while some partners who enter my office may have one glaring dependency—gambling, alcohol, sex—many render the pain of living in a troubled relationship more tolerable by spreading their unmet needs out over several less virulent dependencies, like a water spider perched over a stream on many thin legs. A drink or two here, some overspending there, a flirtation or fantasy in the office—no one issue is enough to fuss over, but their cumulative effect keeps the partner from entering into the tumult of full engagement. A "disengaged" couple complaining of too little intimacy, for example, might do well to interrupt their pattern of splitting a bottle of wine or more most nights over dinner and then finding themselves drowsily in front of a TV show. Countless couples I've seen over the years experience a jump in emotional and sexual intimacy on the heels of one or both partners addressing their relationship to food and weight. Trying to facilitate a couple's move toward one another without first addressing the props supporting their status quo is therapeutically spitting into the wind.

In cases where serious disorders are involved—alcoholism, domestic violence, sexual compulsivity—years of recovery may be required before the couple can focus authentically on anything else. However, just cleaning up such negative circumstances, while necessary, is still not in itself sufficient. Beyond "sobriety" a stage must be set, a space cleared away, for connection to occur. Partners need a place in which to be intimate. In our overcommitted, work-focused, child-focused culture, intimacy comes last in the time-debit line.

Although they'd been married four years, Julie and Sal, two young, hungry, finance executives, had never lived in the same city. She lived in New York; he lived in Houston—for now. Both had changed jobs, and cities, so frequently, I couldn't remember who was where when, even if they could. They described their relationship as "a new marriage," by which they meant that, for years, they mostly met in airport hotel rooms. In her mid-thirties, Julie started developing a yearning for such traditional notions as children, and a home they could all be in at one time. Sal agreed to work on it, but the problem for me as their therapist was that, not surprisingly, we had a hard time scheduling appointments. Getting them both to Boston on the same day proved as difficult as scheduling the Pope.

"If we could do this," Sal said earnestly, reacting to my frustration when trying to schedule our next session, "we would be at the end of the therapy, not at the beginning." I looked him over coolly. I hate it when clients steal my own lines.

"Isn't this called a 'catch-22?'" asked Julie.

"Look." I feel suddenly avuncular. We all three put down our Palm Pilots and smile at one another. "This ain't gonna go. You need enough commitment to say 'no' to your work demands in order to even get here to *try* dealing with the rest of it. You can't be intimate with each other, or me for that matter, because there's no place for you to be intimate in. Take a week, think it over. Tell me what you want."

The following week they committed to seeing me regularly. It turned out to be the most consistent commitment to their relationship they had yet made, and the turning point of the therapy.

Now the ground has been set. Obvious impediments to the work ahead have been dealt with and brought into recovery. A realistic space has been cleared away in the lives of the partners; the demands of kids, work, outside commitments, have been tempered. Everyone is "on board." Everyone "gets it." No one is there under duress. No one has one foot out the door. At this juncture, I often breathe a sigh of relief, feeling that the most difficult part of the therapy lies behind us. Generally speaking, helping a couple learn relational skills is not as difficult as helping them move to a place where they are ready to use them.

So, then, what does it mean—to learn relational skills? And what are the different challenges faced by men and women as they begin? *Over the course of years, I have distilled five essential capacities: How to hold the relationship in warm regard despite its imperfections. How to speak. How to listen. How to negotiate. And how to stay on course independent of your partner's response. Each of these five skills breaks down a fundamental pillar of patriarchy and replaces it with a relational approach, a new way of thinking, feeling, or behaving. Taken together, these five skills operationalize the new vision of love. They transmute relationality from a way of thinking to a way of life.* In systematizing these skills, my aim was to extend the work of my friend and colleague Pia Mellody.

A central aspect of Pia's system—and the work that is done at The Meadows, a treatment facility based on her model—is the active teaching of five *self-skills* to clients. Traditional therapy holds that character is a fixed structure determined early in childhood whose reconfiguration demands years of painstaking work. Pia's genius was the notion that one could simply teach people how to have better relationships with themselves, teach them how to intervene on their own immaturity, how to, in a word, regrow themselves. Over the years, I have found Pia's system to be extraordinarily helpful in the process of restoring healthy intimacy with oneself, and Pia and I have led seminars together on the restoration of intimacy with self—Pia's emphasis—and with others—mine.

I view Pia's five-point grid as relational, that is, it arms one with the skills necessary to reestablish a good relationship between you and you. One client teased me at the end of a rich individual session by saying that he felt he'd just undergone intense couple's therapy with himself. Inspired by seeing the effectiveness of Pia's skill focus, I went on to organize a core set of five relational competencies designed to fit alongside her five self-skills.

Maturity, or if you prefer, good mental health, simply means that you treat yourself well. Many of us don't. We first learn to have a good relationship to ourselves by internalizing the healthy relationship our parents, and other caregivers, had with us. The five self-skills that constitute adult maturity begin as every child's psychological birthright. If these healthy capacities were not present in our early relationships, they will be missing in our personalities. This rule is inescapable. *A child cannot create mature capacities by himself.* The type and degree of mistreatment a person was subjected to will be a strong determining factor in the type and degree of damage he sustains—until he heals. *Just as we are inclined, in intimate relationships, to re-create the familiar themes we grew up with, we are also predisposed to restore the familiar in our relationship to ourselves; we tend to treat ourselves the way we were treated. It is what we know.*

FIVE CORE SELF-SKILLS
(adapted from Pia Mellody's *Facing Co-Dependency*)

1. Self-Esteem
Holding self in warm regard despite imperfections and limitations

Dysfunction
Shame
Grandiosity

2. Self-Awareness
Knowing one's own experience (thoughts/emotions/sensations) and sharing them politically

Dysfunction
Disassociation
Perfectionism

3. Boundaries	Dysfunction
Ability to protect and contain oneself while remaining connected to others	Too porous (reactive) Walled off (disengaged)

4. Interdependence	Dysfunction
Identifying one's wants and needs; caring for self/letting others care for one appropriately	Overdependence Antidependent; Needless/wantless

5. Moderation	Dysfunction
Experiencing and expressing oneself moderately	Immature (too "loose") "Supermature" (too "tight")

1. *A child should be held in warm regard despite his imperfections.* This is the first birthright. The parents' ability to cherish the child becomes internalized as the adult's capacity to cherish herself; this first core skill is *self-esteem.*

2. *A child's feelings must be validated and put into a realistic perspective.* The parents' ability to welcome a child's thoughts and feelings, without being perfectionistic or denigrating, becomes internalized as the adult's capacity to inhabit her own feelings and share them appropriately; this is *owning your reality.*

3. *A child should be protected and contained without being overburdened or cut off.* The parents' ability to set appropriate boundaries with the child, being neither fused nor disengaged, becomes internalized as the adult's capacity to connect without being overly porous or excessively walled off; this is *having healthy boundaries.*

4. *A child should be taught how to do what she can for herself, and also to lean on others appropriately.* The parents' ability to offer care without excess or neglect becomes internalized as the capacity to be independent when needed and yet also to ask others for help when one should; this is *interdependence.*

5. *A child requires help feeling and behaving age appropriately.* The parents' ability to have fitting expectations, without either unduly

indulging immaturity or demanding unsuitable levels of pseudo-maturity, becomes internalized as the adult's capacity to experience and express herself in a balanced way; this is *moderation.*

Healthy self-esteem, owning one's reality, good boundaries, interdependence, and moderation—these five abilities are hallmarks of a well-adjusted, well-functioning person. Immaturity is an imbalance in any of these five abilities; there is either "too much or too little."

Unhealthy self-esteem can be shame, feeling less-than, or grandiosity, feeling better-than.

When we own our reality we are in touch with our feelings, thoughts, sensations. We are able to share them appropriately, and view our experience in a realistic, human, way—without perceiving ourselves to be gods or monsters. Damage concerning one's reality can be expressed as doubts about one's experience, disassociation, or as judging oneself against a distorted standard—seeing oneself as either bad or defective, or as good and perfect.

Unhealthy boundaries can be either too porous or not open enough.

Unhealthy dependency is a state in which one is either overly dependent, or antidependent, needless and wantless.

Immoderateness can express itself as being either *superimmature,* a "big baby," too loose, or *supermature,* rigidly "adult," too tight.

If we lay out these five skills along with their imbalances, an interesting picture emerges. On one side of the dysfunctional traits lie shame, a sense of oneself as defective, too-porous boundaries, overdependency, and superimmaturity. On the other side lie grandiosity, a sense of oneself as good and perfect, being behind walls, antidependency, and supermaturity. Which side is "feminine" and which side "masculine"? While tremendous variation exists in real individuals, generally women in our culture tend to be pulled toward shame and its attendant issues, and men toward grandiosity and its attendant issues. Even more interesting is the observation that women tend to be pulled *overtly* toward the left, and yet maintain a fair degree of *covert* traits on the right, while the opposite can be said of men. Women clients, the "latents," often struggle openly with issues of shame. Less obvious are the ways in which, by being manipulative, by managing men rather than dealing with them, they also play out hidden issues of grandiosity. Similarly, many women clients appear overly dependent, even love-addicted, in their relationships. But when their partners become emotionally available, their covert discomfort with receptivity comes to the fore. These women, while adopting a stance of pursuit, have been subtly walled off and antidependent all along. That the reverse pattern is true for men was a central concern of *I Don't Want to Talk About It*, in which I discussed men's flight from shame into grandiosity, from the hidden immaturity of too much dependency and vulnerability to a compensatory pose of too little. Pia's scheme of self-skills demonstrates that under the enforced division central to psychological patriarchy, each sex has literally handed over half of itself—a distorted, covert half—to the other, and that neither of the unbalanced domains we call masculine and feminine represents health. What Pia describes as the passage from immaturity to maturity is synonymous with what I describe as deconstructing traditional gender—empowering the woman so that she can lift up from shame and overt dependency, reconnecting the man so that he can come down from grandiosity and out from behind walls. Relational recovery asks each sex to reinhabit the qualities that patriarchy deformed and drove underground. Understanding the five core self-skills reveals that not only in relation to others, but equally in relation to our own marred psyches, the process of restoration and the journey beyond patriarchy are one and the same. Just as Pia's five self-skills offer a practical map for restoring a healthy relationship to ourselves, the five relational skills that comprise the *practice of intimacy* offer a practical map for restoring healthy relationships with those we care about.

CHAPTER THIRTEEN

Relational Esteem

When we lose our balance we die, but at the same time we also develop . . . we grow. Whatever we see is changing, losing its balance. The reason everything looks beautiful is because it is out of balance, but its background is always in perfect harmony. This is how everything exists in the realm of Buddha nature, losing its balance against a background of perfect balance. So if you see things without realizing the background . . . everything appears to be in the form of suffering. But if you understand the background of existence, you realize that suffering itself is how we live, and how we extend our life. So in Zen sometimes we emphasize the imbalance or disorder of life.

—SHUNRYU SUZUKI-ROSHI,
Zen Mind, Beginner's Mind

The first of the five core interpersonal skills is *relational esteem*, which is an exact analog of Pia's first self-skill—*self-esteem*. *Self-esteem* is one's capacity to hold oneself in warm regard in the face of one's own imperfections and limitations, one's capacity to cherish oneself as a flawed, flesh-and-blood, human being. *Relational esteem* is the capacity to hold the relationship in warm regard in the face of its imperfections and limitations, to cherish the relationship as the union of two flawed human beings. I have referred to this capacity throughout as an aspect of *repair*, as *embracing the whole dance*, as *connection in the face of disconnection*.

In Pia Mellody's model, self-esteem is the foundation, the most important of all the five skills and the one from which all others depend. The same is true, in the interpersonal domain, for *relational esteem*. It is the basis for all of the other skills, the path out of disillusionment. Yet it is precisely what patriarchy teaches us not to do.

The essence of patriarchy's romance story is a celebration of love as a form of otherworldly, doomed perfection. When we compare our actual relationship to this idealized fantasy, when we imagine that the couple at the cocktail party, or down the block, is so much more loving, sexual, or problem-free than we are, we have fallen prey to *relational shame*; we experience our relationship as "less than," "worthless," in much the same way that in shame disorders we see ourselves as worthless. Patriarchal love promises a transcendent escape from our own humanity, our aloneness and imperfections. Like all intoxicants, it offers a flight into grandiosity. *Relational esteem*, by contrast, teaches us that deep love arrives not from the avoidance of our own and our partner's imperfections, but precisely as a result of their painful, funny, maddening, endearing collision. *The paradox of real love is that our capacity to sustain intimacy rests on our capacity to tolerate aloneness inside the relationship.*

Patriarchy offers us love as a shell game. Love is the electric bunny in front of the nose of the greyhounds in a dog race, the carrot dangling on a stick. Remember, patriarchy codes intimacy as feminine, idealizing it in principle and devaluing it in fact. In the course of boys' and girls' development, the devaluing comes first. Patriarchal culture insists that children give up the state of wholeness and connectedness in which they flourished during their early years, only later to offer to those who play by the rules an idealized version of the very state of connectedness they were forced to renounce. Love is the prince or princess waiting for us at the finish line if we keep our nose to the grindstone and stick to our appointed gender scripts. Even if we are too sophisticated to admit it aloud, most men and women buy into this promise, and both sexes feel cheated when it doesn't deliver.

The truth is that relationships do not make us happy. Relationships are the

crucible in which we get to work on ourselves, in which we have the oppor-
tunity to stretch, grow, and, if we are fortunate, thrive. Being inside a relationship is like being inside your home. The house you live in does
not, in all but a limited sense, "make" your life happy. Your home is
the place in which your life occurs. Sometimes, that life is joyous,
sometimes, it is painful. In the best of circumstances, your home is
something for which you've worked hard. You've invested a great
deal in it, and it expresses, in a deep way, who you are. It is far better to face life's vagaries rooted in one's home than being homeless.
But having a home doesn't significantly alter the challenges we face.

Our marriages can become our emotional, spiritual homes, the
rooted place in which we can be both happy and unhappy, comforted
and anguished. There is no "ever after," nor would we really want
one. Patriarchy offers the lie of perfect intimacy, but, in fact, *perfect*
intimacy, like *distant love,* is an oxymoron. Just as healthy self-esteem
evolves not from fleeing one's humanity but by cherishing oneself in
the face of our flaws, so, too, real intimacy is not an escape into
unbroken harmony; it grows precisely in the difficult and yet endlessly creative clash of your imperfections with mine.

As the gender-specific sales of self-help books and magazines can
attest, women tend to hold themselves largely responsible for bridg-
ing the chasm between their actual relationship and the cultural ideal.
For many women, *relational shame* triggers personal shame. And yet,
whether they express it openly through complaint or covertly
through withdrawal, many women find themselves bitterly disappointed in their husbands as well as in themselves. Men tend to move
from *relational shame* directly into grandiosity. When faced with
love's disappointments, their socialization pulls men away from
introspection toward blame; they experience themselves as trapped
with a deficient partner. While each sex may manifest in different
ways their lack of proficiency in embracing the relationship's flaws,
neither does very well. But both can learn.

As is true of all five skills, *relational esteem* is not something one has
but something one does. More than a vision, or attitude, it is an
activity that can be taught and practiced. The best guide I have yet

encountered for the practice of relational esteem is Twelve Step's "Serenity Prayer":—*Grant me the serenity to accept the things I cannot change, the courage to change the things I can, and the wisdom to know the difference.* I am not interested in this sentiment as a pleasant homily or a philosophy but as a tool.

Learning to distinguish between what we can and cannot change, taking responsibility for our actions, and then letting go of the rest—these essential operations bring us into "right relationship" to the people around us. They undo the central delusion of patriarchy—that we are in charge of life. Patriarchy is a spiritual mistake, a claim to be over nature and fate. In fact, we are only ever truly in charge of our own actions, and only then on a good day. Yet most of us, schooled in our culture's mores, live precisely the opposite of the prayer's suggestion. We become so involved, mostly in our own heads, with that over which we have no control that we fail to do what we can. "What if I move and he doesn't?" "What if I write my dissertation and they don't like it?" "What if I take a new job and hate it?" We are so busy attempting to manage the result that we fail simply to run the race.

Traditional masculinity teaches men to feel both an entitlement to control and also the burden of unrealistic responsibility. How hard you may have tried pales in importance next to how well you did. I have said that for men, *performance-based esteem* takes the place of healthy self-esteem, but even that puts it too gently. To be more precise, one would need to speak of results-based esteem. Most men have little faith that they will be cherished merely for their efforts. Women's control is most often exerted covertly. In the traditional arrangement, the flower of a woman's efforts is the accomplishments of the men she nurtures—her husband and sons, over whom she has only indirect influence. But women no less than men often take full responsibility for the fate of things over which they do not have full control—their marriages, the adult lives of their children. Whether the form is openly demanding or quietly manipulative, moving from patriarchy into relationality means shifting out of the paradigm of control to one of personal responsibility.

Most couples entering treatment are like a seesaw with a five-thousand-pound guy sitting on one end while his wife is perched in the air on the other side. The husband calls out to me, "Hey, could you get that skinny lady down from up there?" Could I "get" that stuck-up woman to be more loving, less complaining, more sexually open? Or, if it's a five-thousand-pound woman, could I "get' her guy to be more responsible, more available, more sensitive?

If I ask the five thousand-pound man or woman what's wrong with their marriage, I will most likely receive a clear and detailed description of the intimacy issues challenging the person on the other end of the seesaw. What all good couple's therapy has in common, no matter what the therapist's orientation, is an essential redirection. "If you want that 'skinny lady' to come down," says the couples therapist, "perhaps you should try getting up." The therapist knows that "he" and "she" are connected; there is a seesaw called *interaction*, the *relationship*, and that changing one's own behavior is a much more promising strategy than insisting on change from the other.

I remember early on in our marriage, after one of our marathon fights, trailing after Belinda, dogging her from room to room, saying in a well-intended, heartfelt, and utterly misguided way, "Honey, I think we can get over this thing if you'd just apologize." File that one under the heading "Good luck!"

Practicing *relational esteem* reminds us that the dance of relationship is a feedback loop. You do something; your partner responds. That response triggers a response in you, which triggers . . . If you are stuck in a dissatisfactory loop, try a radical shift in *your* position.

Rachel complains about Steve's rude behavior. When he doesn't change, she complains more vociferously. Rather than change her move, she just intensifies it. People do this all the time in relationships. "Can you hear me?" shouts the angry husband, failing to realize that no one in her right mind would be receptive to his sarcastic tone. "Well, then, *can you hear me now?!!!*"

A few weeks after our initial session, things between Rachel and Steve start to go differently. Rachel has had a tough day with stalled writing and obnoxious politics in her department at school. She feels harried and beat and wants some TLC from Steve. Instead,

Steve clicks into problem-solving mode and offers all sorts of help-ful suggestions that, though constructive, have nothing to do with what his wife wants at the moment. The more "helpful" Steve tries to be, the more frustrated Rachel becomes, and the more . . . Before our therapy, Rachel would have given up or blown up, disgusted either way. Now, she pauses.

"Steve," she manages to say. "What you're giving me right now is great stuff, but I can't take it in. It's not what I want. What I want right now is just sympathy, just listen and be a dear, like, 'Oh, you poor sweetie.' You know what I mean? Like a girlfriend."

"But I'm not your girlfriend," Steve protests.

Rachel takes a deep breath. "You can do it, honey," she says, staying on track. "I have faith in you."

And, Rachel reports, miracle of miracles, Steve does.

Rachel has reaped the benefit of applying the serenity prayer to her marriage. Steve was able to change his position after Rachel changed hers. In the past, Rachel would have gone on blithely for a while, pre-tending that Steve was giving her what she wanted, and then she would have moved into complaint. Both of Rachel's accustomed posi-tions, denial and complaint, are reactive rather than proactive. This time, Rachel transmuted passivity into assertion. Rather than meet-ing Steve's disappointing response with ineffective silence or equally ineffective criticism, Rachel coached Steve on how best to deliver for her. When we want to work the change side of the serenity prayer, we ask: *What can I do to help you give me more of what I'd like? How can I move differently on my end of the seesaw?*

Once we push through the idealized romance story, it isn't hard to see that patriarchy's practical template for relationships is techno-logical. We are taught to envision ourselves as positioned above and "working on" our relationship like a mechanic fixing a machine. By contrast, relational recovery offers a template that is essentially eco-logical. We are not above the system working on it, but rather a part of the system moving within it. The only instrument for change we possess, our only tool, is ourselves—where we throw our weight, what we chose to focus on.

The skills we need to "work the relationship" by "working ourselves" inside the relationship are different from qualities prized in the intervention-from-above model—being right, being powerful. That flies out the window when we begin to think relationally. The new skills one needs are creativity, sensitivity, and flexibility. *You work the marriage by making an experimental move, seeing what your partner does with it, and then adjusting your behavior based on his or her response.* While general things can be said about what tends to work, such wisdom must be leavened with a humbling appreciation that at this moment with this person, all bets are off. There is no big book of relational rules. Think of raising children. The very tack that worked like a charm last Tuesday may be a disaster today. *The rule that surpasses all rules is that you must be connected, willing to see what's in front of you, and willing to move if what you're doing isn't working.*

I get angry with Belinda for something she said that I took as harsh criticism. In a former day, Belinda might react to my anger with matching, or even escalating, anger of her own. These days, she would most likely respond by taking responsibility for her imperfect performance and offering to do what she could to repair it. Nine out of ten times, such conciliation on her part evokes reciprocal conciliation on mine. I soften, she softens, and life goes on. One out of ten times—because of something to do with me that she may never even know of—conciliation on her part does nothing, or might even trigger an escalation. No matter how humbly she apologizes, I stay mad, or get even madder. Eventually, Belinda needs to change tacks and stand up to me.

"Hey, listen, honey," she'll say. "I've already said I'm sorry several times. If you're not going to come down off your anger, I can't control that. But I want to tell you that I don't like it and I wish you would stop already."

If calling me on my behavior works no better than conciliation did, her next move would probably be leaving me some space to get over it—whatever "it" might be. These days, I am in enough relational recovery that that usually works. A few minutes to a few hours later, Belinda will most likely get a hug and an explanation. "Sorry, I'm feeling incredibly stressed about . . ." We have moved into repair. In our early years, Belinda would have had neither the patience nor the skill to allow me that space. She would have gone after me, insisting that I explain and change my behavior "right now." The ensuing fight could have lasted for days.

While angry demand never works with me, the stance that does work is uncertain. On Tuesday, conciliation is just the thing. On Wednesday, pushing back is required. On Thursday, giving me space is what works. There's no way Belinda could—and, thankfully, no compelling reason she needs to—know in advance what will work. What works is her *flexibility,* her willingness to try different tacks coupled with *responsiveness.*

A readiness to shift one's position is one of the great, unsung skills of relationship. Some people might label such intentional action "manipulative," but I don't agree. Manipulation means deliberately distorting the truth in order to control another person. Being flexible means that—out of the many possible truths you could pick—you chose to be thoughtful, even playful, in which truth you select. You don't attempt to control the other so much as shift the dynamic by controlling yourself. Just as I distinguish relational flexibility from manipulation, I also differentiate it from accommodation. Sometimes flexibility requires you to shift from acquiescence to confrontation; sometimes, the reverse. You don't lie; you don't deliberately distort; you don't necessarily give in. You just jump out of your accustomed track.

What if nothing works? What if even a therapist cannot redirect the destructive dynamic? Now is the time to set firm limits, even issue an ultimatum. Such a declaration will often be met with the charge that you are "being controlling." But there is nothing controlling about having a limit. You are not telling your partner that he has to change, only that you will not tolerate it. How does one decide whether or not to "bottom line it"? Mentally, or even on paper, you draw up a list of the needs that are being met in the relationship—including such "unromantic" considerations as logistics, help with the kids, finances—and you draw up a list of the needs that are not being met. Taking stock, you ask yourself—either alone, with friends, family, or your therapist—the following critical question: Are enough of my needs being met in this relationship that it is worth my while to grieve those needs that are not?

When contemplating this question, it is critical to remember what patriarchy denies—that even very good relationships often have great gaping holes in them, things that are very bad.

Matthew was in love in his late fifties after two failed marriages and a string of bad relationships. He had worked hard in therapy, had routed out and transformed most of the old ways of thinking, feeling, and behaving that had tripped him up in the past. Life rewarded his good work with a great woman. Lilly was smart, funny, sexy, soulful—and severely arthritic.

"You have to understand," Matthew beseeched me in one session, looking truly desperate. "I grew up with a mother who had MS. My son from my first marriage has spina bifida. I have spent most of my life behind wheelchairs. I don't know, Terry. I just don't know if I can *do* it."

Matthew talked. He came in week after week and talked. His feelings from childhood. His longings for a healthy mother, his shame. His guilt about his son. His secret repulsion. His tortured, wonderful path toward acceptance. And now, this. Maybe it was too much. How much was he to ask of himself? But, on the other hand, Lilly was amazing; he had never felt like this with anyone.

One day Matthew comes in with news. "I'm going to marry that girl," he announces.

"So, you're up for it," I reply.

"Well," he begins, "I don't know if I'd say that I'm exactly up for it, but—"

"Matthew," I cut him short. He looks at me. "Are you up for it?" I repeat.

He contemplates me for a while and then relaxes. His shoulders release, his brow unknits, and he smiles. "Yes," he tells me. "I'm up for it. I want it."

The profound truth that the culture at large hides about acceptance is how much it hurts. Some of the things you don't get in your relationships hurt a little, others hurt a lot. But, if they are important to you at all, then the discrepancy between your boundless desire and the borders of reality will chafe. "Between the idea and the reality," wrote T. S. Eliot, "falls the shadow." The romantic vision promises "shadowless" relationships, but it is precisely by wrestling with the relationship's shadow, with disillusionment, that deep intimacy is sustained. Right after my first son's birth, Belinda suffered a short-lived but severe postpartum reaction. The difference between my expectations of this happy time and the reality spirited me off to a desperate, cruel place.

Coming home to my wife and new baby, I swing open the car door and step out into the parking lot, my body tense against a cold blast of air. Out past the streetlamps, the sky looms, close, bearing down like a storm descending, but there is no storm. Shit, I think. It's just October and it's coming already.

Late fall. Cold and dark, like two neighborhood bullies, crowd out the easy expansiveness of summer, herding us deep into coats, cars, houses, squeezing us down inside ourselves.

I remember the smell of burning leaves. My father towers beside me, massive, his great potbelly thrust out at the night like a dare. He leans against a heavy old rake as sparks dart madly up toward extinction. "Nothing like the smell of leaves," he philosophizes, knocking ash from his cigarette. It all seemed so vibrant to me then. I was his boy, Edgar's boy, eight or nine, standing limply beside him, small against the sheer bulk of him, the light of the fire across a concrete wall, the cold, the aching silence between us like the numbness of my freezing hands and feet. "Nothing like it," I agree, not wanting the moment to end. "Yes, indeed," he replies.

Eventually, all the leaves have been fed into the fire, sparks ascending, the ash left behind. I don't want to go back inside the house. I can't face the emptiness waiting there, my parents' bickering, the incessant TV. I want to stay out here in the crystalline night with flickering warmth against my face and my father's huge shape, his thick silence, beside me. Glimpsing him in the erratic light as he glances up at our back kitchen window, I suddenly sense, wordlessly and dreadfully, that he is as reluctant to move as I am.

It is darker in the house than it is out here.

The sound of a car pulling into the driveway tugs me out of my reverie. I hike my briefcase out of the backseat and shut the car door, craning my neck up toward the windows of our rent-controlled Brookline apartment. From this angle it doesn't look like Belinda has any lights on. I'm anxious to see my son, and apprehensive about my wife. Justin is barely ten weeks old. Labor and delivery were hard on Belinda, hours of pushing, pain, then the fetal monitor started spiking and she was shot off for a fast C-section. I stayed with her, trying not to faint, offering reassurances to her head while observing the doctors and nurses split open her belly and move quickly into her womb. And then there he was, slick with blood. Belinda was nauseated and weak, but happy. They gave him to me, put him in my arms, stuck a bottle of sugar water in my hand, and told me to feed him. I felt panicky, but a nurse reminded me how to maneuver the bottle. It wasn't all that difficult. "Well, you made it," I remember telling him. "I guess you made it."

Holding my son in those first moments, I was inundated with love, overwhelmed. I had never touched such unalloyed tenderness; I was weak from it. I sat down, looking into his tiny face, awed by responsibility for his life.

From the driveway to the back door is a short jog, but the wind blusters, cold. The heft of my briefcase, the handle chill against my bare hand. Inside, up the stairs, our hallway is dim and the light in the foyer is turned off as I put my key in the lock. I am afraid to go in. And I'm angry. Belinda sits splayed like a rag doll, her nightgown draped over her legs, in a huge leather chair in the living room. The whole apartment is dark. At first I don't see her at all, and then when I do I assume she is sleeping. The sight of her face, open-eyed, staring, makes me flinch.

"Belinda?" I whisper, thinking, still, that she might be asleep.

"What?" she answers, wide awake.

"Honey?" I come up beside her, my voice soft, while the muscles in my neck and jaw tighten. "Honey, are you okay?" At this she laughs, bitter and far away. And I hate her.

Looking back, there were many reasons why I hated Belinda. I hated her for being so wretched. It hadn't dawned on me yet that she had a postpartum depression, which she would soon treat and conquer. At the time, her condition felt frightening and endless. I saw her as willfully negative, indulgently wallowing in unhappiness. Here was the greatest moment of our marriage, the crowning glory of our journey toward normalcy, and she seemed to be coming unglued. She was great with Justin, tireless and loving. But as soon as he was down for a moment, a torrent of misery poured out of her. I felt abandoned by her and, beneath that, afraid—afraid that her unraveling would just keep going, that I'd married a crazy woman who would live out her whole lifetime—and mine—depressed and angry, as my mother had. In our first years together, Belinda and I had been a stormy couple, passionately loving and just as passionately going after one another. Having a child was a leap of faith that things would improve between us. Staring down at her in the dark, it suddenly seemed like I'd made the wrong choice. But what could I do? I wasn't about to leave my son. His birth was a nail driven through my foot to the floorboards of our marriage. I was sentenced to spend my days back in the dark house I'd spent my life running from. I articulated none of this. More than unable to say it all to her, I was utterly incapable of admitting it myself. Instead of acknowledging my real feelings, I offered Belinda treacly solicitation peppered with covert attack.

"Is it really necessary to sit here in the dark?" I ask. And she immediately bridles.

"Is it really *necessary* to be so fucking mean?" she throws back at me. I breathe, a long, deep, put-upon sigh. "Here comes the Ophelia scene," I mutter under my breath, but not quite softly enough. "What did you say?" she turns on me, suddenly sharp, snapped out of lethargy.

"Nothing," I lie.

"Do you think I'm *stupid?*" She rounds on me. "I heard that. Your idiot stage whisper . . ."

"Belinda, I—"

"Don't you think I know what you meant?"

"Listen, B., it's just—"

"Do you think you're the only one here who's ever read a book? Do you think I'm illiterate?"

"Honey," I whine, beleaguered, "can't we start this again?"

"I am *not* fucking Ophelia," she says, her voice tremulous with hurt and fury.

"Fine, B. Fine."

"And I'm not fucking *crazy.*"

"Okay, I'm sorry. It was uncalled for, I didn't mean . . . Look, I'm stressed too . . ."

"I'm not *any* of those things, Terry. But you know what you are? *You* are mean. You've been *really* mean, Terry."

"Now, look . . ." My patience starts to unravel.

"You've been mean to me for *weeks* now," She starts to cry. "Just when I need you. I can't . . ."

"Aw, sweetie." I soften.

"I can't *take* it, Terry. I'm having trouble, okay? I know that. I can't deal with a new baby and all that I'm feeling if you're going to do *this* to me, too." Her victim stance angers me.

"What am I doing, Belinda? What? I'm working longer hours than ever; you're not bringing in anything, which is fine, it's fine. I wake up with Justin almost as much as you do. I'm tired; I'm wiped out from no sleep—and I come home to—"

"To what?" she counters, "To your bitch, crazy wife?"

"Belinda, I don't see . . ." I deny it all, even to myself, especially to myself. But she is right. My feelings toward her have somehow congealed into cold forbearance, at best. She repulses me, and I let her know it in a dozen small ways—in the way my eyes remain drawn as I look at her, the way I no longer hold her at night when we sleep, the very civility with which I most often treat her.

"Just leave me alone." She turns away, exhausted. "If you don't want to be here, then *don't.* I don't want you here against your will." Her words sound insane to me, inciting me further.

"Are you telling me to get out?" I up the ante.

"Do what you want." She sighs. "I'm too tired. I can't fight anymore. I've never seen you like this, Terry. You were never like this. I need to rest," she lifts herself up from the chair. "I'm going to—"

"I *can* leave, you know," I say, fury overtaking me. "Is that what you want? You want me out of here?"

She trails off to bed, not even looking at me. "I'm exhausted," she repeats. "Do what you do. Just, don't wake me up . . ." And she's gone.

Incredulous, I storm out of the apartment, spilling my pent-up indignation into the street. "Damn it," I mutter. "*Damn* it!"

I lean against a brick wall, ready to nurse my grudge at her, but, perversely and against my will, what comes to me instead is the memory of falling in love.

We called them "dumpers," not great for body surfing, but beautiful to watch. They crest very high, close to the shoreline, and then the great crash, white foam fanning out along the side, loud, chaotic. I am lying with my head on Belinda's lap. I am thirty-four years old and we have just found one another. Belinda strokes my hair, absently looking out at the ocean, smiling her wide-lipped smile. "Porpoise smile," I call it.

"You know Freud's idea of the 'family romance'?" I burble along. "It is supposed to be every child's fantasy that the family he's in isn't his real family. In truth, the child belongs to some king and queen somewhere."

"Oliver Twist," Belinda says.

"Right, exactly." I look out at the breaking waves. "So when I was a kid, young, kindergarten, maybe, first grade, I remember running out of my house, after some screaming match with my father, or their going after each other. And I'd walk down our street—I was only allowed to go to the end of the block. And I'd think about being an alien."

"You are," she agrees.

"No, listen," I tell her. "Really, I'd imagine that I wasn't human. I remember having this fantasy that light could shoot out of my hands, and that someday some spaceship would come down from the clouds and rescue me, that I'd go back to where I belonged."

"Aw, sweetie," she says, sadly.

"You know, even though I was so alone in that house," I tell her, "the one thing I had my whole life was I *knew* it. Even when I was so young, when kids aren't supposed to see stuff, it felt like I could see everything—my father's despair and my mother's rage, and the darkness that hovered over all of us. You know what I mean?"

"Of course I do," Belinda says.

"There weren't any words for it," I tell her. "Maybe a lot of little kids walk around seeing it all and not saying so—I sure didn't tell anyone—but if I wasn't the only one I didn't know it."

Belinda smiles, perhaps at my earnestness. I sit up, face her, put a hand on her broad cheek. "When I got older," I go on, "old enough to first start thinking about girls, I had this recurrent fantasy. I would be on the school bus, all alien eyes, those bug eyes, and the kids would be doing their kid things, Rowdy, connected in ways I never was. There I am drinking it all in from the sideline, where I always was, and suddenly . . ."

"From across a crowded bus," helps Belinda.

"From across a crowded bus," I agree, "I see her, lonely and sad, like me. And, just like me, she's seeing it all, too, feeling it all. And in one trancelike moment, we see each other. We see each other seeing each other . . ."

"Seeing it all," Belinda finishes for me.

"Yes," I tell her. "Yes, exactly. The one I'd been waiting for."

Belinda flashes her wide-lipped smile and kisses my face. Confronted with her tenderness, I find myself coming undone, tears, runny nose.

"My sweet boy," she murmurs. "My little boy."

"I think what I'm trying to say," I stammer out, equal parts overwhelmed and embarrassed. "I think what I mean to say, Belinda, is that you're that girl."

"Of course I am, darling," she tells me. "I will always be that girl for you. No matter what." She laughs, kissing my face. "Look at us." She cracks up at our tears. "Mister and Mrs. issues and tissues." But even though she laughs, she holds on to me.

"If we forget this," she says later, "we'll come back here. Right back to this spot. So we can remember what we're about."

•　　•　　•

An eddy of wind kicks up swirling leaves and dirt around me, settling as quickly as it comes. Grit sprays into my eyes and makes them water. A moment later, I look up resentfully at the darkened windows of my apartment. This is stupid, I think. This is just stupid. I consider the possibilities. I could go to the paperback bookstore and hang out there a while; I could go to the coffee shop—but the thought of either strikes me as obscenely lonely. I'm tired and cold. I have yet to see Justin. In an instant, I imagine myself back in the apartment, indignantly thrusting a protesting Belinda aside. "I want to see *my* son!" I am yelling. My imagined self-righteousness collapses a few seconds later and I feel ridiculous, out on the sidewalk, with my wife and kid upstairs. Exactly what point, I wonder, was I supposed to be making? I cross the street and perch on a stoop facing back toward the apartment. And slowly, I begin to let creep into consciousness the dawning admission that Belinda is right. I *had* been torturing her, in ways I never even thought I had in me. I knew I could yell and get angry, but this felt far worse—being cold, despising, and all of it denied. I had wanted so much for us to be the happy family neither of us had ever had. I felt so let down by her, awash in her self-preoccupied pain. I experienced her despair as abandoning not just me but my child— who was just a projection of my own vulnerability, anyway, the lonely boy I once was. Alone on the stoop it comes to me in full, how resentful I'd been, even while going through the motions. As I stare up at the blank windows, I sense the heat of a fire rising up against my face in the cold, the crackle of burning leaves. Sadness flickers over me, like firelight.

"I'm not going to do it," I tell my imagined father, as he leans against his old rake, facing away from me, toward the flames. "*You* stayed out here your whole fucking life," I tell him. "You *never* made it back. Not here or anywhere." His hunched shoulders, his worn coat, threaten to undo me. "I'm not staying out here with you," I tell him. "You're on your own." In my mind, he says nothing, Although I can tell he's hurt, I know he'd never let me see it. Too proud, I think. Too stiff. I get up from the steps. Too damaged.

•   •   •

Justin lies quietly in his bassinet, breathing softly. His skin is cool and soft on my lips and he snuffles and turns his face slightly in sleep. I cup his bald head in the palm of my hand. In our bedroom, without speaking, I undress and curl up next to Belinda, two spoons, my arms around her. "You're cold," she complains. "Your face is cold."

"I need you to warm me up," I answer, but she doesn't reply. Her body lies limp in my embrace. "You're right, you know," I say after a while.

"Right about what?" she answers, suspicious.

"Everything," I tell her. "The way I've been acting. How mean I've been treating you." I can feel her stiffen slightly at my words.

"Are you placating me?" she asks.

"No," I say evenly. "No, I'm not."

She turns around to face me, looking at me hard. Then, she begins to cry.

"I'm sorry," I tell her. "I'm really sorry. I just went a little crazy, I guess." To my utter amazement, she forgives me.

"You were horrible," she answers, reaching out for me. "Just horrible. And then, when you kept denying it, it was like a nightmare. I felt so alone."

"I'm sorry, darling." I kiss her wet eyes. "I'm back now," I offer lamely, expecting more anger, but she softens; her body molds into mine.

"That's why I love you," she says, matter-of-fact.

"What?"

"Because you come back," she says. "Eventually."

I stroke her hair. "Thanks for the vote of confidence," I answer. I feel her relax, as her breathing turns rhythmic and deep. I listen to the sounds around me. Her breath, the erratic creaks of our old building, traffic outside. Holding Belinda lying still in my arms, I find myself thinking less about either of us than the baby in the room across the hall, and about the other one we hope will soon follow. I try to imagine what their lives will feel like, unhampered by the unbridled family anguish Belinda and I were each battered by as children. And lying there, far from sleep, feeling raw and fragile, I realize that the only thing standing between their grandparents' misery and the lives that will stretch out before them is us, their mother and me.

There are things you get in a real relationship, and things you do not get. The character of the union is determined by how the two partners manage both aspects of love—the getting and the not getting. Moving into acceptance means moving into grief, without being a victim. You own your choice. "I am getting enough in this relationship," you say, "to make it worth my while to mourn the rest." And mourn we do. Real love is not for the faint of heart. What we miss in our relationships we truly miss. The pain of it does not, and need not, go away. It is like dealing with any loss.

I object when people, especially therapists, talk about "resolving grief," as if grief could ever be so compliant. We humans don't "resolve" grief; we live with it. The pain of our losses recedes, over time, and we get on with our lives. But periodically one may well feel the chill hand on the heart—what we miss, our mortality—its sudden grip like a sharp intake of breath. It is important for us to recall in such moments that we still remain. Grief washes over us and we are left standing. It's okay. Nothing's wrong. It's just a natural part of things. Dead leaves underfoot. A clear autumn evening, the black sky like a vault, the vapor of our own breath in the air, a surprise. "Oh," we say. "It will be winter again soon. It's grown dark so early." And we burrow deep into our clothes for a moment, glad to be heading home.

CHAPTER FOURTEEN

Learning to Speak Relationally

To live outside the law, you must be honest.
—Bob Dylan

The way to keep passion alive is by telling the truth—the truth about what we see, what we feel, what we really want. We don't try to control our unruly desires by backing away from them, pretending they are gratified when they are not, or pretending that they don't matter. Mature love requires us to acknowledge our full experience, our feelings and wants, while making grown-up choices about them. We are conversant with our desires; we experience the lack of those that remain unmet. And yet, we own our decisions as ours, not as an imposition, embracing equally the joy of what we get and the pain of what we do not get.

Sexual passion serves as a good illustration. Can a healthy relationship sustain over time the erotic vibrancy of an early relationship? This is the promise of countless popular books and magazine articles—mostly aimed at women who are less anxious about their own pleasure than their spouse's. We have seen how the accumulation of unresolved injuries make it unlikely that most partners who follow the dictates of patriarchy will remain sexually close for very long. But what about a couple in recovery? If the partners truly commit to working the relationship, communicating with honesty and skill, does sexual passion not wane? The answer is: yes and no. Partners who are able to maintain most other forms of intimacy—intellectual, emotional, physical, spiritual—are, by and large, better equipped to

sustain sexual intimacy as well. But they still have to work at it—
teach each other their likes and dislikes, create a space in which to be
sexual, cultivate skill and tenderness—no mean feat in a culture
that offers couples little respite from outside concerns and respon-
sibilities. Many of the couples I see need help transitioning from their
accustomed side-by-side pattern to turn and face each other again. It
is difficult to pull away from the inertia of a relationship's horizontal
line in order to retrieve the vertical—the experience of being present
in the moment. A weekend away, a romantic dinner, sexual surprises
like an impromptu night in a hotel all serve to help partners shift
focus from the details of their lives back onto one another. And yet,
no matter how creative one is, sex, like any other form of connection,
is not one long unbroken high note. Healthy sexual passion follows
the same rhythm of connection, disconnection, and reconnection that
characterizes every other aspect of relationships. What longevity
brings, for good and ill, is knowledge. Is sex with a known partner as
purely exciting as early-stage fantasy? No, it isn't. While manuals on
technique, Tantric exercises, and G-spot illustrations are all generally
to the good, the great excitement of fantasy is the promise of one's
own larger-than-life projections. As a flawed human, you will not be
able to live up to your partner's most intense fantasies, nor will she
be able to live up to yours. But is this the only aspect of good sex?

The same knowledge of one another that works against the pro-
longation of early-stage excitement associated with fantasy can be a
great benefit to couples who know how to use it. "I wouldn't say that
I feel more passionate toward Steve than I did early on," Rachel tells
me several months into our work together. "But I do feel a *deeper* sexuality emerging—precisely because I am beginning to feel I know
him, feel that it's safe to open up to him."

Sexual passion is about surrender, the willingness to give in to
one's own sensations, and participate in the flow of the other's.
Most partners pull away from one another over time not because of
sex per se, but rather as a result of emotional issues; they carry too
many nicks and scars, too much unspoken hurt, disappointment,
inadequacy, to enter into that level of surrender. It's easy to allow oneself to be that vulnerable with a relative stranger because there are so

few consequences, the vulnerabilities one enters into are so delimited. But to give yourself over to someone who has hurt you; someone you have seen as so flawed, so imperfectly human, someone whose harsh judgment or loss would be hard to withstand—to open your body with a commensurately open heart, not to some idealized lover but to *this* flawed man, *this* woman—given all that you hate and adore about them—that is a difficult and rich experience. Sex from such a place of *knowing love* is as diverse in its moods as we are. Couples with mature sex lives talk about the variation—giggly sex, rushed sex, down-and-dirty sex, cuddly sex, tender sex, slow, sweet nostalgic sex, perfunctory quickies. Healthy couples will predictably encounter periods when there is virtually no desire at all, and other times, long into the relationship, when they can't get enough of each other. Without doubt there will be differences between the partners in appetite, tempo, style. And couples who can communicate and negotiate will generally do better over the long run than those who cannot. Still we must return to a place of truthful acknowledgment. Our sexual longings, like most other longings connected to intimacy, are infinite. That is part of our great beauty as humans. The partners we live with, like ourselves, are finite. And that, too, is part of our great beauty as humans. Does tension exist between our perfect longings and the imperfect world? I mistrust anyone who denies that. But whoever defined real love as devoid of tension? As adults, we stand by our choices—what we are willing to live with, what we are willing to let go of. We fight for our needs and yet we also accept the relationship's limitations—not because we have to, but because we have decided it is worth it.

Relational esteem helps us understand how to speak the truth to ourselves. *Learning to speak relationally* provides a map for telling our truth to others. In order to live beyond patriarchy we must allow ourselves to drop each day to levels of vulnerability, and take risks with our partner's responses, that push us a long way away from the safe, stable, unions of our fathers and mothers. *If we want our marriages to feel more like lover relationships, then we must be willing to take the kind of risks that lovers take. Safe passion is an oxymoron.* This does not give us license to "let it rip." If we want to live in the truth and succeed at it, we must proceed skillfully.

Earlier, I outlined the corrosive effect on relationships of silence—in particular, women's silence. Silence comes in many forms; many of the women clients I see, for example, do, in fact, speak, loudly and vociferously—just not effectively. And while women's silence constitutes a profound degenerative influence, I don't mean to suggest that men are voluble processors of their relationships. Women's silence demands our attention because its roots lie in suppression. When there is much to say and no safe place to say it, the unspoken festers and spoils, becoming a wellspring of chronic resentment. Men, by contrast, are rarely bullied into silence by women, but rather they tend to be less cognizant of interpersonal dynamics. The humorous contrast of men's obtuseness about relational issues and women's preoccupation with them has become such a staple of American wit it borders on cliché. In *Dave Barry's Complete Guide to Guys* a couple is driving home when the woman realizes that they've been together six months. "And then there is silence in the car. To Elaine, it seems like a very loud silence. She thinks to herself: Geez, I wonder if it bothers him that I said that. Maybe he's been feeling confined by our relationship; maybe he thinks I'm trying to push him into something he's not ready for . . . But hey, I'm not sure I want this kind of relationship, either . . . I mean, where *are* we going? Are we just going to keep seeing each other at this level of intimacy? Are we headed toward *marriage?*

"And Roger is thinking: Gosh. *Six months* . . . so that means it was . . . let's see *February* when we started going out, which was right after I had the car at the dealer's, which means . . . lemme check the odometer . . . Whoa! I am *way* overdue for an oil change."

It is not difficult to see oneself and one's partner in such an amusing description, but men's much-vaunted obliviousness may be more apparent than intrinsic. My clinical experience has taught me that "down deep" men harbor just as many disappointments, get their feelings hurt just as often, as women do. Most men are simply unused to identifying, or explicitly dealing with, the broil of emotional turmoil that is a natural part of intimacy. Feelings, "issues," and emotional needs are all disavowed and devalued by the traditional masculine code. If women lose their voices, so do men in a different way. Both sexes need to be empowered to speak.

The necessity to help both partners regain expression illustrates a shift in focus at this stage in the work of repair. In the first phase of recovery, *reconnecting the couple,* addressing the asymmetry in men and women's relational capacities was critical. In this third phase of the work, the *practice of intimacy,* that asymmetry, while still acknowledged, recedes from center stage. As men and women learn the skills they need to live relationally, the fact that women come to the table better prepared than men matters less than that both sexes are not prepared well enough. Both sexes, albeit in different ways, apply the basic mores and assumptions of patriarchy to their relationships, and neither fares very well. The first phase of relational recovery brings the partners into a *willingness* to speak (women) and to listen (men). Once that readiness has been established, both sexes need to learn how. While speaking the truth in any form generally represents a step up from silence, it isn't enough to say that the partners must speak. In order to succeed, they must learn how to speak their truth adeptly.

Here's an example of unskilled speaking:

After weeks of dramatic improvement, Rachel and Steve seem miserable again. One step forward, five steps back. Rachel flops down in her chair, a rag doll, and shakes her head.

"It's been *awful,*" she moans. "*Worse* than awful. We haven't been in one of these for a long, long time. We've been fighting nonstop for *days.*" And then the clincher: leaning close in, Rachel confides, "I think this therapy might actually be making things *worse.*"

Sitting inches away from the vortex of his wife's emotions, Steve appears to have developed an intense interest in the seams of my ceiling. I look them both over for a moment, gathering my thoughts. They haven't looked this bad since they first came to see me— Rachel a martyr; Steve, passive-aggressive and cold.

"So, what happened?" I ask.

"Look, we've both been under a lot of stress," Rachel begins.

"Steve's been traveling a lot, for his business. This is a heavy time of year for him. As I know, let me say. I mean, that's not . . . we've agreed to that. Anyway, I guess it all started . . . the fighting started . . ."

"Tell him about Andrea, Rachel," Steve cuts in, not bothering to shift his eyes from the ceiling, his voice flat, emotionless.

"What?" Rachel bridles immediately. "Am I not telling the story fast enough for you, Steven? I don't need to be the one . . ."

"Go on." Steve waves, impatient.

"I would *welcome* your participation," says Rachel, dripping condescension. Steve snorts.

"You want to put that into words?" I confront him.

Steve shuffles about for a moment. "Let's just say I don't exactly feel 'welcomed in my participation,' " he manages.

"Why is that?" I press.

He makes a sour face, and waves us on again, imperious, resigned. "Go ahead, Rachel." He sighs. "Tell the story." I look at his scrunched-up face for a moment, thinking, Yuck! but decide to chose my battles.

"As you know," Rachel picks up the thread, "Andrea can be a handful. A *spirited* child, as we say in Cambridge."

"Heaven forbid she should be stifled." I join with her.

"Andrea and I have had our ups and downs. But, I think, by and large, we've got a grip. So, last Tuesday, Steve had just come home. Andrea and I were into something. It was just beginning to settle down . . ."

"Not hardly." Steve can't help himself.

"Steven," Rachel rounds on him. "You don't *know*. Andrea and I had been at it for over an hour. There were tears; there were consequences; there were apologies. We were just about—"

"Rachel." Steve fairly lifts himself off the chair. "Andrea was in the corner sobbing, and you were towering over our ten-year-old *screaming*."

"*You* were the one screaming, Steven," Rachel counters.

"That's just not true. I simply told you that berating Andrea wasn't acceptable," he begins.

"I was not *berating* her, Steven. *You* were berating *me*."

"But Andrea told you herself," Steve continues. "I was standing right there. She said—"

"She's a *child*," returns Rachel, exasperated. "Of *course* she'll agree that I'm mean if you give her the opening."

"Rachel." Steve tries to be reasonable. "I am very supportive of you in your dealings with—"

"No, you are not," her anger flashing. "You are *not!* You think I'm *harsh*. You think I'm *controlling.*"

"Don't tell me what I think," Steve retorts.

"And don't tell *me* I'm screaming when I'm not," she shoots back. "You come flouncing in. You have *no idea* what we've been through. And you start acting like the fucking reincarnation of Mr. Spock."

"Doctor Spock," Steve corrects.

"Pardon?" Rachel stops short.

"Mr. Spock's the guy with the ears," Steve says affably. Rachel just looks at him. "'Beam me up, Scotty?'" Steve tries.

Rachel contemplates her husband for a long moment. "You're *such* an asshole," she declares, and then glances over at me. "No, no," she suddenly scrambles. "Sorry. You can *behave* like such an asshole." She crosses her arms. "There," to me. "Is that better?"

I look across at her for a moment, resisting the impulse to smile. Even during a fight, they are somehow appealing, although I imagine right now it's more fun to watch them than to be them. Steve and Rachel both look at me, upturned faces, expectant, a class waiting for the lecture to begin, pens poised, open hearted. I sigh.

Rachel and Steve have gotten snared in what I call a *perception battle*—a contest about reality. Was Rachel inappropriate with Andrea or wasn't she?

"This wall is green."

"No, it's red."

"Sorry, it's green."

Couples get into *perception* battles all the time. They are, without exception, a huge waste of energy. Like a dog chasing its own tail, perception battles go nowhere; they are uniformly irresolvable. Futile arguments over "the truth" provide an excellent example of how both sexes get pulled into using patriarchal values in their relationships, and how those values fail. The core assumption dictating Rachel and Steve's muddy attempts at conflict resolution is the preeminence of *validity*. Was Rachel *setting limits* or was she just *screaming?* Was Steve *undermining* or was he *supportive?* Whose reality is most legitimate? Partners try to "resolve" the difference in their points of view by eradicating it. "If you would only see it the *right* way" is the implicit message, meaning, of course, "my way."

I tell couples like Rachel and Steve that they are trying to apply the scientific method to their fight. Each "argues his case," marshaling evidence; the argument ends, presumably, when both partners accept the superior reality, the one *right* reality, and everyone moves onto the same page.

The traditionally masculine values of science, of measures and proofs, operate marvelously well in the domain for which they were designed. The great achievement of scientific reasoning is inarguable. *But while the idea of objective reality may be just the thing to send men to the moon, or get our buses to run on schedule, it is neither helpful nor necessary in interpersonal relations.* Later in the session Steve is able to drop the "objective" case for his point of view in favor of speaking more intimately. "When I hear you yelling at Andrea like that," he tells Rachel, "I go right back to my mother berating my younger sister." He turns to me to explain, saying, "It was constant, the two of them, and excruciating to watch."

"What would they fight about?" I ask him.

""What would they *really* fight about?" he asks. "It was all about control. My mother dictated to my sister who and what she should be. What to wear, which boyfriends were acceptable. You name it."

"And where was your father?" I ask.

"Ostensibly on the sidelines . . ." He pauses.

"But in reality . . ." I prompt.

"He'd sneak into my sister's room and comfort her, support her rebellion."

I look at him hard for a moment. "Really?" I ask. "Are you being literal? Your father would actually sneak into her bedroom?"

"Well, yeah. Or off in a corner somewhere," he answers. "They had a very 'special' relationship." The way Steven drawls out the phrase gives me pause. I take a few minutes to explore with him the precise nature of their relationship, and, on first pass at least, hear Steve describe it as inappropriately close, what therapists call enmeshed, though not physically incestuous. "And your mother's control," I ask, "did it extend to your father as well as your sister?"

"Not really. He just ignored my mother."

"He never fought with her?"

"No," Steve says. "Why should he bother?"

"You're very smart, Steve," I say. "Finish that thought."

"Why should he fight with my mother? He had my sister to do it for him." He seems to collapse a bit in the chair; his square bulk loses shape.

"You look sad, Steven," I say. He nods his head.

"I felt badly for Sheila, my sister. Night after night the same screaming bouts. I tried to coach her out of it, but she was so stubborn . . ."

"She had a job to do," I tell him. "And you?"

"What?" he asks. "Where did I fit in?" I nod. "I didn't. I stayed out of it."

"How did you manage that?" I ask. Steve smiles, aware of the implications of what he's about to tell me.

"I joked around," he confesses. "Barbed, pointed comments. If any of them tried to mess with me, I'd . . ."

"You used your mind like a knife," I say. He shrugs, aping modesty.

"It's what I had," he says.

"It's what you still have," I reply.

A few minutes later I ask Steve to try speaking to Rachel again about her manner with Andrea, only this time to stay connected to the soft, open place he had come to. "Speak from that," I suggest.

"Rachel," he turns to her. "Whether you're *actually* yelling or not, when you turn on her that way I get really upset. Could you please take that into consideration?" Even more than his wording, the warmth in Steve's voice augurs well for a shift toward repair. This is a technique I use often, asking a partner to summon the energy of warm regard for his partner before speaking. "Remember," I advise in such moments, "that you love her." When addressing difficult matters, changes in tone can do wonders. I ask partners to attend to whether they feel "hard" or "soft," behind a wall or a permeable boundary. You can hear the difference in someone's voice, and partners react at least as much to the quality of the sound as to the spoken content. Recalling his own vulnerability, Steve softens. But Rachel is not ready yet to shift with him.

"What if I disagree?" she asks me.

"You can't," I reply. She's taken aback.

"What do you mean I can't? Don't I have the right—"

"He's talking about some feelings he has when he sees you behave a certain way. How can you disagree with his feelings? They're his."

"I disagree that I 'turn on her,'" Rachel answers.

"That part's mostly irrelevant," I claim. She takes great exception.

"Let me tell you, Terry, it hardly feels irrelevant to me!" she exclaims.

"Well, it should be," I answer, unwilling to budge.

From a relational perspective, the answer to the question "Is Rachel harsh or is Steve overprotective?" is *What does it matter?* Hauling in a panel of experts to listen to Rachel next time she confronts her daughter in order to judge which of their descriptions is most accurate, even were it possible, would still not address the thing Steve needs addressed, which is Steve. "More than who's right," I say to Rachel, "what matters is that your partner, for reasons he's been remarkably lucid and open about, gets into an uncomfortable state, and he is asking for your help with it. You have the right to turn down his request, tell him to go deal with his reaction. That's within your power, although you will have to deal with the consequences. Or you could empathize with his feelings and honor his request. The choice is yours to do with as you please, Rachel. Arguing with him about it, however, won't get you anywhere." She thinks for a minute, crossing her arms.

"And just *why* should I accommodate him?" she asks.

"Maybe you shouldn't," I answer. "I don't know how much this means to you. But, on the surface, it looks like it wouldn't cost you that much to set limits with Andrea a little more calmly."

"You don't understand," Rachel tells me. "It's taken me a lot of therapy to be able to stand up to Steve. I spent years accommodating to him."

"You spent years overaccommodating, if I heard you right," I say. "But, the healthy antidote to that is not underaccommodating." Rachel finally turns to her husband, peers at him for a moment, and suddenly smiles.

"Steven," she says, "if you talked to me the way you just did a moment ago, I'd give you just about anything."

"I'll try," Steve tells her earnestly. We all relax for a moment, but then Rachel's momentum impels her to sell past the sale.

"Instead of the way you normally talk," she goes on, puffing out her chest and dropping her voice by an octave to mock him, "'Now, Rachel. You *know* that Andrea *only* responds—'"

"Come on, honey." Steve gets annoyed. "You don't have to exaggerate, I really—"

"It's okay. It's okay." I head them off, before they trip into their next perception battle. "You're in agreement."

For decades, couples therapists have taught partners to avoid nasty, blaming "you" statements: "You always do *this*. You really are a *that*." Relational recovery goes a step further, asking partners to give up "it" statements as well, forgoing lordly authority in favor of speaking with the humility of a fellow participant. "This may not be *the* reality. But it certainly is *my* reality. And as such, I would like it addressed." Speaking from a place of ownership, from your subjective experience, does not diminish the legitimacy of your point. But most of us latch on to objectivity because we think it augments our authority. In the patriarchal divide, the "objective" lands firmly on the masculine side of the equation, while "mere subjectivity" rests timidly with the devalued feminine. The more completely removed one is from "the personal," the more authority one has. But if we step beyond the confines of patriarchal thinking, someone's point is not diminished simply because it belongs to them. Speaking from the "I," from our personhood, lessens neither our authority nor our responsibility. It offers us a way to reclaim our voices from within the respectful context of connection, teaching us to deal with disagreements not by eradicating our differences, but by managing them. If Steve is uncomfortable with Rachel's tone, and if Rachel is uncomfortable with Steve's undermining, let each of them own their discomfort as theirs, and let their partner attend to it with sensitivity.

Living authentically means leaving behind patriarchy's shadowy world of lies, half-truths, and obfuscation—the unspoken want, the unrisked confrontation, the demimonde of protection. Yet it also means moving beyond the harsh, shadowless glare of "objective" truth, unyielding and stripped from relational context. Unlike the monotone fantasies we were raised with, real love is rife with paradox. The paradox inherent in relational esteem is that our capacity to stay in deep connection rests on our ability to bear solitude inside the relationship. The paradox inherent in learning to speak relationally is that when we step into living the truth we give up the hubris of acting as if we owned it. Only after giving up "the truth" can we learn to speak *our* truth.

CHAPTER FIFTEEN

Learning to Listen:
Scanning for the Positive

The third core skill, *listening relationally*, is comprised of two operations: one inside you, the other between you and your partner. First, there is the actual listening itself, and then, your response. In order to listen well a capacity most in this culture have not developed must be cultivated—a functioning *internal boundary*.

As part of my training as a family therapist, I learned to analyze a family's boundary issues, discerning whether the family was "enmeshed"—overly intrusive, having poor boundaries—or "disengaged"—distant and alienated, having too many walls. It wasn't until I met Pia Mellody, however, that I realized boundary issues could be applied to individuals as well. Her work inspired me to think of boundaries not as a structure, but as a skill—one that could be learned.

An *internal boundary* is to your psyche as skin is to your body. It is where you end and the world begins. It complements your *external boundary*, which is the capacity to determine when, by whom, and in what manner you will touch or be touched. Just as the external boundary both protects us and allows us to connect physically, an internal boundary protects us and allows us to connect emotionally. I sometimes call it a "receptivity regulator"; it modulates the extremes of over- and underreactivity. Most of the partners I encounter have not been taught the art of such balance. Some possess damaged or nonexistent boundaries, others characteristically shield themselves within walls; and others vacillate between both conditions. A poor internal boundary allows other people's feedback, beliefs about you, even, at times, their very emotional state to pierce you to the quick. "How could you *think* that of me?" "I'm so hurt that you feel that way!" or "It depresses me when you get so sad," are hallmark sentiments of someone with a "thin skin," a poor internal boundary.

The complementary boundary dysfunction comes from skin that is too "thick," permitting little to no receptivity. Walls protect you like a fortress; they let nothing in. The subjective experience is one of disconnection, obliviousness, or indifference. You can use virtually anything as a wall—wall of anger, wall of silence, wall of words. Walls insulate you from whatever another might say or feel. Some of the partitions are egregious—rage, drunkenness, TV clickers. Others are more subtle, like humor, caretaking, even pleasantness. Using walls of good manners, for example, is one of the great British upper-class traditions—"Oh, how *very* nice!" which translates as, "Drop dead. I can't wait to get out of here."

It doesn't take a lot of reflection to notice that this issue sorts by gender, with women needing to learn how to decrease their sensitivity to the environment and men how to increase theirs. Further reflection, however, breeds greater nuance. Men appear overtly walled off. And yet, my clinical experience aligns with research demonstrating men's marked physiological responses to interpersonal tension. Behind men's walls often lies someone who is overly sensitive. Similarly, women who appear highly reactive may hide covert walls.

In contrast to the excesses of poor boundaries or walls, a healthy boundary is supple; it allows you to be both protected and yet connected at the same time. As your partner speaks, whatever emotion she throws at you goes *splat* on the outside of your internal boundary. Imagine this psychic shield as resting about arm's length away, encircling you. Safely ensconced within your boundary, you cast a cool eye on what's being asserted, point by point. If the material rings true for you, or if some portion of it seems true, you relax your boundary and let *that* in—"Yes, I did that," or "I know I can sometimes be that way"—you "own it" inside yourself. That portion of the material that does not seem true you simply let drop, like an egg sliding off glass and landing on the floor. You understand that such inaccurate descriptions of you are important information *about the speaker.* This does not constitute ignoring your partner's thoughts or feelings, even if what she's saying does not resonate with your truth; that would be using a wall. At its best, the feeling one has inside an internal boundary is one of relaxed, secure interest. You remain actively engaged, standing toe-to-toe with your partner, working hard to sift through each point or feeling she shares, determining—in your own mind—what you will take in as yours and what you will leave out as hers. This is an entirely subjective exercise. Trying to determine what is or is not "valid" is not the point. You must choose what rings true *to you.* On the other hand, if feedback from one person is matched by similar feedback from others, perhaps you have a blind spot. At the least, it is important to note the impact of your behavior on others, no matter what your intentions might have been.

Projections are human. We make up things about one another all the time. You needn't feel shame about someone's misperception, nor grandiose because your partner "got you wrong." Healthy self-esteem and a good boundary work together. Going neither "one down" nor "one up," you hold both yourself and your partner in warm regard while accepting nothing that inaccurately describes you.

Visualizing an internal boundary works like this. Picture a place—it could be real or imaginary—in which you have a sense of relaxation, a feeling of "I'm enough and I matter." Then drop the imagined place, and stay centered in that state of "enoughness" for a moment. Imagine a shield encircling you. It can be realistic or fanciful, a screen of flowers, a force-field, or a glass dome, but you must be able to view with crystal clarity whoever stands before you. Be certain that your internal boundary remains impermeable; nothing can get past it unless you choose to let it. The nastiest comment, the most raw feeling—an emotional atom bomb could go off and you would remain unfazed. Inside your circle you can afford to be open, spacious, curious, relaxed.

•   •   •

The important thing to remember about practicing an internal boundary is precisely that it is a practice, similar to getting physically fit. Understanding the concept of exercise is one thing; doing it is quite another. Although it takes months, even years, of slow, steady effort before an internal boundary becomes consistent, most people experience an exhilarating glimpse of its effects within a few weeks.

"I couldn't wait to come see you." Jane, a twenty-seven-year-old elementary school teacher, flops down in her chair, flushed and grinning. "Michael and I just spent the weekend off by ourselves. My mom took Daniel and we went off to Maine. It was great, but boy, was I nervous. You know that over the last six months, maybe even the last couple years, since Daniel was born, Michael and I just can't be alone together for more than a few hours without some zinger. He just *has* to get me. Then I react, and then *he* reacts, and, without fail, we wind up in the same stupid fight. Well," she warms, "*this* time I was determined. You'll be proud to hear, I stayed present. I didn't go away inside myself like I have before. I was there with him, but that poison dart was not getting in. So, we get through the first day, not a problem. Next day, he says, 'Let's go for a drive.' Okay, my sensors go off. I put up my little force-field. We pull over, looking out on this hill. He starts talking to me about his life—his feelings since Daniel, pressures at work. At first, it's fine, it's great in fact, and then, all of a sudden, he lobs one at me. We don't even need to go into the details but, just believe me, it was mean. And you know what?" she smiles. "It went *smack*, just like that. And I did the most amazing thing." She pauses.

"Which was?" I'm happy to ask.

"Nothing," she answers, utterly pleased. "For probably the first time in at least two years. I just sat there. This is about you, I kept telling myself, it's not about me one way or the other. And we moved on! He talked a little more about his work. I was supportive, tried to be, felt it, anyway. And then we drove back. No fight, no rigamarole. We had a nice weekend!"

"You seem surprised," I say.

"But it *worked*." Indeed, she is surprised. "I've been walking around practicing this stupid thing for days and it actually *did* something!"

I call what Jane did "learning to use an internal technology." She had discovered the thrill of realizing that one's relationship to one's own internal state need not be a passive one. Over the years, I have found that this one skill of defining boundaries, all on its own, particularly when practiced by both partners, can radically transform a relationship.

The lack of an internal boundary inevitably leads to control or withdrawal. If there is no membrane between you and whatever external stimulus gets thrown at you, then you attempt to regulate your own level of comfort or discomfort by managing the stimulus. ("I could be happy, if only you were less angry.") When control fails, the only other option is withdrawal. This was Jane's technique before she came to see me. The paradox here is that it was the increased healthy distance afforded by an internal boundary that allowed Jane to move back into more closeness. Therapists often talk about "breaking down walls." But attempting to deprive someone of protection is a fool's errand. Replacing the crudeness of a wall with a more permeable form of safety is a crucial step toward relational health.

Our first impulse, once we achieve some mastery of boundaries, is to share the results of our sifting and sorting with our partners. "Well, you got this right, but *this* was totally off base." We also have a natural desire to explain ourselves, "Well, yes, I was late picking Johnny up, but you have to understand. First, the transmission dropped right out of the car and then . . ." All of this would be well and good if the objective were for you and your partner to share your divergent thoughts on any given matter. And, indeed, most of us wrongly assume that such equal communication is the objective. But when we address tough issues, we need to remember that the point of speaking and listening is not individual expression but relational repair. Using an internal boundary is a skill you use inside yourself. With a functioning boundary in place, you are ready to address the issue between you and your partner. The relational skill needed for this next step is perhaps the most disciplined of the five, and the one at starkest remove from the mores of patriarchy. I call this third skill *scanning for the positive.*

If someone voices discomfort about something, particularly if it's about you, her primary interest rarely lies in learning about your side of things. This is a point that is just as relevant to businesspeople as to marital partners. When someone is addressing difficult issues, more often than not her primary interest will be *her* concerns, not yours. When we listen relationally, *we place ourselves at the service of the speaker.* While it's seldom voiced, the truth is that the person you're listening to really doesn't care all that much at that moment about you one way or the other. She wants to know if you care about her. Do you get to come back with an explanation, how things "really were"? Well, perhaps sometime later. After you've addressed her concerns, you can provide your ideas about what happened. But ask yourself if that is really necessary, and even if it is, begin with solicitation— scan for a response that furthers repair.

I come home after a hard day of listening to clients and run smack into a wife who is fit to be tied.

"I'm totally annoyed with you," Belinda greets me. "You told me this morning you'd take out the trash. Forget that! You said you'd call the painter. He just called my office wondering why he hasn't heard from us. And you left your *son* waiting after ballet for almost thirty minutes wondering where the hell you were! Terry, Alexander was really *upset.*"

"Honey, I—"

"I tried to tell you this last week, Terry. Ever since you wrote that damn book, you've been more and more preoccupied. Your head's getting so big I'm not sure it will fit through the door. You know, people are going to stop liking you, Terry. They may already not like you, for all I know."

On the brunt end of Belinda's tirade a visceral wave of hurt indignation washes over me instantaneously. I am in major boundary failure. In the early years of our marriage, I would have met anger with anger. "Who do you think you are talking to me like this? I work hard," I would have protested. "I come back to *my* home . . ." Blah, blah, blah. Would I have been right? Well, actually, yes. This is no way to greet a husband. Justice would have been on my side! But I often say to the couples I see, *"You can be right or you can be married. What's more important to you?"* When we step out of patriarchy into relationality, simple notions of justice, like ideas about objective truth, are no longer the central concern.

Later on in the marriage my response at such a moment would have grown more sophisticated. "You know, honey," I'd start. "I really want to hear you out, but it's hard to listen when I feel badly treated by you. Could we speak together in a respectful manner so that I can . . ." By that point, I could well have been dodging pots. I was still busy telling Belinda that she was wrong, still trying to control her—and shift the focus from me. It was really a reiteration of "Who do you think you are, talking to me like that?"—only slicker.

Nowadays—on a good day, at least—when I feel that hot wave sweep over me, a voice in my head calls out: *"Freeze! Don't say a word! Don't move a muscle!"* And then I breathe, slowly, perhaps glancing down at the floor. I visualize my internal boundary (better late than never), and *think* for a minute. *Second consciousness* is kicking in.

I often speak to couples about the critical importance of *whoosh*. *Whoosh* is the visceral wave, the conditioned reflex, that washes over us instantaneously. For some it is fear, for others, shame, and others still, anger. I grew up in a raging household. Whenever someone sticks something in my face my reflexive response is a desire to knock in their teeth. That's where *second consciousness* comes in. The voice in my head shouting "Freeze!" is the voice of maturity, the functional adult part of me. I have been speaking of intimacy as a daily practice, but a more precise description would be intimacy as a moment-to-moment practice. Any occasion when a more mature part of oneself cuts into an habitual, dysfunctional reaction is an instance of recovery. It is an example of what Belinda has called *relational heroism*, those moments when every muscle and nerve in your body is pulling you toward your old set of responses, and yet a new force lifts you up off the accustomed track toward deliberate, constructive action—toward repair. Just as intimacy's degenerative course is comprised of thousands of small moments of disconnection, relational recovery is comprised of such moments of grace. They are the atoms of regeneration.

As I stand in my kitchen, listening to Belinda's complaints, I first feel *whoosh*, and then, quick on its heels, the voice of reason. Once the intensity of my physical reaction quiets a bit—my signal that it is safe to open my mouth—I respond.

"Belinda, you're right," I say. "And I'm really sorry. I did promise to take out the trash and I spaced on it. I didn't succeed in reaching the painter, and I'm sorry you were bothered with it. I feel terrible about being late for Alexander; I know he was upset. And I think I have been more preoccupied since the book, less present with you and the kids in some ways. Now, here's what I want to do. I'm going to go right upstairs and apologize to Alexander, as best I can. I'll take out the trash and call the painter. And I will really do my best to get a grip and be more responsible." And off I go.

As one might well imagine, there are quite a few other things I would have been more than happy to add. I already had apologized to Alexander. I'd called the painter several times; it wasn't my problem if he refused to answer my messages. If I was more preoccupied after my book it was in part because I was about three times busier than I had been before; busy, among other things, working harder for the family, a change she seemed loath to acknowledge. And also . . . oh yes, who the hell did she think she was . . .?

Using an internal boundary means sifting through what you hear for that portion that is true for you. *Scanning for the positive* means sifting through what you hear for those things you can *agree to and give*. Most of what Belinda threw at me would not make it past my internal boundary. Her accusations struck me as exaggerated, distorted, and delivered from a one-up, unloving place. But, like jewels in a trash heap, there were points in her speech that were true. By sheer force of discipline, these were the only points I chose to respond to. I had strained through the 85 percent of her diatribe that seemed like nonsense, and given back the 15 percent that I could admit to. I owned it, apologized, and, most important, took action. Perhaps Belinda would accept these actions, perhaps not. That was up to her. About all the rest—the inaccuracies, explanations, bad behaviors she'd brought to the table as well—what purpose would disputing them have served? Whether or not I addressed these things later, *this was not my moment; it was hers.*

Scanning for the positive is a kind of unilateral disarmament. For men it often feels like submission. One frequently hears that men are frightened of intimacy. I don't believe that is true. I think that many men don't know what intimacy is. The one-up, one-down world of masculinity leaves little space for tenderness. One is either controlled or controlling, dominator or dominated. *When men speak of fearing intimacy what they really mean is that they fear subjugation.* In a visceral way, most men in our culture experience vulnerability as opening themselves up to be overrun. *Scanning for the positive* means that in a moment like the one I describe with Belinda, when you feel someone's fangs at your neck, you bend further forward, exposing even more of your skin.

I have come to trust, after years of working with this issue, both in my own life and with clients, that such leaning into vulnerability often works as a kind of jujitsu, effectively disarming your attacker. I have also come to trust that owning one's part with humility does not abase one, nor does it invite reprisal. But acquiescing at such moments goes against men's most fundamental training—as though, by not "standing up for themselves" they collude with their own castration. And here we have come to a crisis point in recovery for many of the men I treat—for if speaking requires the courage to assert, listening requires the courage to receive. And emotional receptivity is the antithesis of traditional masculinity. Helplessness, weakness, dependency—these are qualities men are taught to fear and despise, particularly within themselves. The myriad variations of dominance, the endless displays of "power over," in boardrooms, staterooms, bedrooms, hide the dread of another's power over us. The one place a man may with impunity turn for succor, for "shelter from the storm," is his "helpmate," his wife or girlfriend. But what of those

moments when she herself becomes the storm? What of his vulnerability then? *Scanning for the positive* is a particular instance of a profound shift, from being "over" to being "with," from delusion to
humility. Speaking relationally requires us to have a firm sense of self
to bring to the table. *Listening relationally* requires the capacity to relax
that self enough to be permeated and moved. The fundamental
issue in honest speaking is *relational empowerment,* assertion within the
union. The fundamental issue in listening is surrender. Using a
boundary, instead of a wall, means that you choose, at times, to drop
your shield, to take in. Loving passionately means having the capacity to protect yourself and yet also the willingness to deliver yourself
into someone's hands, trembling and vulnerable, open to hurt—to
being left, betrayed. In that "still point of the turning world" one is
equally self and union. *But patriarchy takes aim at both elements—
damaging women's ability to maintain the self, and men's capacity to relax into
union.*

"You do not have to walk on your knees for a hundred miles
repenting," writes the poet Mary Oliver. "You only have to let the soft
animal of your body love what it loves." Mostly, when men in our
culture speak of a return to their animal natures, they portray a
regression to savagery—"nature red in tooth and claw." But this
woman poet reminds us of a different side, the delicate wisdom of our
biology. Patriarchy bids us to place ourselves above nature, disowning our mortal bodies. But real passion demands our return to
the pleasures and fragility of a tender animal. Learning to listen relationally, listen with cool heads and clear boundaries, listen with the
quietness of the heart and the gentleness of the body, means having
a self so developed it can afford to yield.

CHAPTER SIXTEEN

Staying the Course:
Negotiation and Integrity

The fourth core relational skill is *negotiation*, a topic about which much good literature already exists. I ask the couples I work with to distinguish between three modes of negotiation: *invitation, request,* and *demand.*

Of the three forms of negotiation, invitations are the least restrictive, the easiest to decline. Acceptance of someone's invitation rests solely on your own desire. An invitation asks, "Would you like to?"—talk, go out, make love. An answer of yes or no is simply a matter of asking yourself what you want. A savvy inviter understands that one increases the odds of acceptance by making his invitation . . . inviting. "Let's go to the gym and work out together (which I know you hate), and then we can see that new foreign film (that you love)." This isn't manipulation—there's nothing underhanded about it. It's just being smart. When invitations are declined, partners should review their invitation before getting angry at the declinee. If you brought up a tough issue at midnight, you might want to rethink your timing rather than blame your partner's uncommunicativeness.

Unlike invitations, requests have nothing to do with the recipient's desires. If invitations translate as "Would you like to?" requests translate as "Would you do this for me?" There is nothing wrong with requests so long as the balance in the relationship remains relatively even. Like invitations, requests can range from the utterly banal "Would you please pass the salt?" to the extraordinary "Would you please enter a five-week rehab program?" Unlike invitations, requests are not easily declined, although they are, ultimately, declinable. When one says "no" to a request, the reason for declining must be commensurate with the reason for the request. "Could you pass the salt?" could well be met with "I don't want to move for a minute. The count's three and two and it's bottom of the ninth." On the other hand, "Could you go into rehab?" could not be well met by the same answer. In loving relationships even terribly important requests may be declined, but only for terribly important reasons.

Of the three modes of negotiation, demand is the most restrictive. Here, declining is not an option. Healthy couples reserve demand only for emergencies—"Grab that kid off the balcony!" or bottom lines— "You can never strike me again." To help clarify the difference between these two modes, I ask partners to distinguish between their wants and their needs. A need is a survival requirement—either for you as an individual—water, air, food—or for the relationship—a good sex life, sobriety, a reasonable level of trust. By definition, needs are bottom-line issues.

Many women partners, who are used to having to turn up the volume in order to get their wants attended to, speak the language of need when they really mean want, and their men—ever sensitive to issues of subjugation—instinctively react to the implicit pressure rather than to the nature of their partners' requests. Blocked from direct expression, many women also turn to habitual forms of complaint. Here is another distinction worth noting—a complaint is not a request. Moving partners from complaint to request is often a huge step toward furthering their capacity for repair. I call complaint a *negative past focus.* It tells your partner what you didn't like about what he has done. Request, by contrast, represents a *positive future focus.* Instead of trying to satisfy your desires by criticizing what you did not get, you ask, simply and directly, for what you want.

Requests can be particularly difficult for women for two reasons. First, the traditional socialization of girls renders desire illegitimate, pulling them toward equating pleasure with selfishness. Second, it is safer to complain than to hold firmly to a request, safer for the individual—since you ask for nothing, you cannot be disappointed—and safer for the couple. Empowering the woman, the very first stage of relational recovery, often requires a jump ahead to this fourth skill. The shift at the beginning of therapy from complaint to firm request almost always throws the couple into crisis. Crisis is what I'm after at that stage, an opportunity to open up the stultifying status quo. But I am also there to help the man tolerate the shift, without withdrawal or retaliation. While many women and men do manage to incorporate the change of women's increased empowerment on their own, particularly younger couples, the great majority cannot. Without sufficient support from without—therapists, friends—the shift to requests and legitimate demands can be an arduous one.

An accepted invitation, request, or demand is a contract. Contracts can be large or small, from "Hand me that cup" to "Till death us do part." Contracts can be renegotiated whenever they need to be, but they cannot simply be broken. Generally speaking, breaking a contract—whether by lying, manipulating, or patronizing—is an internal boundary violation and will do serious damage to the relationship. Over the years I've seen countless passive-aggressive men who "yes" their wives to death and routinely fail to follow through. To these men I plead "Dare to say 'No!' Don't make contracts you don't really agree to." Many of these clients combine elements from their own trauma histories with societal stereotypes and transpose to their marriages the idea that women are a raging storm, far too wild and frightening for reasonable negotiation. And, indeed, they may have chosen partners who fit that description—and who fit it even more as years of their irresponsibility roll on. In such cases the woman partner must be brought down from ineffective, often offensive complaint and demand, while the man must be brought up from cowering under the negotiation table and encouraged to sit down at it.

A good contract is precise and closed-ended. Couples often get into trouble when they think they have walked away from a conversation with a settled agreement, while their spouses think nothing of the kind. Just as in a business agreement, the clearer you are, the better the odds that you'll get what you want.

Identifying our wants and needs, bringing them maturely back

into the relationship, and navigating the sometimes joyous, sometimes raw, process of negotiation—these are the component parts of
artfully managing our desires.

The final core relationship skill has been implicit in all of the others.
I call it *relational integrity*. Al-Anon calls it "detachment from outcome." Learning *relational integrity* means managing your end of the
seesaw, knowing that what he does on his end is nothing over which
you have control. It corresponds to Pia Mellody's self-skill of *moderation*—the capacity to experience and express oneself moderately
without being either excessively immature or mature, a big baby or
a stiff. The relational correlate to individual moderation is the capacity to stay moderate in the face of your partner's immoderateness.

Saint Augustine once claimed that the reward of patience is
patience. When I work with partners, I sometimes say that the yield
of their increased capacity for intimacy is an increased capacity for
intimacy. They are not in all cases compensated for their efforts with
a rescued relationship. While I have an avowed preference for keeping couples together, especially if there are young children involved,
my aim is not maintaining a marriage at all costs. I work to augment
each partner's ability to be close. If they end up being intimate
with one another so much the better. But if that is not to be, then they
each get to take their hard-won skills and forge a better relationship
with someone new. They will also break the dysfunctional legacy
they were about to hand down to their children. The best course of
action, in any case, lies in attending to one's own behavior, leaving
one's partner to deal with his own.

"We've broken up five times already," admits thirty-one-year-old
Henry. Broad-shouldered, with hair the color of wet sand, he has
an Oklahoma cowboy's face. His grin shows off white teeth and
dimples.

His wife, Natalie, seems unimpressed. Dark, aquiline, with black
eyeliner and purple lipstick, she's pure New York, SoHo. Impatient,
she takes over the conversation. "We've been together for over ten
years," she raps out, her voice a deep, husky staccato to his drawl.

She's sexy, aggressive, and not to be messed with. "I've dragged him off to my therapist. He's dragged me to his. We've been in counseling on and off for virtually our entire relationship." She looks balefully at her young husband. "If there weren't children . . ." she trails off. Two kids, I find out, four and eight, both girls, the light of their lives. For a moment, abrasive Natalie is overcome. She turns her face to the wall, wiping her eyes. I indicate the tissue box next to her but she ignores me.

"What happened?" I ask Henry. "How come she's so pissed off?" Henry stares at his shoes, bangs flopping over his face. He plays with the crease of his pants, glancing up through a curtain of hair, and smiles shyly.

"I'm a liar," he tells me.

Despite his good looks, his charm and winning sincerity, Henry was a fake. Although his geniality and intelligence got him into the "right" schools, he didn't do nearly as well in them as he'd told her he had. In fact, he hadn't exactly "moved around" a bit, as he'd claimed when they first met; he'd been bounced. Henry talked his way through business school, talked his way into and then back out of a number of high-profile jobs. And he was close to talking his way out of his marriage. Forever on the trail of "putting a few deals together," Henry watched his classmates get rich on dot coms and venture capital, while he haunted the clubhouse and golf links having "meetings." For all of her artist's trappings, Natalie maintained the conventional notion that her husband might actually hold down a job. Faced with an underfunctioning spouse, Natalie followed a course not uncommon to wives. She picked up the slack by overfunctioning and then despised him for it. She claimed not to mind the burden of his unemployment nearly as much as his cover-ups and lies.

"For three months last year Henry took a briefcase every morning, telling me he was off to consult to a VC firm," she sighs. "Imagine how it felt running into him one afternoon when I was picking out a book with Robbie at the public library. 'Oh, look, hon. Here's Daddy!'" Hangdog Henry doesn't say a word. "First, I couldn't believe it," she says. "I really thought he was making deals. He did make one a few years ago."

"To the tune of three hundred thousand," Henry chimes in.

"So, I thought, Okay, he's one of those entrepreneurial types; he'll come through. But then it went on, year after year."

Henry frowns. "I've had some bad luck," he says.

She turns on him, exasperated, "Henry, will you please come clean? At least in here?" She turns back to me. "So first, it was denial. Then I really felt bad for him. I love Henry. It was pathetic, the lengths he'd go to. But after years of it, I just . . ." She trails off. "I've got a *family* to raise," she says. "I just can't take this anymore."

It was Natalie who kept them afloat. A talented designer and a good businesswoman, Natalie had built her own design studio, which now housed a staff of young talent.

"I do the front-end piece," Natalie tells me, exuding quiet assurance. "I interface with clients, get where the need is, evolve a concept that will work for them. The studio executes. We're doing all right."

"They're doing great," Henry corrects. His pride seems genuine.

"Henry's been very supportive," Natalie admits. "He's been wonderful, actually. He's pored over designs with me, written my business plan. When I'm traveling or up to my ears, he's the one who looks after the kids, drives them around, packs their lunches." She smiles wanly. "He's a much better mother than I am," she says.

An achievement crash-out in the world, at home, Henry is a relational star. He is deeply connected to his kids' inner lives, their schoolwork, their friends. He is the social switchboard for the family. "He's like having a girlfriend," Natalie smiles. "He remembers birthdays, for God's sake, not just mine. I mean, like someone down the street. He'll send flowers to a neighbor's sick *uncle.*" Natalie mock-shudders.

"It sounds like he'd make someone a wonderful wife." I go along with it.

"Sure," Natalie raps back, "if that's what 'someone' wanted."

I find myself thinking, Oh, I don't know. I've seen worse arrangements in my time. But clever Natalie has leaned forward, anticipating my thoughts.

"*Good* wives," she enunciates, "don't *con their partners.*"

•   •   •

Over the course of twenty years' practice, dozens of Henrys have graced my office, promising young men of varied ages who never quite make it out of the starter's box. These are the agile antiheroes who once reigned in our popular consciousness before corporate values rolled over them—Holden Claufield in *The Catcher in the Rye*, James Dean in *Rebel Without a Cause*. These are the sensitive lost boys who stand outside patriarchy, marginal, yes, but not really pushing that hard to "get in."

Patriarchy offers our daughters the choice of cooperation and blessings, or defiance and ostracism. If you think forty years of feminism has put an end to girls' subjugation, you should have a frank talk with a thirteen-year-old. Patriarchy offers our sons the choice of emotional stoicism and success in the world, or wholeness, connection, and failure. With virtually no model for healthy integration—of competence and connectedness—in either the culture at large or in many boys' lives, some boys and young men, like Henry, chose relationality over achievement, emotional competence over worldly gain. Faced with the prospect of induction into the lonely code of masculinity, these tender boys become gender-protesters. Society generally calls them "losers." They have a knack for washing into a therapist's office.

In the courtship stage, women are drawn to such men because they are more open then most. Disillusionment sets in on the day they realize that these men have neither the talent nor much inclination to take care of themselves—let alone others—in the traditional sense. Some are simply enfants terrible, falsely empowered, demanding narcissists. Others, like Henry, are big-hearted and generous, and quite responsible in their own way. But all of them are "illegitimate"—bastard sons of the patriarch, *refuseniks* in the gender war. And illegitimacy carries its price.

If women under patriarchy must claim their power surreptitiously, a man like Henry must disguise his heart's ambitions as well. Few men openly declare "I'm more interested in developing emotionally, putting my energies into relationships, than I am in doing particularly well in the world." This is not a widely accepted pick-up line. The truth is that Henry is really rather happy horsing around with his friends, picking up the kids from school, and making their lunches each evening. His problem is that for years he has disguised his preference, to himself and others, with endless false promises, unrealistic projects, overreaching schemes, and outright falsehoods. And if Natalie has complained or even pressed him for details, Henry responds by flailing about, angry and sullen, as though he had been terribly victimized. For close to eight years, Natalie answered his indignation with hers. And they have had terrible fights—screaming, yelling, throwing-things fights—storming out of the house, chasing each other in cars, much of it, to their abject shame, in front of the children.

"I've done everything." Natalie shakes her head. "Everything I can possibly think of. We're both in therapy. We're both on medication. You would think . . ." She can't finish.

We try putting it back together a piece at a time. We draw up a list of internal boundary violations—yelling, name-calling, shaming someone, being sarcastic or patronizing, making commitments and breaking them, lying, manipulating—and contract to take all of those behaviors off the table. They contract as well to call "time-outs" if either or both of them "lose it." As a final measure, we agree that they will physically separate for a while if they are powerless to stop their abusive behaviors. "That wouldn't mean the end of the marriage," I reassure them, "or even a major setback as far as I'm concerned. We'd still meet here together and we'd figure out how each of you could do enough individual work to get a grip. All it means is that your primary commitment right now is to stop exposing your kids to this level of fighting." They readily agree.

Faced with the prospect of separation, sobered by the thought of damaging their kids, Natalie and Henry truly committed to ending their miserable behaviors with one another. So far, the therapy had helped them move into *appropriate shame*—out of the cycle of grandiose comfort with actions they had no business being comfortable with, or the flip side—bouts of paralyzing toxic shame.

Appropriate shame is a middle ground that clients often have to be taught, a space of remorse proportionate to one's offensive behaviors, with an emphasis on making amends. In the past, Henry had vacillated between self-indulgence and overwhelming despair. Neither state was very helpful to his wife and children.

Henry worked on his shame-filled and yet entitled avoidance, and Nathalie worked on her rage. But their chronic fighting finally stopped as they increased their capacity for *relational integrity*. There had been periods before when each had pledged, with passionate sincerity, to stop their verbal violence. Good intentions carried them for a while. But no one goes from war to perfection. Sooner or later, someone would slip, anger begot anger, and their recovery would unravel. What broke their cycle was hard-won proficiency at staying moderate in the face of the other's immoderateness.

Anyone can behave with skill and integrity when their partner is doing the same. What makes us grown-ups is the capacity to *remain* skillful, even when our partners act like full-fledged lunatics. Staying on course, maintaining your program, when things are going well is like riding a bicycle downhill. It's quite pleasant, wind in your hair. And you may work up a bit of a sweat. Staying seated in maturity when your partner is acting like a big baby is like riding uphill. In the blast of his yelling, withdrawal, distortions, you dig down deep, switch into low gear, and crank. It isn't particularly pleasant. You may not even be sure how much longer you can keep going. But the exercise builds great relational muscles.

"But if I don't put pressure on him," Natalie protests, "he just stomps away and nothing gets settled."

"Bring that in here," I answer, "and we'll deal with it. But ultimately Henry will do what he does."

When you face the prospect of focusing exclusively on your own behavior, the greatest fear is not that you will fail but rather that you will succeed and your partner won't follow. If one of the partners moves into recovery and the other refuses to join him, dissolution is most often just a matter of time. This is a daunting prospect. The poet e. e. cummings once wrote: "dying is fine) but Death / o / baby

/ i / wouldn't like / Death if Death / were / good." Fighting bitterly
over what you're not getting is one thing. It's quite another to let go
of the battle and tend to your own progress, accepting that the relationship's fate is out of your hands. Learning to let go of outcome, as
frightening as it may be, brings along with it great relief and clarity.
It teaches you when to insist and when to back off. Throughout the
discussion, I have stressed the importance of closeness. But responsible distance is also a part of mature engagement.

Although you might wish to remain seated in your functional adult
self, intimacy inevitably activates unhealed aspects of your personality. The part of you that is motivated to learn relational skills and
practice them is, unfortunately, not always the one in control. When
closeness triggers trauma most of us are flooded with the feelings we
had when the injury first occurred—the *wounded child*—or we may
respond by shifting to that young part of ourselves that compensated
for the hurt—the *adapted child*. Neither of these aspects of self—the
wounded one or the adapted one—is greatly motivated to exercise
relational skills. The wounded child—the residual part of us that was
on the receiving end of abuse or neglect—most often feels overwhelmed, frightened, and powerless. The adapted child—an immature version of an adult that we cobbled together as best we could—is
usually too rigid, too black-and-white, to care; that part of us would
rather be right than intimate. The reactivation of both immature
parts of our character—our injuries and our defenses against them—
is inescapable in close relationships, a part of our humanity. It is useful to understand that when you or your partner are in one of these
immature states *nothing will be solved*. The only issue, when one or
both of you flies into an immoderate response, is shifting back into
the functional adult. Don't be seduced by the content. I tell my
clients "You don't argue with someone who's drunk." First, you
wait for them to sober up, and only then should you deal with the
issues. Trying to resolve matters in such heated moments is a fool's
errand because the part of the person who's fighting with you has no
real interest in resolution. *Relational integrity* means learning to back
off at such times. Give your partner the space to recoup. And then,

when you can both remember that you love one another, or, at the least, can treat one another with respect, try again.

In the months that followed, Henry and I took on the issue of his avoidance, and Natalie, while clear about Henry's effect on her, loosened her efforts to control him. Both held fast to their resolve not to escalate in the face of aggravation, and, barring a few skirmishes here and there, they did rather well. As we spoke together about Henry's relationship to the traditional male role, the tug of war between them moved from the shadows out into the light. They both began to define Henry as a "different kind of man." Moving toward a new marital contract, they shifted from their accustomed inarticulate dance of position and counterposition to a complex discussion of what Henry really wanted and whether their marriage could accommodate it.

"Maybe you *should* be a house-husband for a while," Natalie ventures in one session. "*Take care* of the kids and the house. I like working. We can just make it official."

I wish I could report that Henry discovered himself teaching urban underprivileged kids, or painting, or mounting a dot com of his own, now unburdened. But the truth is not so tidy. He has, for what it's worth, begun consulting with a career counselor and he seems to be serious about the process. Whether or not he succeeds in finding a place for himself in the world, for the time being, at least, his wife is considerably less angry with him. Henry has stopped lying.

It is hard to remain adult when your partner's acting like a big bully or a big baby. Just as when you scan for the positive—giving up the desire to "correct" your partner's "distortions" and offering instead whatever you can—choosing to maintain integrity, even as your partner indulges, doesn't feel "fair." It isn't. In healthy relationships everyone gets to be a jerk sometimes, but, mostly, we have to take turns.

I claimed earlier that the great paradox of intimacy is that our capacity to remain close rests on our ability to tolerate solitude inside the relationship. All of the five skills designed to implement a shift from patriarchal mores to relationality have in common an increased capacity to bear that solitude. Relational esteem is the most obvious; it is fundamentally about reminding yourself to summon the energy of warm regard even as your partner disappoints. But the others are no less centrally concerned with widening the band of acceptance. Shifting from speaking "the truth" to "my truth" means giving up the dream that we can live in some imagined twinship called "agreement." Cultivating an internal boundary allows intimacy precisely because it affords distance, protection. It is a concrete demonstration of the difference between real intimacy—which is about two free-standing individuals who choose to share with one another—and immature fusion. Scanning for the positive requires us to live in the little grief of not "being understood" by our partners as we choose, instead, to help them feel understood by us. Contracting means entering into the loneliness of sometimes not getting what we want. And even though it is true that maintaining your commitment to skilled behavior happens to be your best means of keeping the relationship vital, at bottom, that's not why you do it. Fundamentally, you preserve your maturity for your own sake, because you deserve it, whether it makes your partnership better or not. And, perhaps, you remember that your children are watching.

In the whirlwind of a close relationship, you can rest assured that every fear you have available will eventually be realized, every wound revisited. That is passion's fire, which has the power to mend or consume. Most men and women, ill-prepared, sooner or later retreat from that fire. They speak of "making peace," but really mean losing heart. Some settle; some kick against their traces; some turn to other things, other people, for comfort. There is another way. Nietzsche once wrote that a great artist needs a heart on fire and a head of ice. Hot passion requires cool skills. Relational recovery offers something that lumbering patriarchy cannot begin to approach— craft, the discipline of loving artfully. Entering into that craft means giving up the delusion of "being over"—"in control" of our partners, our own natures, our fate. We surrender instead to the humbling knowledge that we are not over anything; we are merely, humanly, *with*. With is fine. With suffices. Despite its limitations, or, more precisely, by our coming to terms with its limitations, our love, though imperfect, sustains us.

SELF SKILLS	RELATIONAL SKILLS
1. Self-Esteem Holding self in warm regard despite imperfections and limitations	**1. Relational Esteem** Holding the relationship in warm regard despite imperfections and limitations (harmony/disillusion-ment/repair)
Dysfunction Shame Grandiosity	*Dysfunction* Control > revenge > resignation
2. Self-Awareness Knowing one's own experience (thoughts/emotions/sensations) and sharing them politically	**2. Speaking Relationally** Contract before speaking; speak from the "I" (multiple subjectives); move from complaint to request (negative past to positive future)
Dysfunction Disassociation Perfectionism	*Dysfunction* Objectivity battles
3. Boundaries Ability to protect and contain oneself while remaining connected to others	**3. Listening Relationally** Listen with an internal boundary; respond by scanning for the positive (lead with agreement, not argument)
Dysfunction Too porous (reactive) Walled off (disengaged)	*Dysfunction* Defensiveness/argumentative-ness/walls

4. Interdependence
Identifying one's wants and
needs; caring for self/letting
others care for one appropriately

Dysfunction
Overdependent
Antidependent/needless/wantless

5. Moderation
Experiencing and expressing
oneself moderately

Dysfunction
Immature (too "loose")
"Supermature" (too "tight")

4. Contracting
Moving from "win/lose"
to relational wisdom

Dysfunction
Zero/sum power struggle; needs
are not directly expressed;
contracts left too open-ended or
vague

5. Relational Integrity
Staying moderate in the face of
your partner's immoderateness
(detachment from outcome)

Dysfunction
Answering immature behavior
with reciprocal immaturity
(either complimentary or
symmetrical)

CHAPTER SEVENTEEN

What It Takes to Love

"Sometimes, I just feel so deflated." Damien peers at me hard.

He doesn't look deflated, I think to myself, meeting his stare; he looks grim. A competitive rower in college, now in his late thirties he is tall and athletic looking. With assured movement and a long, chiseled face, Damien is all edge, a knife-blade of a man, sharp, fast, aloof. Even now, after months of recovery, he radiates a searing intelligence mixed with cold judgment. Sitting across from his unyielding gaze, I feel suddenly that my office is shabby, my desk a mess. Because I am his therapist and not a colleague or friend, I take careful note of the insecurity he inspires—neither backing away from it nor retaliating. If I feel this way, I think to myself, no doubt, so do others. Where did he learn it from, I wonder, this talent for shaming? Who did he see do this, growing up? Who did it to him?

"I think things are better between Judith and me," Damien adds, "slowly getting better. But . . ." he trails off. "I'm still out of the house."

This was my first session with Damien alone. Coming into Boston for a business trip, he had called to ask if he could "drop by." Six months earlier, he and his wife, Judith, had come from San Francisco for two days of intensive, "turnaround" work. For a few years now, I have offered such consultation/intervention for couples on the brink, like them—relationships about to dissolve despite therapy—often despite several therapies—back home. After spending time with each of the partners by telephone, speaking with their therapists, and reviewing background material I ask them to prepare, we meet for two back-to-back, full days of treatment. At the end of that time, so our contract goes, we agree that they are either on their feet or divorcing. Colleagues at the Family Institute of Cambridge have face-tiously named such out-of-town offerings "Terry's Last Resort." A group of students once gave me a banner to put over my door read-ing "After this, it's Lourdes." Although really it should read "After this, it's lawyers."

Damien Seeger was one of my guys—smart, driven, wounded, and clueless. His own father was stunningly blind—a drinker, a carouser whose manner at home ranged from unavailable, to coldly indifferent, to outright demeaning if pushed. All this was peppered capriciously with unexpected bouts of sentimental "deep bond-ing"—boozy fishing expeditions, sporting extravaganzas, and, as his son got older, whorehouses. Growing up, Damien thought his father a god, and would have done anything to win his approval. Damien's mother was less impressed. She divorced her boy of a hus-band when Damien was ten, and surrounded herself with a circle of well-meaning, strident, self-described "feminists," all of whom adored Damien for being the sweet, sensitive boy who seemed so unlike "those horrible men." Young Damien was pampered and stroked until, in his teens, he began showing signs of being a lot less unlike "those men" than his mother and her circle had hoped for.

Until finally escaping to college, Damien shuttled between the modest circumstances of his radical, blue-stocking mother and the decadent opulence of his hard-partying, demonic father. In drastically different ways, both parents used him; neither saw their son as a sep-arate entity with his own tastes and needs. Torn by their contradic-tory demands, Damien grew up convinced that he was a profound disappointment to both of his parents, and that he had never really belonged to either. It did not surprise me to learn that, as a teen, he had attempted suicide.

It was Judith who saved his life.

"We were an island of two," Damien told me, sitting next to his wife in our first session. "I had been looking for her my whole life."

They met as freshmen in college. Judith was an idealistic early education major, out to change the world. The oldest of five, daugh-ter of an alcoholic father and a long-suffering mother, she seemed born and bred for the caretaker role. To her, Damien was an audacious rebel, full of self-loathing and genius. To him, she was home. "She saw me," Damien remembered, "*really* saw me, in ways no one else ever had." But Judith's "safe harbor," it turned out, didn't offer her troubled young lover a place to rest so much as a corporate springboard.

Young Damien didn't merely step onto the usual masculine conveyor belt; he dove for it. Rocketing through the ranks of a small, respected consulting company, Damien eventually managed to outflank the firm's owner—a man who had welcomed him and cultivated his talent. Damien repaid his mentor by buying the business out from underneath him.

"My first 'score.' " He smiles ruefully. "I guess no good deed goes unpunished. I mean," he shifts in his chair, "the guy made out financially. He just retired a little early."

"What a fine, warm young man you were," I reflected.

"Scorched-earth policy," he told me. "No prisoners." He looked away. "I burned a lot of bridges," he said.

Damien had worked brutal, eighteen-hour days, proud to demand more of himself than he asked of his staff. The company grew tenfold. "It wasn't a business to me," he said. "It wasn't even a substitute family." I waited obediently through the pregnant pause. "It was an *empire.*"

Empire building drew him away from his wife, and his new son, Sam, far more often than not. He had no real friends outside of work, and no interests beyond a compulsive exercise regime. Even saying that Damien "buried" his feelings would have seemed too "squishy" to him. "I was a samurai," he told me, with no hint of mockery. "I would have done well in the military, the CIA. Combat suits me."

And what of his human needs? Had he succeeded in encasing them completely? Throughout his meteoric rise, with the intense recklessness I'd seen in others like him, Damien, as he once bluntly put it, "fucked anything that moved."

"We'd make a deal," he explained, "with some business leader in his chalet in France, and while he and our lawyers were off signing papers, I'd be screwing his wife in their greenhouse." Given how hard he worked "for his family," and how ubiquitous behavior like his seemed to him in his high-flying circle, Damien hadn't been precisely clear, he confessed, why such license wasn't just granted to him as a matter of course. "It was nothing beyond sheer appetite," he told me. "You might as well get upset that I go to the bathroom. It meant that little."

"I'm sorry to hear that," I told him.

It was only a matter of time until something blew up, and it did when a young female colleague filed a sexual harassment suit that, to Damien's profound surprise, was not taken as frivolous. His company weathered it. But the feelings of neglect, mistrust, and resentment that Judith had silently harbored for years ripped through their marriage and fractured it. Judith threw him out. That was close to a year before I met them. For a lot of men, the story would have ended there. Eventually, the old wife would have been replaced by a new one, the womanizing toned down, if not stopped altogether; everyone would have "gotten by." But, as Damien told it, more than being tossed out, the look of profound repulsion he saw in Judith's eyes suddenly snapped him awake.

"It was like I looked up all at once from the carnage," he told me. "I was blood soaked in My Lai. I was in some brothel with my father, some orgy, naked and covered in filth. And I lift up my head and suddenly there is my wife and my baby, standing there on the sideline, staring at me, not a word, just their look. And I felt mortified. No," he corrects himself, "I felt *horrified*. Viewing myself through their eyes, I saw myself, *recognized* myself, as grotesque. Something had gone terribly wrong. In *me*," he clarifies. "Something was broken." And yet, even as he describes his epiphany, he remains impassive.

"Damien," I ask, "are you feeling anything as you say this?"

He shakes his head. "No," he answers, while his eyes fill.

"And if those tears in your eyes could speak," I push a little, "what would they say?" He just shakes his head, far away, like someone remembering war. I force myself to lean back and breathe. "We're in this," I remind myself, "for the long haul."

• • •

Armored as he was at the start, Damien proved, nonetheless, to be as passionate in the pursuit of repair as he had been in his path toward destruction. He read voraciously. He sampled several different therapies. He admitted, and started dealing with, childhood injuries. He found, took to heart, and earnestly engaged in treatment for sexual compulsivity. And it was there, in the addictions community, that he first learned about "covert depression," and me. By the time I met the couple, Damien had a good six months of early-stage recovery under his belt. And Judith had been far from still in her own right. She had worked hard on her "codependency"—in individual therapy, adult children of alcoholics' meetings, and an empowering women's group. Individually, they had moved quickly and well. As a pair, however, each new heartfelt stab at marriage counseling only seemed to further their conviction that the bond between them was irretrievably shattered.

"If it weren't for Sam, I know I wouldn't be here," Judith tells me within an hour of our first meeting. "But we do have a son together . . ." She shakes her head. "I'm not sure that I ever loved Damien," she reflects later on in the session. "That may wind up being the dealbreaker. I know I *felt* like I was in love at the time. But now I'm not sure either of us knows what real love is. Maybe I loved him, maybe it was just my pathology."

"Why do you question your own feelings like that?" I ask her.

"Because," she turns toward me and smiles, a smile of inexpressible disappointment, "it isn't only that I don't trust my husband," she says, glancing his way, "which, of course, I don't. I mean, really, how could I? How could I ever trust him again?" She shifts in her chair. I get the feeling she's said all this before. "But," she goes on, "I'm afraid it goes much deeper. You see, I don't trust *me* either. I don't trust *me* with him. I'm not sure what my motives were—or are—anymore. Right now, I'm not certain of much of anything."

I look at her as she speaks, her petite, precise, delicate features; there is also something sharp about Judith, like her husband, but it doesn't detract from her warmth. Damien trains his intelligence on you like a beam too bright. But Judith draws you in with hers. You *want* to hear what she'll say. I watch her turn her face toward the window—embarrassed, pained.

"You never in a million years thought it was going to be like this, did you?" I guess, softly. She shakes her head, overwhelmed. "I'm sorry," I tell her. She nods, quietly cries, dabs at her eyes.

"It's my own fault," she answers. "How naive was I? What did I *think* he was doing all that time in those planes, those hotel rooms? What do they *all* do?" She sounds peevish, young. I wonder if Damien hears in her the voice of his mother, his mother's friends.

"I would do anything to make this better," Damien tells me, head bowed, his enveloping cloud of grandiosity, ambition dissipated by the gust of impending loss. "Tell me where to crawl, what mountain to climb," he says, guileless, sad. "I want my family back, my wife. I want to make her love me again."

His sudden simplicity startles and moves me. "She's angry, Damien," I say tenderly, as Judith silently cries. "And she's hurt. But more than any of that," I tell him, "she's scared. Am I wrong?" to her. She nods.

"Scared of me?" he asks, vulnerable, small.

"Scared of going back," I reply.

Both Judith and Damien had worked very hard since the first time I had met them. Each had followed through with the complex treatment plans we'd drawn up together. Each had at least the beginnings of a strong, loving community of helpers and fellow travelers to mentor and support their fledgling new skills. Damien had been sexually "sober"—that is, able to answer for himself—for close to a year; a year he'd spent, as he put it, despondently, "in exile."

"I don't know what more I can do," he tells me, more open, more vulnerable than I'd ever seen him. "I just want to come home."

I look across at him and smile. "A friend of mine once said," I repeat myself from an earlier session, "that everyone's either blatant or latent. I promised you the first time I met you that once you dealt with your blatant dysfunctions, were you then to stand with your arms open wide, saying, 'Hey, sorry, for all of those terrible years.

Here I am now!' your wife would most likely *not* swoon in your arms. Do you remember my telling you that?"

"A year's a long time to wait," he answers.

"It's less time than you took acting out—" I begin, but he cuts me off.

"I know that, and you're right. You're right. But nevertheless . . ." He smiles, a warm, sly smile that brings me up short. I think it's the first time I've ever seen it. My God, I think to myself, he's thawing out.

"Terry, you promised me." He leans toward me, conspiring, playful. "You *promised* me you would help." I look at him for a time and he looks right back, no demand, no intimidation—and no wall.

"*Please*," he asks. "Would you *please* help me?"

For a moment, I glimpse what his mother and her friends must have seen, what he had, no doubt, burnished as bait for his women, but which stood clear and simple between us now as he placed himself in my hands. I see his sweetness. "You've come a long way in a short time," I say aloud. He just smiles, waits, humble. "Of course I will, Damien," I tell him. "I will do what I can."

"I call it *transmission–reception work*," I tell Judith, who eyes me with mock suspiciousness from her chair. At Damien's request, she has flown in to join us. She is here, though, if not precisely under duress, then at the least trailing "strong reservations."

"I'm not sure this is the time yet," she tells me, "to think about putting it back together." She fires her first shot across my bow.

Although they don't know it, and certainly it would be hard to explain to an onlooker, Judith and Damien are actually heading toward the end of their treatment. We had had three more hard-working, daylong sessions after the initial intervention six months earlier. And it appears they have each learned quickly and well. Together, we deconstructed their idealized, romantic dreams of relationship as they took in a new model of intimacy. Both are assiduous in their daily practice of the five core self-skills and the five core relationship skills as well. Their self-esteem is better; they are able to speak more skillfully than ever before, to listen, and even negotiate.

And yet, despite all their progress, Judith—hurt, mistrusting, and, for the first time in their marriage, holding the cards—has not been willing to let Damien back in, physically or emotionally.

"I think it is time, Judith," I tell her bluntly later on in the session. She tilts her head, quizzical, playing at not understanding my meaning. I consider her for a moment, small, pretty, precise. "I think it's time to relent."

Here's the pattern. Judith says, "All I want from Damien is for him to tell me he loves me."

I say, "Well, Damien?"

Damien goes, "Aww, honey. I love you."

At which point, Judith responds, "Sure, you just said that because he told you to."

When *B finally* gives to *A* the things *A* has been desperately, hopelessly pleading for, do you think *A* welcomes such progress with open arms? Well, sometimes, perhaps, but not very often. Typically, *A*, just as *B* predicted she would, greets her partner's improvement with a repertoire of responses I call *disqualification moves*. "Ah, you did it," she might say, "but you didn't really mean it." Or, "Okay, you did it, but you did it so poorly!" Or, "You're doing it now, but the minute I take the pressure off, I know you're heading right back into your old nasty ways." Or, failing all else, the classically simple, "This is too little, too late."

In order for passionate connection to be restored between men and women, two things need to happen. Men must recover the relational skills and appetites that they were deprived of, *and then women must respond when they do.*

"It's been a year, Judith," I tell her, while Damien looks on, giving the two of us all the space we may need. "If you're still not ready, so be it. We can talk about that and deal with it. But that's about you, your issues. The time for us to be hammering away at Damien's 'untrustworthiness' has passed. I don't say this glibly. And I wouldn't say it about anyone. But I'm telling you as your therapist. This is about as much trustworthiness as you get in this world."

•   •   •

There are a lot of understandable reasons why sincere partners, begging for change, are loath to acknowledge the miracle when it actually occurs. They've been duped before and they're tired of feeling like suckers. They've built up their hopes countless times and don't want their hearts broken again. They fear that if they relax their grip on their partner's throat, he'll "get comfortable" and stop working. I could go on. It's a long list. The problem, of course, as I explain to Judith, is that no woman can reasonably expect her man to sustain his efforts at reconfiguring virtually everything he has ever learned while she remains cold and unmoved.

"But it's *his* work," Judith protests. "It's about him. He needs to do this for himself."

"That's just not true," I push back. "I know it's the politically correct thing to say. I know you hear it all the time—'He has to get well for himself, not just to win you back'—but that's simply not how I see it," I tell her.

She gets mad. "Look," she rounds on me, "I've been manipulated enough—"

"This isn't about manipulation," I cut her off. "There's a legitimate place for one's being motivated by the wish to restore one's own family." While I was speaking to Judith, it felt as though I were addressing as well the legions of helpers and friends—some of whom I'd recommended—who supported her *individual empowerment* without pushing her further toward *relational empowerment*. Okay, Judith was powerful now. Great. But unless she planned to leave her husband forever, sooner or later that power had to be integrated back into her marriage. When recovery programs, growth movements, even feminism implicitly posits individual strength as something set against closeness, softness, they unwittingly replicate the central polarity of patriarchy itself. Every boy learns that you can be *either* strong *or* connected. Judith, where she now stands, breaks no new ground; she's just switching roles. Strength *in* connection, on the other hand, *that* is *terra nova* for both sexes.

Some individuals will "get empowered" and empower themselves right out of potentially workable relationships. Women who reclaim their lost power will often receive a great deal of implicitly antirelational support for taking a position I facetiously describe as "I was weak. Now I'm strong. Buzz off!" *Relational empowerment* invites instead the sentiment "I was weak. Now I'm strong. Let's be intimate." Whether it has been men retreating from their marriages to bond with one another in the woods, individual psychotherapy, codependence recovery, or feminist support groups, so far the main focus of "personal growth" has been just that—personal. I believe that bringing our growth *back into our relationships* is the necessary next step, not just for individuals like Judith but also for the various empowerment movements and for mainstream culture as well.

"You're behind a wall," I tell Judith, "a wall of mistrust and anger. That's okay. It is functional to put yourself behind a wall for protection when someone is being offensive. It's like the principal of self-defense. But, like self-defense, when the attack stops, you need to stop. It's time to let that wall soften back into an internal boundary, something supple, responsive." She shifts in her chair. "See, Judith, once the offending behavior has stopped, if you still choose to remain behind your wall that's no longer about protection. It may masquerade as security, but it's really covert revenge."

"Well, that's fine." Judith tosses back her dark hair, ready to take me on, cool, rational, arguing the case. "But you assume that the offense is, in fact, over, Terry. You tell me, 'Well, Judith, it's time to start trusting him now. Do it because I say so. After all, I'm your therapist.' Well, thanks. I'm happy to hear that you trust him. But, what if I don't?"

"You know, trust—" I blithely begin, but she cuts me off, in no mood for reassuring generalizations.

"Do you *know*..." Her voice begins to quaver. She's angry at me, and at herself for crying. "Do you have *any* idea how many lies he's told me over the years?" Pain fills the space between us. I back off, humbled. Who was I, really, to tell her anything? What if I bullied her back into the marriage only to set her up? Suppose, years later, he went ahead and dragged them both through it all over again?

"Judith," I say softly, "do you want out, then?"

"No," she wails, "but . . . but. . . Oh, *shit.*" She turns away from me. "What is it you *want* from me? How do I start to trust him again, after so many lies?"

"I don't know," I answer quietly. "You tell me, Judith."

"But, *I* don't know," she cries, utterly frustrated with me. "I *did* trust him once. And it turns out I was crazy. So how do I even go about *deciding* anymore? Do you understand what I'm saying?"

"Of course I do," I answer. "But, Judith, I think you do have what you need. A lot of people go hunting for some sort of 'proof of trustworthiness.' There are even therapists who recommend this; hiring a private detective and so forth. But, you know, there's always that doubt," I tell her. "I think that's the wrong way to go. I think you just feel it, in your gut. You feel whether or not he's really in recovery, if it's holding him, if he really means it."

"My gut wasn't all that helpful before," she says, pouting.

"I think it would have been, if you'd paid attention," I answer. "I don't think the instrument, your intuition, was faulty. You disassociated from it. You didn't want to know. You were in la-la land."

She looks hard at her husband. "How do I know you won't do this again, Damien?" she asks, eyes narrow, angry. "How can I even think . . ."

Damien spreads his hands, about to answer, but I intercept him. "You don't," I tell Judith. "Any more than he knows about you, or me, or anyone else."

"But I didn't . . ."

"There are no guarantees here," I answer. "We could all be gone by tomorrow. You take your best shot." Her anger seems to ratchet up each time I speak. It's clear that she's tired of listening to me; she wants to deal with her husband.

"Why?" she asks, furious. "Why should I ever believe you again?"

"Look," Damien reacts, "if you can't do it, Judith, then just—"

"That's not going to be helpful," I head him off.

"Tell me *why?*" she repeats, vibrating with anger, on the edge of screaming, or crying, or both.

"What can I say, honey?" he starts.

"Don't *'honey'* me, Damien." She's snarling now, raw, nothing demure about her any longer. "Don't placate me! Help me out here," sarcastic, taunting. I've never seen her like this. "Help me out, Damien. How am I *supposed* to trust you?"

"I'm not sure what to say," he answers softly, afraid of her.

"Should I trust you like I did when you were in Hong Kong? When I was putting together Sam's crib, his room, and you were off getting hand jobs in massage parlors?" Her face is scrunched up with contempt; disgust contorts her. "Or, how about the time . . ." I stop listening for a moment, thinking hard. My first instinct is to step in; I don't understand the savagery of her tone—not because the hurt she carries doesn't warrant it, but because we've been through all this already, months ago, several times. She's done this venting, raw and angry, both to Damien's face in my office and on her own. Until this moment, I'd always taken her rage at face value, part of the marital wound she carried, but I now guess at something behind it, stoking it, keeping it inflamed.

"I will *not*," she is saying, pointing at him. "I will not let you off the hook. You're *not* just going to get away with this, Damien!"

I glide my chair next to her, as she faces her husband. I don't look at her, but sit side by side. "Judith," I say, peering hard at Damien. "Judith, who are you talking to?"

She looks at me, startled, offended. "I'm talking to the man who, for evidently the whole of our marriage together, . . ."

"Okay," I say, "I understand that. But I was wondering if there wasn't someone else along with Damien that you were speaking to just now. Someone behind his chair as you spoke." I see her pause, take it in, a slight recoil. Her pointing finger swivels from Damien to me. "You really are . . ." she starts, smiling that bitter smile. "Oh, you're good, you're good." She has begun to cry.

"Who got away with it?" I ask her quietly.

"Like we haven't been through this," she throws out at me, but even so, her head bends and she cries.

"Go on," I say softly. "Let it go."

"He was such a *bastard* to her!" through her tears.

"Your father?" I ask. She nods, bent over, messy. I give her a wad of tissues and scoot Damien out of his chair. I put the empty chair down firmly in front of her. "Ready?" I ask. She nods, even before I set up the role-play; she's warmed up. She wants to get at it.

"Tell him," I say to her. "Put your father in that chair and tell him. What was it that you saw him do?" We had talked over this part of her history before but we had never moved it toward a role-play. She is hungry for the enactment and barely waits for me to finish my instructions. Bent over, she spits out in a low snarl, "You *bastard!* You *bastard!*"

"Tell him what he did to her," I coach.

"You . . ." She pauses a split second, gathering strength. "You *fucked* with her, Father. You *tortured* her. You played with her *mind.*"

Gone is any semblance of restraint, propriety; a little street fighter has swept into its place. "How?" I prompt. "Tell him how he did it."

She turns to me, breaking role. "He lied. All the time, lies. He was a politician. Very well known, respected, all that . . . *shit.*" She pauses.

"Go on," I urge her.

"But it was all *bullshit,*" she says, locking back onto the empty chair. "Underneath, he was just a drunk, a disgusting drunk, who did whatever he pleased."

"Meaning?" I ask, but she brushes my question aside.

"When she tried confronting him—Mother. When she caught him out in some bullshit lie, he'd just gaslight her, tell her it wasn't true, call her a bitch, say she was crazy. It was astounding."

"Were there other women?" I ask.

Again, the smile, knowing, sardonic. "Who knows?" she replies. "Women, men. We'll never know. He could have done it with zebras for all we know. Sure, other women. Why not? When he wasn't too . . . incapacitated."

"And you?" I hazard a guess, struck by the intensity of her hatred. I expect that she'll need me to clarify the question, but she knows what I mean. Impossibly, her smile broadens, and her eyes glitter even more coldly.

"You can't really say that," she answers. "Incest? Not really. He was so drunk. I doubt he even knew who I was. Believe me, he wasn't hard to ward off. Although *Mother,*" she says the word like it has quotation marks around it, "she seemed unable to stand up for herself."

My ears perk up. "Say that again?"

Her face sets, grim. "She never knew how to stand up for herself," she repeats.

I look at her a moment; the delicate features of her face, jewel hard. "You mean sexually?" I ask.

"I mean every way," she answers.

A world of questions hangs in the air. "Ask your father to leave the chair for now and bring in your mother," I tell her. She shakes her head. "No?" I ask. "Good. You have the right to pass, Judith. But, maybe you could just tell me why . . ."

"I don't want her here," shaking her head. "I don't want to talk to her."

"Okay, that's —"

"I don't want to *deal* with her," she says, ignoring me. "I don't want her tears, her histrionics. My mother was an invalid," she tells me. "In-*valid.* She had her dogs, her pills, her bedroom. I don't want to feel her feelings for her. I don't want to be her darling. I don't want to fight her fight."

"You fought with your father?" I pursue.

Again, the smile. "Not at first, at first I was his princess."

"And then you hit adolescence," I guess.

"Even before. Years before. As soon as I started thinking for myself."

"How often did you fight?" I ask.

"Every night," she says, simply.

"How bad were they," I inquire, "the fights?" Damien stirs in his chair, about to speak, but I shush him.

Judith looks hard at the empty chair. "Bad," is all that she says. "They were bad."

"Judith," I speak to her softly, "look at your husband." There's so much in her story, so much more to flesh out, learn about, say. But this is enough for now. What we have suffices to do the next piece. "Look at Damien," I repeat. It's clear that she doesn't want to, embarrassed suddenly, brought back to this place from wherever she'd gone. She looks at him, as he sits on the floor, leaning against the wall, his face all concern for her. "Tell me what you see as you look at him," I ask her.

"I know what you want me to say and it's true," she answers me, quick, a little breathless.

"Say it then," I reply. "Say it to him."

She sits up, folds her hands on her lap, gathers herself—and then turns away. "I can't deal with this," she mutters.

"Look at him, Judith," I bring her back. "Take a good look. There's a reason why you fell in love with this man."

"I just . . ." She shakes her head, defeated.

"Do you think your father would ever enter into treatment?" I ask her.

"No," she smiles.

"Have you ever been able to tell him the truth or feel that you have been heard?" She shakes her head. "Has he ever been accountable to you? Ever made amends?"

"Damien," she straightens up again, and then falters.

"Tell him, Judith," I press. "You both deserve it."

"You're not my father, Damien," she tells him, and they both start to cry. Facing one another, not touching, not speaking, powerfully locked by their gaze, grief washes over them. "You've been a bastard," she goes on. "Damien. You know you have. In your own right. A lying, cheating fuck." She lowers her eyes. We wait. "But you're not my father," she tells him. For a long while she sits, crying softly, arms limp at her sides.

"I'm sorry," Damien whispers. "I'm so dreadfully sorry." Judith glances up at me from her chair, her body straining toward her husband.

"You want to go?" I ask. She nods. "Go," I say. "Go!" She crosses the room to Damien, who gathers her up in his arms. They rock together, holding tight, too overwhelmed to speak.

Healing is the last phase of the process. Healing occurs when the blatant one—for our purposes, "he"—after considerable learning and effort—begins, like Damien, to deliver, and then the latent one, "she," feels his change *and welcomes it*. Progress and response begin to chase each other like kids on a playground, self-reinforcing, or, said differently, having fun. The more responsible he shows himself to be, the more relaxed she becomes, and the more relaxed she becomes . . . Vicious cycles transform into "charmed circles," wherein skill breeds skill, and intimacy invites more intimacy. But even healing has its consequences. Opening up our hearts in the present means reopening our heart's wounds from the past. For Judith to take possession of the happiness she'd worked hard to earn, some open ledgers had to be settled. It was time for her to give up the fight she'd had on her mother's behalf, the only template for relationship she'd ever known. In *daring to be happy*, she abandoned the wretchedness of both her parents—"leaving" her father "off the hook," and leaving her mother to her own resources. It so happened that Judith's parents were still miserably alive. But her work would have been much the same even had they been dead. She, like her husband, was psychologically upwardly mobile. They were moving into a world of health that was literally beyond their parents' imagination. Crossing that border feels to many of us who surpass the constricted, hurt lives that came before us like abandonment.

When I work with clients about this issue I speak of it as "keeping a parent *spiritual company*." Keeping spiritual company means uniting with them by inhabiting the same kind of world that they live in—a fighting world, or a mistrustful one, a country with no rules, or one so rule-bound no one can move in it. Crossing out of patriarchy into healthy relatedness means, for most of us, leaving behind that particular version of patriarchy that riddled and deformed our families. Usually, we emigrate. Those in the old land from which we hailed seldom choose to make the same journey.

Soon after our session, Judith had a dream, in which she encounters her mother in a burning building. She tries to lift her mother up onto her shoulders but the smoke overwhelms her. "I can't leave you here!" she cries in her dream. "But it's what I *want* for you," her dream-mother answers. "I'm your *mother*. You're my *child*. Don't you think I want you to escape?"

• • •

In the final phase of treatment as new patterns of putting out and receiving begin to take hold, as the upset engendered by intimacy is faced, the couple is ready to wean from our therapy. Conventional psychology uses the language of "internalization." The skills, the containment, the very kindness the partners once leaned upon me to provide—it would be said—they now come to incorporate. They can do that now, the punch line would go, "all by themselves." But I am a relational therapist. I don't believe anyone does much of anything "all by himself." The couple in this final phase transitions from the acute work of restoring intimacy to the lifelong challenge of preserving it. Their last task will be creating a network around each and both of them for support, stimulation, and guidance. Every one of us who is committed to the cultivation of intimacy needs to create such a subculture around us, a community that understands and nurtures our values—as mainstream culture does not. Existing friendships can be deepened as we reveal ourselves more honestly and invite the same. Men's groups, women's groups, workshops, service to others—anything helps so long as it lifts us out of the lie of better than/less than, and reinforces our growth in connection.

It is a tough, antirelational world out there. The old terms have been with us for a very long time. We should expect to get caught up in them sometimes, losing our way. That's when help from those who know and love us is essential. Women have been quite successful in building an empowerment subculture. Adult men now stand in desperate need of similar nurture—as do our growing sons. Recalling the support our daughters enjoy in their efforts to be whole, and contrasting that to the daunting lack of support for our sons, we see how much work lies ahead of us in helping boys. And couples need such a community of nurture as well—other adults we can speak to honestly, who will neither deny our pain nor push their own agenda.

It is time to extend the net of empowerment that has begun to encircle girls to both sexes, time for women and men to join with one another and lift a veil that has covered us both. Doing whatever I can to help foster the growth of such a relationship-cherishing subculture has become my life's work. And there are legions out there just like me—researchers, educators, clinicians, each, in his or her way, giving voice to one clear, simple, message:

Patriarchy is over. We needn't live like this any longer.

ENDNOTES

Introduction

17 *The relatively stable divorce rate:* R. Schoen and N. Standish, "The Footprints of Cohabitation: Results from Marital Status Life Tables For the U.S. 1995" (Population Research Institute, September 2000). See also T. C. Martin and, L. L. Bumpass, "Recent Trends in Marital Disruption," *Demography,* 1989, vol. 26, pp. 37–51.

17 *Our sense of community is breaking down:* R. D. Putnam, *Bowling Alone* (New York: Simon & Schuster, 2000). See Also J. P. Robinson and G. Godbey, *Time for Life: The Surprising Ways Americans Use Their Time, Second Ed.* (University Park: Pennsylvania State University Press, 1999). T. Caplow, H. M. Bahr, J. Modell, and B. Chadwick, *Recent Social Trends in the United States: 1960–1990* (Montreal: McGill–Queens University Press, 1991).

18 *Since the publication of my previous book:* T. Real, *I Don't Want to Talk About It: Overcoming the Secret Legacy of Male Depression* (New York: Scribner, 1997).

18 *The latest research on boys and their development:* W. Pollack, *Real Boys* (New York: Random House, 1998). See also W. Betcher and W. Pollack, *In a Time of Fallen Heroes: The Re-Creation of Masculinity* (New York: Atheneum, 1993). See L. R. Brody, "On Understanding Gender Differences in the Expression of Emotion," in S. Ablon, D. Brown, J. Mack, and E. Khantazian (eds.), *Human Feelings: Explorations in Affect Development and Meaning* (Hillsdale, NJ: Analytic Press, 1993); J. Garbarino, *Lost Boys: Why Our Sons Turn Violent and How We Can Save Them* (New York: Free Press, 1999).

19 *So wrote a seemingly normal Atlanta stockbroker:* Excerpt from a letter apparently written by Mark O. Barton and left in the Barton home, *The New York Times Editorial Desk,* "The Shootings in Atlanta," July 30, 1999.

20 *But early feminists like:* B. Friedan, *The Feminine Mystique* (New York: Norton, 1963). G. Steinem founded *MS* magazine, New York, 1972.

21 *The latest empirical research on both early infant relations:* A. Ganley, *Feminist Therapy with Male Clients,* in M. Bograd (ed.), *Feminist Approaches for Men in Family Therapy* (Binghamton, NY: Harrington Park Press, 1991) See S. Bem, "The Measurement of Psychological Androgyny," *Journal of Consulting and Clinical Psychology,* 1974, vol. 42, pp. 155–62. See also I. Broverman, S. Vogel, D. Broverman, F. Clarkson, and P. Rosenkrantz, "Sex-role Stereotypes: A Current Appraisal," *Journal of Social Issues,* 1972, vol. 28, pp. 59–78.

21 *Adult optimal health:* D. Ornish, M.D., Love and Survival: 8 Pathways to Intimacy and Health (New York: HarperCollins, 1998). See D. Spiegel, J. R. Bloom, H. C. Kraemer, and E. Gottheil, "Effect of Psychosocial Treatment on Survival of Patients with Metastatic Breast Cancer," *The Lancet*, 1989, vol. 2, pp. 888–91.

21 *Studies demonstrate that young children:* R. Levant, *Masculinity Reconstructed: Changing the Rules of Manhood at Work, in Relationships, and in Family Life* (New York: Dutton, 1995) See also L. Brody and J. Hall, *Gender and Emotion*, in M. Lewis and J. M. Haviland (eds.), *Handbook of Emotions* (New York: Guilford, 1993); L. Brody, "Gender Differences in Emotional Development: A Review of Theories and Research," *Journal of Personality*, 1985, vol. 53 (2), pp.14–59; R. Buck, "Non-verbal Communication of Affect in Preschool Children: Relationships with Personality and Skin Conductance," *Journal of Personality and Social Psychology*, 1977, vol. 35 (4), pp. 225–36; W. Betcher and W. Pollack, *In a Time of Fallen Heroes: The Re-Creation of Masculinity* (New York: Atheneum, 1993).

22 *"Not in entire forgetfulness/And not in utter nakedness/But trailing clouds of Glory,"* W. Wordsworth, *The Poetical Works of Wordsworth*, Cambridge Edition (Boston: Houghton Mifflin, 1982).

CHAPTER ONE

25 *Women marry men hoping they will change:* B. Arndt, quoted in *Sun Magazine*, no. 291, March 2000.

33 *One of the few stable statistics:* R. Schoen and N. Standish, "The Footprints of Cohabitation: Results from Marital Status Life Tables for the U.S. 1995," (Population Research Institute, September 2000). See also T. C. Martin and L. L. Bumpass, "Recent Trends in Marital Disruption," *Demography*, 1989, vol. 26, pp. 37–51.

35 *"Our souls are love":* From the poem *Ephemera*, W. B. Yeats, *Collected Poems* (New York: Macmillan, 1961).

38 *Over 70 percent of divorces:* A. Applewhite, *Cutting Loose: Why Women Who End Their Marriages Do So Well* (New York: HarperCollins, 1998).

38 *Gender roles have been rigidly defined:* J. Demos, *Myths and Realities in the History of American Family-Life*, in H. Grunebaum and J. Christ (eds.), *Contemporary Marriage: Structure, Dynamics and Therapy* (Boston: Little, Brown, 1976). H. Braverman, *Labor and Monopoly Capital: The Degradation of Work in the Twentieth Century* (New York: Monthly Review Press, 1975).

CHAPTER TWO

43 *Traditional socialization teaches girls to filter their sense of self-worth:* C. Gilligan, *In a Different Voice: Psychological Theory and Women's Development* (Cambridge, MA: Harvard University Press, 1982); L. M. Brown and C. Gilligan, *Meeting at the Crossroads* (New York: Ballantine Books, 1992); P. Orenstein, *Schoolgirls: Young Women, Self-Esteem and the Confidence Gap* (New York: Doubleday, 1994); M. Pipher, *Reviving Ophelia: Saving the Selves of Adolescent Girls* (Putnam, 1994); S. Shandler, *Ophelia Speaks: Adolescent Girls Write About Their Search for Self* (HarperPerennial

Library, 1999); T. Real, *I Don't Want to Talk About It: Overcoming the Secret Legacy of Male Depression* (New York: Simon & Schuster, 1997).

43 *Greek myth of Narcissus and Echo:* Ovid, *Metamorphoses,* trans. A. Mandelbaum (New York: Harcourt Brace, 1993).

49 *In her classic study:* A. Hochschild, *The Second Shift* (New York: Avon, 1989).

53 *Research tells us that all human beings:* J. Bardwick, *Psychology of Women* (New York: Harper and Row, 1971).

54 *To paraphrase David Habersham:* D. Habersham, "Pretty, Polite, and not too Smart," *The New York Times Book Review,* September 11, 1994, pp. 15–18. The review is of *Schoolgirls: Young Women, Self-Esteem and Confidence Gap,* by Peggy Ornstein (New York: Doubleday, 1994).

54 *"Girls lose relationship in the service of maintaining relationships":* L. M. Brown and C. Gilligan, *Meeting at the Crossroads* (New York: Ballantine, 1992).

54 *If you ask an eight-year-old girl:* Quote by Catherine Steiner Adair, Director of Education, Prevention, and Outreach of the Harvard University Eating Disorders Center.

55 *A notable exception is Dana Crowly Jack who speaks in chilling terms about the correlation of wives' pent-up anger at their husbands and their expressed rage toward their children, particularly sons:* D. Crowly Jack, *Silencing the Self: Women and Depression* (Cambridge, MA, Harvard University Press, 1991).

CHAPTER THREE

58 *From the film* Good Will Hunting: Distributed by Miramax Films, 1997.

60 *Recent research tells us that boys from:* J. Chu, "Learning What Boys Know: An Observational and Interview Study with Six Four-Year-Old Boys." (doctoral dissertation, Harvard Graduate School of Education, Cambridge, MA: 2000). Note from Ms. Chu: "My study shows that boys as young as four years old are capable of being fully present in their relationships in the sense that they are self-aware and keenly attuned to others as they negotiate their interactions. However at this age, there are signs that these boys are learning to nuance their behaviors and become more savvy in their interactions, in ways that seem effectively to shield or detract from their genuine presence in relationship. I wish to emphasize that these boys do not shut down or lose their relational capabilities at this time. These boys are learning not to reveal or act on their relational capabilities largely in response to cultural messages (as conveyed through their interpersonal relationships) about what is considered acceptable and appropriate behavior for boys. However, there is evidence—in this study and in my study of adolescent boys—that their relational capabilities remain intact, even though they may become less apparent" (personal communication).

See also W. Pollack, *Real Boys* (New York: Random House, 1998); O. Silverstein and B. Roshbaum, *The Courage to Raise Good Men* (New York: Viking, 1994); R. Levant, *Masculinity Reconstructed: Changing the Rules of Manhood at Work, in Relationships, and in Family Life* (New York: Dutton, 1995). See also L. Brody and J. Hall, *Gender and Emotion,* in M. Lewis and J. M. Haviland (eds.), *Handbook of Emotions* (New York: Guilford, 1993); L. Brody, "Gender Differences in Emotional Development: A Review of Theories and Research," *Journal of Personality,* 1985, vol. 53 (2), pp.14–59.

While various researchers have pointed to this early period as traumatic for boys, my thoughts concerning the implications of the difference in the age in which relational injury occurs for the two sexes were stimulated by conversations with Carol Gilligan.

60 *Trauma research indicates:* B. van der Kolk, (ed.), *Psychological Trauma* (Washington, D.C.: American Psychiatric Press, 1987); S. Ablon, D. Brown, J. Mack, and E. Khantazian (eds.), *Human Feelings: Explorations in Affect, Development and Meaning* (Hillsdale, N.J.: Analytic Press, 1993).

61 *In his work on couples, researcher John Gottman:* J. Gottman, "Predicting the Longitudinal Course of Marriages," *Journal of Marital and Family Therapy,* 1991, vol. 117, pp. 3–7; J. Gottman and R. Levenson, "The Social Psychophysiology of Marriage," in P. Noller and M. A. Fitzpatrick (eds.), *Perspectives on Marital Interaction,* pp. 182–200 (Clevedon, UK: Multilingual Matters, 1988); J. Gottman, *Seven Principles of Making Marriage Work* (New York: Crown, 1999).

62 *In* Maternal Thinking: S. Ruddick, *Maternal Thinking: Toward a Politics of Peace* (Boston: Beacon Press, 1989). This reference and its import were pointed out to me by my colleague at the Family Institute of Cambridge, Jeffrey Kerr, LICSW.

CHAPTER FOUR

73 *On the "masculine" side:* "In reality, girls and boys, women and men are more alike than they are different but as Rubin says, societies impose a 'sameness taboo' on them. Together with race ethnicity and social class, *gender categories* are institutionalized cultural and social statuses." Quote from Preface in J. Lorber and S. A. Farrell (eds.), *The Social Construction of Gender* (Newbury Park–London–New Delhi: Sage Publications, 1991). From the work of G. Rubin, *The Traffic in Women: Notes on the "Political Economy" of Sex,* in R. R. Reiter (ed.), *Toward an Anthropology of Women* (New York: Monthly Review Press, 1975).

73 *Which one of these two "sides" is healthy:* See C. West and D. H. Zimmerman, *Doing Gender,* in J. Lorber and S. A. Farrell (eds.), *The Social Construction of Gender* (Newbury Park–London–New Delhi: Sage Publications, 1991); J. Gagnon and B. Henderson, *The Social Psychology of Sexual Development,* in J. M. Henslin (ed.), *Marriage and Family in a Changing Society* (New York: Free Press, 1985).

74 *But in 1983, sociologist Joseph Pleck:* J. H. Pleck, *The Myth of Masculinity* (Cambridge, MA: MIT Press, 1981).

74 *Initially Bem and her colleagues called this ideal "androgyny":* "I do not think, however, that the concept of androgyny adequately conveys that masculinity and femininity have no independent or palpable reality. Androgyny inevitably focuses more on the individual's being both masculine and feminine than on the culture's having created the concepts of masculinity and femininity in the first place. Hence, androgyny can legitimately be said to reproduce precisely the gender polarization that it seeks to undercut, and to do so even in the most feminist of treatments.

"In 1977, to convey more forcefully that masculinity and femininity are cultural lenses that polarize reality, I shifted the focus of my research from the concept of androgyny to the concept of gender schematic information processing, or gender schematicity. Simply put, gender schematicity is the internalizing of the gender polarization in the culture. . . ." S. Bem, *The Lenses of Gender: Transforming the Debate on Sexual Inequality* (New Haven and London: Yale University Press, 1993), p. 125.

75 *What makes a good morani*: Morani was the word used for *warrior* in the Masai village at Lake Natron. I am unsure of the spelling, although I have seen the term *Iimoran* used to denote the plural, *warriors. Maasai*, text Tepilit Ole Saitoti, photographs Carol Beckwith (New York: Harry N. Abrams, 1980).

77 *In* I Don't Want to Talk About It: T. Real, *I Don't Want to Talk About It: Overcoming the Secret Legacy of Male Depression* (New York: Scribner, 1997).

78 *Violence* is *boyhood socialization:* For a fuller discussion and further references, see T. Real, *I Don't Want to Talk About It: Overcoming the Secret Legacy of Male Depression* (New York: Scribner, 1997).

78 *"the great divide":* O. Silverstein and B. Roshbaum, *The Courage to Raise Good Men* (New York: Viking, 1994).

78 *As sociologist Nancy Chodorow:* N. Chodorow, *Reproduction of Mothering: Psychoanalysis and the Sociology of Gender* (Berkeley: University of California Press, 1978).

81 *What pioneer feminist psychologist:* J. B. Miller, *The Healing Connection: How Women Form Relationships in Therapy and in Life* (Boston: Beacon Press, 1997).

81 *The Old Testament:* New American Standard Bible.

CHAPTER FIVE

85 *"Many of us know":* R. Bly, *Iron John: A Book About Men* (Reading, MA: Addison-Wesley, 1990).

89 *"My mother's strength":* J. Baldwin, *No Name in the Street* (New York: Dial Press, 1992).

90 *Since Carol Gilligan's groundbreaking research*: L. M. Brown and C. Gilligan, *Meeting at the Crossroads* (New York: Ballantine, 1992).

90 *"It looked authentic":* Adapted quote from the documentary film *All Men Are Sons*, directed by John Badalament. This extraordinary film follows the lives of six men as they speak about masculinity and their fathers. The film culminates with all six men gathering together for the first time in a cabin in the woods with me for a day and a half to work deeply on the impact that the relationship with their fathers has had on their lives.

93 *Pia observed that there wasn't one form of childhood abuse:* P. Mellody, *Facing Co-Dependence, What It Is, Where It Comes from, How It Sabotages Our Lives* (HarperSanFrancisco, 1989).

CHAPTER SIX

97 *"Come thick night":* W. Shakespeare, *The Tragedy of Macbeth* (New Haven: Yale University Press, 1954), p. 16, verse 51; p. 49, verse 47–48; p. 14, verse 52.

98 *In Stanley Kubrick's film: Full Metal Jacket*, Warner Bros., 1987.

98 *In writing about his reasons for making public:* Daniel Ellsberg was interviewed in AARP's *Modern Maturity.* "My Private Vietnam, What I Had to Do," *Modern Maturity*, May–June 2000. From his position in the Rand Corporation Ellsberg had access to top-secret material about decision-making in Vietnam, which he

submitted to the Senate Foreign Relations Committee. This material later became known as the Pentagon Papers.

101 *But when Freud heard his female clients:* See J. M. Masson, *The Assault on Truth, Freud's Supression of the Seduction Theory* (New York: Penguin, 1985); *A Dark Science: Women, Sexuality and Psychiatry in the Nineteenth Century,* compiled by J. M Masson (New York: Farrar, Straus and Giroux, 1986).

102 *A century later:* C. Gilligan, *In a Different Voice: Psychological Theory and Women's Development* (Cambridge, M.A.: Harvard University Press, 1982); L. M. Brown and C. Gilligan, *Meeting at the Crossroads* (New York: Ballantine Books, 1992); J. L. Herman, *Trauma and Recovery* (New York: Basic Books, 1992); D. C. Jack, *Silencing the Self: Women and Depression* (Cambridge, M.A.: Harvard University Press, 1991).

114 *The choreography of patriarchy:* For discussion related to this see, in C. West and D. H. Zimmerman, *Doing Gender,* in J. Lorber and S. A. Farrell (eds.), *The Social Construction of Gender* (Newbury Park–London–New Delhi: Sage Publications, 1991).

CHAPTER SEVEN

117 *Researcher John Gottman tested out:* J. Gottman, *The Seven Principles of Making Marriage Work* (New York: Crown, 1999); J. Gottman, The Marriage Clinic (New York: W. W. Norton, 1999).

117 *Derisively dubbed by journalists the "Yes, dear," study:* T. H. Maugh II, "Study's Advice to Husbands: Accept Wife's Influence," *L.A. Times,* February 1998, Home Edition, Section: Part A, pp. A–1. K. Parker, "Stating the Obvious, a New Growth Industry," *Jewish World Review,* June 16, 1999.

119 *"One can say":* G. Bateson, *Steps to an Ecology of Mind: Collected Essays in Anthropology, Psychiatry, Evolution and Epistemology* (San Francisco: Chandler, 1972).

119 *An essential component of all couple's therapy:* A. Dienhart and J. M. Avis, *Men in Therapy: Exploring Feminist-Informed Alternatives,* "Critique of Family Therapy Practice: How Five Models Work with Men," pp. 29–36, and M. Bograd, *Female Therapist/Male Client: Considerations About Belief Systems,* in M. Bograd (ed.), *Feminist Approaches for Men in Family Therapy* (Binghamton, NY: Harrington Park Press, 1991); J. Libow, P. Raskin, and B. Caust, "Feminist and Family Systems Therapy: Are they Irreconcilable?" *American Journal of Family Therapy,* 1982, vol. 10, pp. 3–12.

120 *In her classic article:* V. Goldner, "Feminism and Family Therapy," *Family Process,* 1985, vol. 24, pp. 31–47.5.

120 *A client, enamored of the book:* C. P. Estes, *Women Who Run with Wolves: Myths and Stories of the Wild Woman Archetype* (New York: Ballantine Books, 1992).

121 *Treading lightly on their male clients' issues:* A. Dienhart and J. M. Avis, *Men in Therapy: Exploring Feminist-Informed Alternatives,* in M. Bograd (eds.), *Feminist Approaches for Men in Family Therapy* (Binghamton, NY: Harrington Park Press, 1991); M. Bograd, "Family Systems Approaches to Wife Battering: A Feminist Critique," *American Journal of Orthopsychiatry,* 1984, vol. 54, pp. 558–68; D. Luepnitz, *The Family Interpreted: Feminist Theory in Clinical Practice* (New York: Basic Books, 1988); F. Pittman, "Gender Myths: When Does Gender Become Pathology?" *The Family Therapy Networker,* 1985, vol. 9, pp. 24–31.

132 *While medication can transform:* K. R. Jamison, *An Unquiet Mind* (New York: Knopf, 1995).

CHAPTER EIGHT

137 *"When we lose our balance we die":* S.Suzuki-Roshi, *Zen Mind, Beginner's Mind,* T. Dixon (ed.), (NY and Tokyo: Weatherhill Inc., 1970, pp. 31–32).

140 *"My wife . . . and I didn't hate each other . . .":* J. Taylor, "Divorce Is Good for You," *Esquire,* May 1997, pp. 52–59.

140 *"It's a long way to walk":* J. Updike, *Too Far to Go: The Maple Stories* (New York: Fawcett Crest, 1979).

148 *"My name is Lester Burnham":* The film *American Beauty,* Dreamworks, 1999.

149 *"This is the dead land":* T. S. Eliot, *The Hollow Men,* in *Selected Poems,* verse 3, p. 78 (New York: Harcourt Bracc and Co., 1936).

153 *When women speak frankly about their sexual fantasies:* See N. Friday, *My Secret Garden: Women's Sexual Fantasies* (New York: Pocket Books, 1973).

153 *If romance is the great seller among women:* One billion dollars is spent annually on pornography on the Internet. *U.S. News and World Report,* March 2000.

153 *But as pioneer sex therapist:* D. Schnarch, *Passionate Marriage: Love, Sex and Intimacy in Emotionally Committed Relationships* (New York: W. W. Norton, 1997).

153 *One recalls the famous Victorian journal:* quoted in *Sun Magazine,* no. 291, March 2000.

CHAPTER NINE

155 *A woman can be proud and stiff:* W. B. Yeats, *Crazy Jane Speaks to the Bishop,* in *Collected Poems* (New York: Macmillan, 1961).

156 *Thus begins Europe's earliest secular verse:* William IX, Duke of Aquitaine, in *Medieval Song* (ed.), J. J. Wilhelm (New York: Dutton, 1971).

157 *Katharine of* The English Patient: M. Ondaatje, *The English Patient* (Toronto: McClelland and Stewart, 1992).

157 *Romeo and Juliet in sweltering Verona:* W. Shakespeare, *The Tragedy of Romeo and Juliet* (New Haven: Yale University Press, 1954).

157 *Jack and young Rose:* The film *Titanic,* Paramount Pictures, 1997.

158 *In the beginning:* J. W. von Goethe, *Faust* (New Haven: Yale University Press, 1992).

158 *Sir Gawain rides from King Arthur's court:* Yvain in *Chretian de Troyes, Twelfth Century Selections, Arthurian Romances,* translated by D. D. R. Owen (London: Dent, 1987), p. 315: " 'What? Will you now be one of those,' my lord Gawain said to him, 'who lose in merit because of their wives? Shame on him, by Saint Mary, who marries and degenrates as a result! . . . Break the bridle and the halter, and let's go tourneying together so you don't get a reputation. . . .' "

158–159 *And patriarchy glorifies the values and attitudes of masculinity:* R. Levant, *Masculinity Reconstructed: Changing the Rules of Manhood at Work, in Relationships, and in Family Life* (New York: Dutton, 1995); J. Bardwick, *Psychology of Women* (New York: Harper and Row, 1971).

159 *As far back as 1978:* J. Pleck, *Working Wives/Working Husbands* (Beverly Hills: Sage Productions, 1985).

161 *For the Roman Stoics, the word* passion: See E. Auerbach, *Literary Language and Its Public in Late Latin Antiquity and in the Middle Ages*, trans. by R. Manheim (Princeton: Princeton University Press, 1965).

164 *Edward Tronick and his team at Children's Hospital:* E. Tronick, "Emotions and Emotional Communication in Infants," *American Psychologist*, vol. 44 (2), pp. 112–19, 1989; E. Tronick, J. Cohn, "Infant-Mother Face-to-Face Interaction: Age and Gender Differences in Coordination and Occurrence of Miscoordination," *Child Development*, vol. 60 (1), pp. 85–92, 1989; E. Tronick, "The Development of Rapport," *Psychological Inquiries*, vol.1, pp. 322–23, 1990. I am indebted to Carol Gilligan for first acquainting me to Dr. Tronick's work, acquainting me, in fact, to the very moment I quote here. It was Carol Gilligan as well who emphasized the importance of this research as it bore upon adult relationships, as in other words, affording a new paradigm. This is but one example of the enormous influence her thinking and our collaboration have exerted on my work.

165 *In* I Don't Want to Talk About It: T. Real, *I Don't Want to Talk About It: Overcoming the Secret Legacy of Male Depression* (New York: Scribner, 1997).

165 *My personal favorite is Perceval:* W. von Eschenbach, *Parzival* (Goppingen: Kummerle, 1989).

166 *A generation ago, women researchers:* J. B. Miller, *Toward a New Psychology of Women* (Boston: Beacon Press, 1976); C. Gilligan, *In a Different Voice: Psychological Theory and Women's Development* (Cambridge, MA: Harvard University Press, 1982); L. M. Brown and C. Gilligan, *Meeting at the Crossroads* (New York: Ballantine Books, 1992); Stone Center, *Women's Growth in Connecting: Writings from the Stone Center* (London/New York: Guilford Press, 1991).

167 *Armed with the skills of "close analysis":* D. Stern, *Interpersonal World of the Infant: A View from Psychoanalysis and Developmental Psychology* (New York: Basic Books, 1985).

167 *Ed Tronick, and others:* E. Tronick, H. Als, L Adamson, S. Wise, T. B. Brazelton, "The Infant's Response to Entrapment Between Contradictory Messages in Face-to-Face Interaction," *American Academy of Child Psychiatry*, vol. 17, pp. 1–13, 1978; E. Tronick, T. B. Brazelton, H. Als, "Structure of Early Face-to-Face Communicative Interactions: Its Developmental Functions," *Sign Language Studies*, vol. 18, pp.1–16, 1978.

CHAPTER TEN

169 *I visualize the obscure process of that mate selection:* "Object relations thoery and marital studies," *British Journal of Medical Psychology*, XXXVI, pp. 125–29, 1963.

170 *Psychoanalyst Ethel Person:* E. Person, *Passionate Attachments: Thinking About Love*, W. Gaylin and E. Person (eds.), (New York: Free Press; London Collier Macmillan, 1988).

171 *From Plato in the* Symposium: Plato, *The Symposium on Love or the Banquet, a Dialogue of Plato*, trans. Percy B. Shelley (Mount Vernon, NY: The Peter Pauper Press, 1945).

177 *And, in the end, old King Laius:* Sophocles, *Oedipus Rex*, ed. by R. D. Dawe (Cambridge; NY: Cambridge University Press, 1982).

178 *Psychoanalyst H. V. Dicks remarked:* H. V. Dicks, *Marital Tensions, Clinical Studies Toward a Psychological Theory of Interaction* (New York: Basic Books, 1967).

178 *James Framo, the father of couple's therapy:* J. Framo, "The Nature of Marriage," American Family Treatment Association Conference, 1984.

178 *Marriage's "exquisite design":* C. Verge, "Couple's Therapy Intensive Training," Family Institute of Cambridge, Watertown, MA.

CHAPTER ELEVEN

183 *"Between the idea | And the reality":* T. S. Eliot, *The Hollow Men,* in *Selected Poems* (New York: Harcourt Brace and Co., 1936).

188 *"Do you read the comic strip 'Broom Hilda'?":* Actually, it was not a client, but my friend and colleague, Dr. Carter Umbarger, who first shared this with me.

190 *As in Albee's battling couple:* E. Albee, *Who's Afraid of Virginia Wolf? A Play* (New York: Dramatists Play Service, 1962).

190 *Pedestrian pair in the film: War of the Roses,* Warner Bros., 1989.

190 *Research informs us that:* J. Gottman, *The Seven Principles of Making Marriage Work* (New York: Crown, 1999), J. Gottman, *The Marriage Clinic* (New York: W. W. Norton, 1999).

195 *I am reminded of the old biblical story:* "Exodus," The Old Testament, New American Standard Bible.

CHAPTER TWELVE

197 *"Pale sunlight | Pale the wall:* Rumi, from the poem "Dissolver of Sugar," *The Essential Rumi,* trans. by C. Barks, *et al.* (San Francisco: HarperCollins, 1995).

198 *To use Susan Faludi's term,* stiffed: S. Faludi, *The Betrayal of the American Man* (New York: W. Morrow and Co., 1999).

202 *A central aspect of Pia's system:* P. Mellody, *Facing Co-Dependence, What It Is, Where It Comes from, How It Sabotages Our Lives* (HarperSanFrancisco, 1989).

203 Chart: Five Core Self-Skills; *Ibid.*

206 *Pia's scheme of self skills: Ibid.*

206 *That the reverse pattern is true:* T. Real, *I Don't Want to Talk About It: Overcoming the Secret Legacy of Male Depression* (New York: Scribner, 1997).

CHAPTER THIRTEEN

207 *Pia's first self-skill:* P. Mellody, *Facing Co-Dependence, What It Is, Where It Comes from, How It Sabotages Our Lives* (HarperSanFrancisco, 1989).

CHAPTER FOURTEEN

225 *"To live outside the law":* B. Dylan, from *Blonde on Blonde,* Columbia Records, 1966.

228 *In* Dave Barry's: D. Barry, *Dave Barry's Complete Guide to Guys* (Ballantine Books, 2000).

CHAPTER FIFTEEN

237   *I learned to analyze:* S. Minuchin, *Families and Family Therapy* (Cambridge, MA: Harvard University Press, 1974).

237   *It wasn't until I met:* P. Mellody, *Facing Co-Dependence, What It Is, Where It Comes from, How It Sabotages Our Lives* (HarperSanFrancisco, 1989).

246   *"You do not have to walk on your knees":* M. Oliver, *Wild Geese,* in *New and Selected Poems* (Boston: Beacon Press, 1992).

CHAPTER SIXTEEN

247   Invitation, request, *and* demand: I owe this distinction to my colleague, Dr. Richard Lee, at the Family Institute of Cambridge, Watertown, MA.

250   *Saint Augustine once claimed:* St. Augustine, *St. Augustine's Confessions, with an English translation by William Watts, 1631* (Cambridge, MA: Harvard University Press, 1960–61).

253   *Holden Caufield in* The Catcher in the Rye: J. D. Salinger, *The Catcher in the Rye* (Boston: Little Brown, 1951).

253   James Dean in *Rebel Without a Cause:* Warner Bros., 1955.

INDEX

289

Terrence Real has been a family therapist and lecturer for more than twenty years. The author of *I Don't Want to Talk About It: Overcoming the Secret Legacy of Male Depression,* he is a member of the senior faculty at the Family Institute of Cambridge, and is a Director of the Gender Relations Program at the Meadows Institute in Arizona. He lives with his wife, family therapist Belinda Berman, and their two sons, Justin and Alexander, in Newton, Massachusetts.